THE ELEPHANT IN THE BO

THE ELEPHANT IN THE BOARDROOM

The causes of leadership
derailment

Adrian Furnham

First published 2010 by
PALGRAVE MACMILLAN

Palgrave Macmillan in the UK is an imprint of Macmillan Publishers Limited,
registered in England, company number 785998, of Houndmills, Basingstoke,
Hampshire RG21 6XS.

Palgrave Macmillan in the US is a division of St Martin's Press LLC,
175 Fifth Avenue, New York, NY 10010.

Palgrave Macmillan is the global academic imprint of the above companies
and has companies and representatives throughout the world.

Palgrave® and Macmillan® are registered trademarks in the United States,
the United Kingdom, Europe and other countries.

ISBN 978-1-349-31092-0   ISBN 978-0-230-28187-5 (eBook)
DOI 10.1007/978-0-230-28187-5

This book is printed on paper suitable for recycling and made from fully
managed and sustained forest sources. Logging, pulping and manufacturing
processes are expected to conform to the environmental regulations of the
country of origin.

A catalogue record for this book is available from the British Library.

A catalog record for this book is available from the Library of Congress.

CONTENTS

LIST OF FIGURES AND TABLES

FIGURES

TABLES

PREFACE

There is no shortage of books on leadership. One calculation puts the number of books with "leadership" in the title at well over 100,000. Certainly, business and management sections of bookshops groan under the weight of them.

They differ enormously. Some of them are historical analyses of great leaders; others biographies of particular – often living – individuals. There are also many autobiographies – mainly of politicians and businessmen – thought, at least in their own minds, to be great leaders. There are books on explorers, political leaders, great generals and religious leaders. They attempt, in the main, through a description of their life and deeds, to seek out the very factors that lead them to be great leaders in the first place.

But "greatness" is time and culture specific. Each generation appears to have its own heroes and "great leaders". Just as one man's meat is another man's poison, so one person's outstanding leader is another's spin-doctor or charlatan. This is partly caused by a sort of revisionism that occurs after a great person has faded from view. Sexual peccadilloes, decisional errors, bullying influence techniques seem to get written about some years after a great leader has "passed on" or even "passed over". In a more objective and sober light, their weaknesses are revealed.

Thus, over the past decade, we have seen the emergence of books and papers on the dark side of leadership. They have been called variously Bad, Derailed, Destructive, Evil, Failed, Incompetent, and Toxic.

These are, of course, not the same in aetiology and manifestation. Some are morally corrupt; others are just low in talent. Some are subclinically disturbed; others just over-promoted. Some seem, at any rate, evil or at least deranged.

This book is about potentially great business leaders: often people thought to have, and indeed having, great skill, charm and determination. It is about people often initially fated and fêted to be high-flyers, talented or those with potential who get noticed and promoted. Nearly all derailed leaders have an impressive CV: a history of achievement and success. But something went wrong. To rise to the top of any organization takes ability and effort: it often takes great determination and great skill. Leaders of organizations need to be courageous and bold, self-confident and socially skilled, and many other things beside. By contrast, bad managers make poor decisions, can't motivate their people and fail to learn from past mistakes. They fail on the basics: finding, forming and motivating a team to fulfil worthwhile and appropriate goals which they articulate as clear targets and challenges.

Failed and derailed leaders don't deliver: they are poor executors of their goals. They don't deliver, they shirk or make poor decisions and quite simply don't get things done. They don't follow good management practices, they don't put the right people in the right jobs, and they don't confront poor performance. Often, the most direct issue is people problems and communications. It is then, no wonder, that interest in the concept of emotional intelligence at work has been so intense.

Followers play their part in derailment. Some conspire with immorality by turning their gaze away. Others demand and expect too much of any individual and place unfulfillable burdens on them. Still others provoke so much stress that leaders buckle under the burden. Successful organizations tend to be well managed. There are good management practices and procedures: operations are monitored and improved – incentives are equitable performance goals which are set regularly and realistically. Good management is integral to organizational performance.

The cost of management failure is high: it has been variously estimated to between one and two million pounds/dollars/euros per "senior manager". These are largely "guesstimates" but are nevertheless realistic given all the factors that need to be taken into account, such as the cost to recruit, select and train replacements and all those who left the organization because of that particular manager. Bad managers are stress carriers for all those around them. They are a mental and physical health hazard. They alone can break and destroy whole organizations.

The question is the incidence of failure. Various writers have made estimates, some based on organizational data and others on simple statements to individuals such as: "How many bosses that you have worked for would you be willing to work for again?" Hogan, Hogan and Kaiser (2009) reviewed 12 published estimates which showed the range 30–67% with a mean of 47%. They claim: "we suggest that two thirds of existing managers are insufferable and half will eventually fail" (p. 5).

It is not important to be psychologically or psychiatrically trained to understand the issue and the book. The idea is this: as part of growing up, most people discover their abilities and predispositions. In certain situations, and faced with certain tasks, they tend to be uncomfortable, insecure and stressed. How they cope with those can lead to long-term failure. Further, we all develop ways of seeing the world. These may be called schemas or strategies. They may be realistic or a little odd. But they endure and shape how people respond to everyday situations. Derailed leaders often have a monkey on their shoulder and a distinctly "different" view of the world, as we shall see.

Some of the sections in this book have appeared in chapters in other books I have written, edited or contributed to. But I have been thinking about this topic for some time now and the vast majority of the content of the book reflects recent ideas and ponderings.

I have various people to thank for inspiration that went into this book. First and foremost must be Bob Hogan, who has pioneered this area. He is an extremely well-read, thoughtful, academic iconoclast, fearless in his attacks on those whose ideology or poor research "justifies" their ideas. I read all his books and papers avidly.

Others have helped in various ways – my brilliant and talented PhD students (Dino, Joanna, Tomas, Viren) as well as old friends (David, Chris). But of course I have as always to thank, most of all, Alison and Benedict.

London   ADRIAN FURNHAM

For Benedict, my fine son of whom I am so proud

PART I

1

RESEARCHING DERAILED, INCOMPETENT AND FAILED LEADERS

INTRODUCTION

This book is about an open secret. Many of our high-flying, supposedly talented and certainly well-remunerated business, political and public services leaders derail. Some go to prison, most "just" get sacked, others have breakdowns. They suddenly resign to "spend more time with their family". Previously hungry for media attention they are suddenly "unavailable for comment". Many cause irreparable damage. High-flyers crash and burn; worse they take everyone down with them. They are a major cause of stress.

But there is a puzzle at the heart of this phenomenon: most were (supposedly) carefully recruited and selected. Further, they had most impressive CVs. They were well known as "stars"; "wunderkinds"; "highly talented"; "golden boys and girls". Clever, confident and ambitious, their careers seemed to give no hint of what was to come. The cost of failure is high. Hogan and colleagues (2009) quote estimates of $1 to $3 million as the cost of a failed executive.

So what goes wrong? Why are their flaws, later so obvious to all, not spotted at recruitment, selection and promotion stages? What are the lessons to be learnt from the study of leadership derailment? Can it be prevented or cured? What responsibilities do the followers have? This book attempts to answer some of these and other related questions. There are some related issues few would dispute: good leaders have a tangible effect on all aspects of organizational performance, some are clearly better than others; the cost of failure can be very high.

DERAILMENT: PASSÉ, POPULARIST, PASSING LEADERSHIP FAD?

Skeptics are, perhaps rightly, cautious of new fads. In the massive (and unpoliced) leadership literature themes come and go. Is the derailed leader an old foe or a new fad? Is this just another way to interpret the leadership literature not so much as the "Great Man" but the "Bad Man" approach. From heroes to outlaws?

Certainly over the last decade a string of books have emerged on bad, toxic, destructive "dark side" managers. To some extent there is some evidence of faddishness. While serious scholars have found inspiration and explanation for derailed leaders in personality disorders (Kets de Vries, 2003; 2006a; 2006b; Hogan, 2007b), others have jumped on this bandwagon (Dotlich and Cairo, 2003).

Is this likely to be the next theme in the leadership literature? Leadership writers have cast about in history and theology and now they are turning to psychiatry to say something new. There have been studies on why people are fired and lists of the habits of spectacularly unsuccessful people.

However, there are three reasons to believe that this is not just another "flash in the pan" for the leadership literature. *First*, it really is a neglected, unspoken-about topic that has simply surfaced as a serious issue. More leaders fail and derail than become great successes. Yet the emphasis in the literature seems always to have been on the minority of good or great leaders. A high number of leaders are "let go" early; many are sacked; others end up in prison.

Derailment and dark side leadership really is the *Elephant in the Boardroom*: the taboo topic. It is as if having been made CEO, the "chosen one", it is assumed, has been carefully selected and groomed for greatness. It often comes as a surprise that these high-flying wunderkinds are not mere mortals but self-aggrandizing, reckless, egoists. People want to know how it happens that derailers are chosen in the first place.

Second, this literature does include the idea of the "dark triad" embedded in the "toxic triangle". It is about not only the pathology of individuals but also how they can hypnotize followers and abuse situations to bring about such chaos. The "great man" or trait approach to leadership has quite rightly been accused of ignoring social factors. The derailment literature, for the most part, does not fall into this trap because it describes and explains how such obviously flawed individuals can have such an impact. Toxic leaders have allure. We get the

4

politicians we deserve. It is totally wrong to see the full explanation "within the individual". Social forces of many sorts proscribe and prescribe who rises to the top and when. Again and again, the idea is of the situation being "ideal" for dark side leadership to occur. In times of change, even chaos, and in times of ambiguity and uncertainty followers will elect strong leaders characterized rather by their boldness, adventurousness and charisma than by their wisdom.

Third, the derailment literature is clearly interesting and important because of its emphasis on screening and therapy. Derailing and derailed leaders can destroy organizations and whole countries. But the literature is clearly practical because it highlights various derailing leaders by the factors that push them over the edge. There are now valid and useful psychometric instruments that can detect those likely to derail. This is as much about prevention as cure. It is, further, deeply practical and useful. It explains what to look for, and when, and why dangerous behaviors are likely to occur.

TERMINOLOGICAL INEXACTITUDES

The work on leaders who fail is marked by a number of different terms. The choice of the terms seems relatively arbitrary and the personal favorite of a writer or of people in a particular discipline. Technically they do have slightly different meanings. The following is an incomplete list from an ever-growing group of words used in this area.

- **Aberrant (leaders)** This emphasizes abnormality, atypicality and deviance from the right or normal type. It has two themes: both unusualness and also a departure from acceptable standards. That is, it has a statistical *and* moral side to it.
- **Anti-social (leaders)** This echoes the immoral nature of leaders who can be anti-social in the way selfish people may be, but more likely the way delinquents are anti-social. More importantly, perhaps, it echoes the new term for psychopath: anti-social personality disorder.
- **Dark side (Triad) (leaders)** This is to contrast the bright and the dark; the outside, the obvious and the straightforward with the inside, the obscure and the devious. Dark implies evil, dismal and menacing. The triad suggests three separatable constituents of evil.
- **Derailed (leaders)** This emphasizes the idea of being thrown off course. Trains on tracks derail. Leaders set fair in a particular

direction deviate from the path, unable to move forward. It is sometimes hyphenated with the next word in the dictionary – namely, *deranged* – which implies not only a breakdown in performance but also insanity.

- **Despotic (leaders)** This is taken from the historical literature emphasizing the misuse and abuse of power by oppressive, absolutist leaders. It emphasizes the autocratic type or style of leadership.
- **Destructive (leaders)** Used by historians in this context to look at the impact of a particular leadership style, it speaks of the ruining, spoiling or neutralizing of a group or force led by a particular person.
- **Incompetent (leaders)** This is used to suggest inadequate, ineffective, unqualified. It implies the absence of something required rather than the presence of something not required. Incompetent leaders are ineffective because they are lacking in particular qualities.
- **Malignant (leaders)** These are leaders who spread malevolence, the antonym of "benevolence". Malevolence is misconduct, doing harm such as maliciously causing pain or damage. Malignant leaders, like cancer, grow fast and are deadly.
- **Toxic (leaders)** This refers to the poisonous effect leaders have on all they touch. Toxic substances kill rather than repel. Again this refers to the consequences of a particular leadership style.
- **Tyrannical (leaders)** Tyrants show arbitrary, oppressive and unjust behavior. Tyrants tend to usurp power and then brutally oppress those they command.

Crudely these can be categorized as bad, sad and mad: *Bad* (dark side, despotic, destructive, malignant, toxic and destructive) implies their behavior or leadership style is evil, amoral, unjust; *Sad* (incompetent) implies that these leaders simply do not have the skills or abilities for the job; whilst *Mad* (aberrant, anti-social, derailed) suggests that the leaders are mentally unstable or psychologically maladjusted. Each will be explored in this book.

SOCIAL FORCES

It is easy to commit an attribution error in studying leaders. *First*, to try to understand leadership entirely as a set of intrapersonal factors and forces neglects the often powerful forces that impact on all leaders. *Second*, it can be attractive, depending on your perspective, to differentiate between good and bad leaders by explaining the origin of the former to be personal ability, temperament and morality, and the latter social forces over which they had little or no control.

Social psychologists insist that bad systems cause bad situations and processes that "approve", even demand, bad behaviors which are the manifestation of derailment.

It is too easy to stereotype writers and researchers for taking an overly "inside" or "outside" view. Even those well known for their work on personality correlates and determinants are happy to recognize the power and importance of other factors.

Some like Zimbardo (2007) want to downplay altogether the "bad person" cause. He and his fellow travellers argue that bad systems cause bad situations that sanction bad behavior – even in good people. This is to reverse the causal chain that bad people seem to cause bad situations and bad systems/processes lead to failure. Zimbardo (2007) wants to explain how "good" people do evil deeds. He does so with experimental and observational evidence.

Most of the toxic management literature, however, seeks to understand not so much how people become evil but, rather, how they become insensitive, arrogant, selfish and over-rash. However, it would be as short-sighted "straw-manning" to suggest that personality psychologists who stress internal factors totally ignore situational factors as it is to suggest that social psychologists refuse to accept the possibility that intrapersonal factors play a significant role.

Groups, as much as individuals, can be pathological. It is not uncommon for them to show dependency on a strong, hopefully wise, leader. Anxious, insecure and immature followers throw themselves on leaders waiting to be told what to do. They follow orders happily, but initiate nothing.

Senior management groups can also see the world as hostile and threatening. Their tendency is to see people as good or bad, friend or foe; sometimes to fight or to befriend. In essence, they externalize issues or problems by consistently blaming others for all their problems. It can also make them completely uncritical of the in-group, the "good guys", and very intolerant of those who do not share this view. Further anxious, alienated managers may form small groups or dyads in the hope that it will lead to synergy and their feeling more effective.

Essentially, groups adopt culturally prescribed defence mechanisms. These become an acceptable way to see the world. They become part of the corporate culture and deeply engrained in all the activities of the organization. In this way, one finds pathological organizations that may be overly suspicious or compulsive, or detached.

Padilla, Hogan and Kaiser (2007) use a simple but powerful analogy familiar to all those attempting their fire-fighter badge in the Boy Scouts. Combustion, heat and fire can start and continue only with three factors: fuel, heat and oxygen. Remove one of these and there is no fire in the first place. These factors have their equivalent in the toxic triangle, the first of which is the destructive, derailing, toxic leader. Next come the susceptible naïve or conformist followers and third, the conducive culture or environment that pre- or proscribes certain behaviors.

A few studies have begun to look at how managers relate to those above and below them, and how this in turn relates to derailment. For instance, Gentry and Shanock (2008) used a mix of equity and social exchange theory to come up with a "trickle-down" theory. Most middle managers by definition manage both up and down. The data suggest that they "pass down" their sense of fairness, justice and the like from those above them. If they are themselves put at their ease they do the same for others. Managers repay their staff by the way they themselves are managed. Thus the forces of derailment trickle down.

In short, you can understand derailment by focusing only on the characteristics of the leader. It is important to look at those who choose, obey and follow that leader as well as the context in which the whole process occurs.

CENTRAL ASSUMPTIONS

The central thesis of this book is based on five assumptions. The evidence for these axioms will be reviewed. They are derived from different sources and different disciplines.

Bad, mad, sad leader

The "first" is that it is important to distinguish between three fundamentally different causes of leadership as noted above. The first is sad management or leadership. Sad is incompetent. Sad, in this sense, is about poor judgment; about a lack of fundamental skills; about being rigid or dogmatic.

Sad leaders often fail because they are appointed by qualification rather than experience, or by nepotism or simply poor selection criteria. They fail because they are too short-term oriented or unable to understand or use office politics. They fail because they are conflict-averse, or micro-managers or emotionally uninsightful.

They fail most simply because they were unable to get things done. They make bad appointments of people whom they do not hold accountable for their performance. They cannot, do not or will not make timely decisions. They ignore market realities. In short, they are not good at handling business complexity; they cannot motivate and develop staff and/or they lose their way. Sad managers are, to sum up, incompetent.

Nearly forty years ago the psychologist Laurence Peter described the famous Peter Principle: "In any hierarchy, individuals tend to rise to their levels of incompetence". Although Peter's book was rejected by 13 publishers, when it was finally published, it became an immediate best-seller. Indeed, Peter made the concept of incompetence popular long before competence or incompetence was on anyone's mind.

Peter (1985) also set out a number of wickedly funny and often politically incorrect principles related to his general theme. Thus he noted:

> The *Competence* Principle: The way to avoid mistakes is to gain experience. The way to gain experience is to make mistakes.
>
> The *Sexist* Principle: Most hierarchies were established by men who monopolised the upper-levels, thus depriving women of their rightful share of opportunities to achieve their own levels of incompetence.
>
> The *Levitation* Principle: When a foundation of a pyramid erodes, the top can still be supported on nothing but money.
>
> The *Evaluation* Principle: Either super incompetence or super competence may be offensive to the establishment.
>
> The *Investment* Principle: Fools rush in where wise men fear to trade.
>
> The *Expectative* Principle: What happens is not only stranger than we imagine, it is stranger than we can imagine.

Peter (1985) deserves credit for writing the first books on managerial incompetence; they are full of wry and witty, and unfortunately true, observations. For instance:

> Individuals may be selected on a basis of competence, for their entry-level jobs, but as they move up they tend to become arranged just as

distribution theory would predict: the majority in the moderately competent group, with the competent and incompetent comprising the minorities, as illustrated in the graph.

There are two rare types of individuals who do not fit into this structure: the supercompetent and superincompetent. A supercompetent is usually someone who sees a better way of doing things.

(pp. 72–3)

Courtis (1986), in a book entitled *Managing by Mistake*, which also looked at sad management, noted "basic and essential management principles are being flouted everywhere ..." Mistakes made by incompetent managers fall crudely into five categories:

1. *errors of omission* (failure to act or communicate)
2. *errors of commission* (doing things you ought not to have done)
3. *qualitative errors* (doing the right thing inadequately or by the wrong method)
4. *errors of timing* (doing the right thing too early or too late)
5. *credibility errors* (doing the right thing, at the right time, but in such a way as to irritate everyone or discredit the action)

(p. ix)

Courtis believes that the corporate oversight of many boards of directors would be unnecessary if managers were doing their jobs correctly. The specific problem, according to Courtis, is that managerial incompetence causes employee stress, which then leads to illness and absenteeism, which in turn leads to greater costs to the company. Vicious circles like this are a function of managerial competence levels.

Whilst sad managers are the result of bad appointments, "mad" managers are the real focus of this book. They are not mad in the ordinary sense but near madness or subclinical pathology. This makes them both attractive and successful at times but ultimately leads to their derailment. Their dark side, usually well under control, comes out in times of stress and derails them.

Of the leaders who derail, most are not sad, but bad or mad. Sad, incompetent managers are too easy to spot. Often they do not have what it takes to rise up in the organization. It is bad and mad managers, who frequently are both, who are the real derailers. Bad managers – bullies, despots, tyrants – thrive in times of chaos, flux or uncertainty. Their toxicity and wickedness may quickly become apparent. Beware the bright, handsome, educated, conscience-free, supremely self-confident managers. They have the dark triad which will be considered in due course.

However, it should be recognized that life is not easy for any senior executive in the "limelight" in good times or bad. Kets de Vries (2006a) notes that there are consistent issues or themes which often "haunt" CEOs and have to be dealt with before changes were really possible. They include:

1. **Loss:** Often of a person, but also a job or indeed the hope of a job. This often leads to depression, grieving and psychosomatic illnesses. The CEO needs to break the depressive cycle, reframe the situation and "move on".
2. **Anxiety:** First becoming number one, then, paradoxically, coping with that position with the different demands as a public figure, decision-maker, etc.
3. **Interpersonal conflict:** Many with work colleagues but also friends and family. They are often the result of non-reciprocal expectations about their relationship. Initiating and sustaining authentic, meaningful and supportive relationships is clearly not simple.
4. **Symptomology:** By this, Kets de Vries (2006) means psychosomatic-type illness, behaviors and responses to stress, from insomnia to highly specific phobias. Stress causes the symptoms that lead to further distress which need to be managed.
5. **Developmental imbalance:** This refers to specific expectations being unfulfilled. It is usually about an unhappy or inadequate transition between roles.
6. **Life imbalance:** This is work–life balance where executives become increasingly estranged from their spouses, children and wider family.
7. **Questions about meaning:** This refers to doubts about the wisdom of the sacrifice made for worldly success. Perhaps selfishness and an over-exciting life have meant they are neither part of the community nor really contributing to it.

For Kets de Vries (2006a) the solution is unhooking false connection, which is about understanding the effect of the past on the present to see some of the discrepancies between self-rated abilities and reality and adopting a more appropriate thinking style that may involve catastrophizing helplessness or biased thinking. It also involves scrapping an imaginary list of "should"s, referring to how they think they and others should behave.

Once "insight" has come, Kets de Vries (2006a) recommends that executives regularly ask themselves three sets of questions which keep them from going astray:

1. What habitual defences (coping mechanisms) do I use to cope with stress and do they need changing?
2. How do I express and experience emotions and could I do this more appropriately?
3. How do I see myself and how honest, accurate is that perception?

The moral is simple: leadership is difficult and puts great demand even on the most talented. These pressures can easily "push people over the edge" to reveal some pathology or lack of integrity.

Subclinical pathology and the spectrum hypothesis

With very few exceptions, human characteristics are normally distributed among the entire species. Whether this comes to physical characters like height, human abilities like creativity or throwing a ball or psychopathology, we get a bell curve.

By definition, most people are "average" and in the middle, but a few are at the extremes. Just as very tall or short people can have significant physical problems, the same is true of personality traits. Thus very conscientious people can be plagued by obsessive compulsive disorder. Similarly, those very low on conscientiousness may find it difficult to keep a job because they are so unreliable.

Perhaps the best way to consider the issue is through the concept of self-esteem. This trait is dimensionally normally distributed among humans.

Most people have sufficient self-esteem or self-respect. Whilst they may periodically wrestle with self-doubt, they feel "OK" about themselves. Few leaders have low self-esteem though many have, quite naturally, some self-doubt that they hide but which may come into focus at unexpected times. Some leaders have average self-esteem. Most have high self-esteem. They believe in themselves and others likewise. It seems a requirement for recruitment, selection and promotion. Indeed, it is self-fulfilling.

The issue, however, is at the high positive end of the spectrum. When does high self-esteem become clinical narcissism? Where is

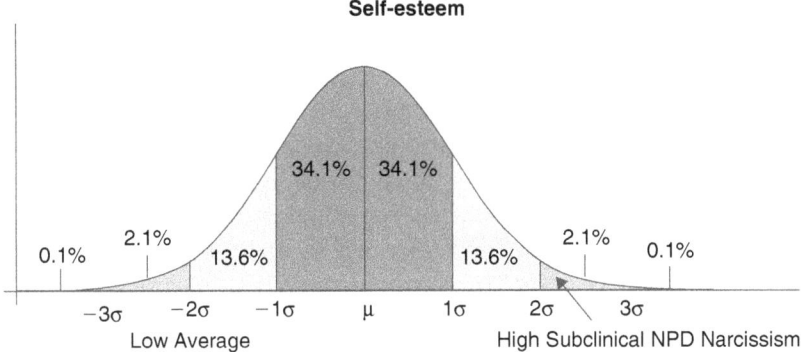

Self-esteem

34.1%   34.1%

0.1%   2.1%   13.6%   13.6%   2.1%   0.1%

−3σ   −2σ   −1σ   μ   1σ   2σ   3σ

Low Average   High Subclinical NPD Narcissism

Key: NPD – Narcissistic Personality Disorder

Figure 1.1 **The bell curve**

that thin line between healthy self-respect and belief and deluded narcissism? We shall see in Chapter 5 that, paradoxically, many clinical or subclinical narcissists have serious self-doubts and a range of unhealthy strategies to boost their self-esteem.

The psychoanalyst Karen Horney (1950) saw the essence of neurosis as a continued, self-defeating defence process. Neurotics create idealized self-images that mask underlying feelings of unworthiness, unattractiveness, unlovability. They devote more and more psychic energy to pretending and self-presenting as this perfect person. But as the idealized self grows more grandiose and distinct from the real self, they lose contact with their real feelings as well as their capacity for change and growth. Even if they attain some goals that are part of the idealized self-image, neurotics will not be satisfied. Further, the more neurotics make unfulfillable claims for deference and recognition to support the ego-ideal, the more enraged they become when it is not delivered.

Some leaders appear supercilious when threatened, others demand obedience and praise. High self-esteem is sometimes subclinical narcissism as manifested in pomposity, bullying and outrageous acts by leaders which is aimed to get followers to respect them and fuel their narcissism.

The spectrum hypothesis suggests that extremes of normality indicate abnormality. That is, healthy/unhealthy, mad/sane, adjusted/maladjusted are not categories but dimensions. Being extreme even on some apparently healthy trait may well indicate a problem. Being very creative may indeed indicate schizotypy, being very cold an indication of schizoid personality disorder. Unusually high or low scores make people not only different but inflexible. People in the middle, the vast majority, tend to be more adaptable. Most great leaders have extreme characteristics. They can, on occasion, be a great help and a great blessing. They can also be a curse because when leaders are under stress they can, in effect, be major derailers.

The interesting point about the personality disorders or dark side "traits" is the extent to which they can so easily be put on a dimension with a positive spin. Thus, arrogance is the flip or shadow side of confidence; melodrama the excess of charisma; volatility the extreme of energy, and excessive caution the excess of logic and analysis. Extreme critics become paranoid (habitual distrust) and very independent people aloof. Eccentrics can look like brilliant entrepreneurs, and mischievous people as creative innovators. The passive-aggressive can at first appear to have political savvy and even perfectionists can look really diligent.

The issue is now called "the spectrum hypothesis". It means that extreme normality is non-normality. By definition, people at extremes are rare/few and therefore not average or normal. Even factors thought to be beneficial and healthy can occur at extremes. Healthy high self-esteem becomes narcissism; out-of-the-box creative thinking becomes schizotypal; sociable, optimistic extraversion becomes impulsive hedonism. Lubit (2004) illustrates this idea in Table 1.1.

Kaplan and Kaiser (2006) express the same idea in their warning against positive psychology called "Stop overdoing your strengths". They talk about balance in the "what" and "how" of leadership. They see the tension in the strategic approach, which is future-oriented and creative, with the operational approach, which is about present efficiency, order and results. Similarly, they discuss the how of leadership, which contrasts the forceful style (giving directions, making decisions, holding people accountable), with the enabling style, which stresses inclusion, empowerment and support. It is not unusual, indeed now even encouraged, to overuse strengths because it leads to "lopsided" leadership. Kaplan and Kaiser note that the stronger one's preferences are for one particular style of leadership, inevitably so is one's distaste for its opposite. They also illustrate their idea by the famous inverted U curve showing that both too much and too little forcefulness leads to better team effectiveness.

This idea, whether called optimal or balance, is hardly new but needs to be discovered every time some management fad advocates a new "magic bullet" solution.

TABLE 1.1 Comparison of healthy self-esteem and destructive narcissism

Characteristic	Healthy self-esteem	Destructive narcissism
Self-confidence	High self-confidence in line with reality	Arrogant, self-absorbed, narcissistic
Desire for power, wealth, and admiration	Desires power but also cares about morality, other people, and personal relationships	Seeks extraordinary levels of success; pursues them at all costs; lacks normal inhibitions to their acquisition
Response to frustration	Able to deal with frustration with some setbacks, irritations, drawbacks	Frustration threatens self-esteem and leads to rage in which judgment goes awry and quite unpredictaby acts destructively to self and others
Relationships	Real concern for others' welfare, wellbeing and contribution	Concern limited to expressing socially appropriate response when convenient; devalues and exploits others without guilt, remorse or recompense
Attitude toward authority	Generally acceptable and respectful	Submits to authority rarely, superficially, hypocritically, either when temporarily idealizing a superior or believing that submitting will lead to concrete benefit; sees self as exempt from ordinary standard rules
Ability to follow a consistent path	Has values; follows through on plans, predictable	Lacks values; easily bored; often changes course
Foundation	Healthy childhood with steady growth of self-esteem and appropriate limits on behavior toward others	Traumatic childhood undercutting true sense of self-esteem and self-worth; learning that he or she does not need to be considerate to others

Source: Adapted from Lubit (2004).

The dark triad

As will be discussed at length in Chapter 3, whilst psychologists have looked at personality types and traits, psychiatrists have been more interested in personality disorders.

A number of books and papers on difficult, disturbed, dysfunctional or toxic leaders, managers or employees are clearly influenced by the literature on the personality disorders. It is no wonder authors are frequently psychologists (Miller, 2008), psychiatrists (Lubit, 2004) or psychoanalysts (Kets de Vries, 2006a). The "clinicians" emphasize "mad" whilst the sociologists, historians or social policy writers emphasize "bad" (Kellerman, 2004).

Hogan, Hogan and Kaiser (2009) used Horney's (1950s) early threefold classification of neurotic needs to classify the personality

15

disorders and explain how they relate to management derailment. They were:

1. Moving *towards* people in controlling anxiety by social contact and building alliances
2. Moving *away* from people – trying to manage anxiety and insecurities by avoiding people
3. Moving *against* people – managing self-doubts by dominating and intimidating people.

Prior to the dark triad of personality noted by Paulhus and Williams (2002), others also argued for a composite, subclinical trait or behavioral pattern linked to leadership failure.

Gustafson and Ritzer (1995) conceived of the concept called "aberrant self-promotion". Interestingly, they identify the same three related traits/disorders but weight them, rather than combine them, that is, see them as separate. Their starting point was the well-established two factors associated with clinical psyhopathy: grandiosity (lying, deception, lack of empathy, guilt and remorse) and socially deviant behavior (parasitism, impulsivity). They were interested in understanding subclincal pathology. They note:

> Aberrant self-promoters (ASPs), as hypothesized here, are individuals who, like psychopaths, exhibit such characteristics as exploitativeness, need for dominance, lack of empathy, and lack of guilt and who, *in addition*, violate accepted social norms, although the ASPs behaviour may or may not be technically illegal. In short, the difference between the ASP and the psychopath is one of *degree*, not *kind*. We have chosen the label "aberrant self-promoter" to underscore our theoretical position that these individuals' primary *raison d'être* is to further their own self-interests. Because such self-promotion is far less restrained than the achievement – or success-oriented behaviour generally accepted by western culture and because we believe the consequences of such self-promotion to be unremittingly negative, we have chosen to call it "aberrant".
>
> (p. 148)

They argue, interestingly, that the fundamental construct underlying the ASP is narcissism:

> In contrast to being motivated by the same factors that engender impression management, the hypothetical, narcissistic ASP does not

so much *want* to be liked as take for granted that he or she *is* liked, admired, or envied. In addition, ASPs, as we envision them, *assume* others will think them competent. Thus, the motives underlying impression management and aberrant self-promotion are presumed to be different, even though the behaviours themselves may overlap.

(p. 150).

Likewise, they note the similarity to the concept of Machiavellianism:

To the extent that "high Machs" are manipulative and are insensitive or indifferent to socially desirable responses, they are similar to the conceptualised ASPs. Nevertheless, we posit important differences between Machiavellianism and aberrant self-promotion. In general, Machiavellianism would seem to be more closely linked to the narcissistic, exploitative personality aspect of aberrant self-promotion than to the ASP's antisocial behaviour *per se*. ASPs, as conceptualized here, routinely subvert the organization's objectives in order to promote and protect themselves. In summary, although ASPs may engage in manipulative *behaviour* indistinguishable from that of a Machiavellian, a "pure" Machiavellian disengages from such behaviour when circumstances contraindicate it; the ASP, presumably, does not.

(p. 151)

The Personality Disorders Framework is in part an organizing structure for this book. Indeed it has inspired many researches in this field including Hogan and Kets de Vries. However, those working in the area have highlighted *three components* of the stereotypically derailing manager.

Canadian psychologists first identified what they called "dark triad of personality". Paulhus and Williams (2002) suggested three components make up the Dark Triad: two of those are technically personality disorders (Narcissism and Psychopathy), whilst another is a "regular" albeit dark personality trait (Machiavellianism).

Indeed, it has been demonstrated that these traits are intercorrelated. Another term for the Dark Triad is *subclinical psychopathy.* In this sense it is very similar to the idea of the successful psychopath.

The three interrelated features of the dark side are:

1. arrogance, self-centeredness, self-enhancement
2. duplicitousness, cynicism, manipulativeness

3. emotionally cold, impulsive thrill-seeking and frequently engaged in illegal, dangerous, anti-social behavior.

Yet Machiavellians differ from clinical Narcissists and Psychopaths because of the lack of extreme clinical behaviors. Indeed, Babiak and Hare (2006) described psychopathy as the *mean side* of the Dark Triad. Dark side managers cheat and lie; they plagiarize and are known for their social deviance. But it is usually never extreme enough to warrant imprisonment nor even dismissal. They are characterized by constant, low-level, deviousness.

Most researchers have found that, when measured separately, there does seem to be a reasonable correlation between these three traits. Certainly the data suggest that there is always an overlap between Machiavellianism and Subclinical Psychopathy, though two studies have *not* found that these two traits correlated with Narcissism (Lee and Ashton, 2005; Vernon *et al.*, 2008). Overall, however, there seems sufficient evidence that these three features are sufficiently related to describe the Dark Triad as a recognizable syndrome, type or disorder. In the 2002 paper Paulhus and Williams note:

> Despite their diverse origins, the personalities composing this "Dark Triad" share a number of features. To varying degrees, all three entail a socially malevolent character with behaviour tendencies toward self-promotion, emotional coldness, duplicity, and aggressiveness. In the clinical literature, the links among the triad have been noted for some time. The recent development of non-clinical measures of all three constructs has permitted the evaluation of empirical associations in normal populations. As a result, there is now empirical evidence for the overlap of (a) Machiavellianism with psychopathy, (b) Narcissism with psychopathy, and (c) Machiavellianism with narcissism. Given such associations, the possibility arises that, in normal samples, the Dark Triad of constructs may be equivalent.
>
> (p. 557)

This research has stimulated other investigations in the area. Jakobwitz and Egan (2006) note that it could be argued that all three traits can confer some social advantage on individuals. They found, as predicted, that dark side people tended to be both disagreeable and lacking in conscientiousness. They believe the primary "normal" trait identifier of the dark side is low agreeableness, tough-mindedness, non-empathy and coldness. A secondary feature is high on Neuroticism and low on Conscientiousness, which leads to bad decision-making because of both an impulsive need for gratification and a sense of entitlement.

Vernon *et al.* (2008) conducted a genetic investigation into the Dark Triad. They report that there are genetic studies on both psychopaths and narcissists so that it may be expected to find some clear indicator of the heritability of the dark side. They found, as had previous studies, that psychopathy's and narcissism's components/traits were clearly heritable but that Machiavellianism's was much less so. Later they note:

> as for fundamental personality features, our findings suggest that in non-clinical samples, members of the Dark Triad share a common core of disagreeableness. Thus the root of their social destructiveness is disturbingly normal – even banal. In combination with disagreeableness, the minimal anxiety of psychopaths may make them the most treacherous of the three – even within the normal range of personality found in our sample. Our more recent work has supported this fear. A wide variety of self-report and behavioural measures of antisocial behaviour were significantly predicted by psychopathy but not Machiavellianism or narcissism.
>
> (p. 561)

They argue that Machiavellian-like behaviors are to some extent learnt rather than transferred genetically.

The question is, therefore, where those behaviors are learnt: at home, school and the workplace. Some schools are known effectively to encourage Machiavellianism even if they purport to do the opposite. The same is true of workplaces where managers sometimes, in order to survive personally, act in ways that are ruthlessly and cynically Machiavellian.

Jonason *et al.* (2008) noted that researchers on the Dark Triad have suggested that, paradoxically perhaps, it could be seen to be advantageous. Being cool under fire means anxiety does not effect one in adverse conditions. Being socially confident allows one to make many acquaintances. As a result, they looked to the "short-term mating strategy" in men.

More recently, Hodson and colleagues (2009) showed how dark side personalities are highly prejudiced. Dark side personalities endorse social dominance views.

The argument is this: Dark Triad traits facilitate exploiting others in short-term social contexts because:

- Narcissists are agentic, dominant, eager for power
- Machiavellians can be exploitative charmers
- Psychopaths have an exploitative nature.

"People of the Dark Triad" are high in self-interest but low in empathy. They are therefore not interested in, well suited for, or good at, long-term relationships where a degree of reciprocity is called for. They get found out and so prefer a "hit-and-run" strategy.

Thus it may be expected that dark triad people are promiscuous; sexually coercive; prone to, and have, unrestricted socio-sexuality. They are, the authors argue, likely to be more interested in short-term mating. Inevitably, this strategy works better for men than for women. It is no wonder then that some of our best-known and often revered great leaders have turned out later to be so sexually active and promiscuous.

Hodson and colleagues (2009) tested their hypothesis by looking at the dark side and four measures of mating. The more dark side traits a young male had, the higher he scored on:

- socio-sexuality – liberal, open sexual attitudes and behaviors
- number of sexual partners
- seeking behavior for a short-term mate.

People with dark side traits have more casual sex. However, the authors most interestingly speculate about the adaptive success of this strategy. They argue from an evolutionary perspective that having the Dark Triad profile may be highly adaptive because it leads to more productive success and that is heritable. Thus, Dark Triad individuals have more sexual partners and, therefore, more chance of reproductive success and the passing on of their genes. Thus, from an evolutionary point of view, one would expect the genes to be more likely to be perpetuated.

The second section of this book is indeed dedicated to the three components of the Dark Triad.

The toxic triangle

The fourth assumption is that there are always three components to the issue of derailment. They each play a crucial part in the unfolding of the drama. They are the nature (ability, personality, values) of the leader;

the nature (hopes, fears, motives) of those that follow him/her; *and* the particular socio-political and economic environment of the time.

Would Hitler have been a successful political leader in Britain? Would Churchill have been elected Prime Minister had war not been declared? What made Gandhi's style of leadership so successful? Who followed Mother Teresa and why? Would white South Africans have "accepted" anyone other than Nelson Mandela?

Social psychologists have talked about the "attribution error". It means that observers tend to explain the behavior of others in terms of the personal characteristics (abilities, personality, moral values) whilst they tend to explain their own behavior in terms of external situational forces acting upon them. Their argument against differential or personality psychologists is that they overestimate individual causal factors whilst simultaneously underestimating external social factors. Thus, both successful and unsuccessful leaders are described and "explained" in terms of their personal make-up whilst less is made of the social forces that helped or hindered them. These include the group dynamics of the top team.

Famous social psychological studies have made this point. The celebrated Milgram obedience study showed how "nice, normal, adjusted, educated" people were coerced into doing evil acts. The same theme has been pursued by Zimbardo in his work on behavior in prisons. He argues for the banality of both evil and heroism. That is, that powerful and often underestimated social pressures can induce the most ordinary individual to commit acts of evil and courage; selfishness and kindness; egocentrism and selflessness. Further, that these acts, particularly heroism, are far from rare or exceptional.

Social psychologists in particular, but also management theorists, have noted that destructive or toxic leadership requires three components: the confluence of a particular type of leader, follower and environmental factors. Padilla and colleagues (2007) argued that destructive leadership is a process that depends on a very particular *toxic triangle*. They note that bad leadership can be put on a single dimension which is effectively the sad–bad dimension, though they do state (2007: 17):

1. Destructive leadership is seldom absolutely or entirely destructive: there are both good and bad results in most leadership situations.
2. The process of destructive leadership involves dominance, coercion, and manipulation rather than influence, persuasion, and commitment.

3. The process of destructive leadership has a selfish orientation; it is focused more on the leader's needs than the needs of the larger social group.
4. The effects of destructive leadership are outcomes that compromise the quality of life for constituents and detract from the organization's main purposes.
5. Destructive organizational outcomes are not exclusively the result of destructive leaders, but are also products of susceptible followers and conducive environments.

The central idea is that the followers "conspire" with bad leaders and particular situations. They encourage, allow, and even require, destructive leadership styles rather than prevent them. Dictators, on the other hand, run roughshod over their "followers", ignoring their petitions and needs. Further, they change the situation (political environment) to suit their needs. By definition, destructive leadership destroys. It can lead to a demoralized workforce, environmental disasters, and failed countries. Whole economies can be brought down by single individuals (i.e. Robert Mugabe).

Padilla and colleagues (2007) argue thus: leadership is "a functional resource for group performance; it involves influencing individuals to forgo, for a limited time, their selfish, short-term interests and

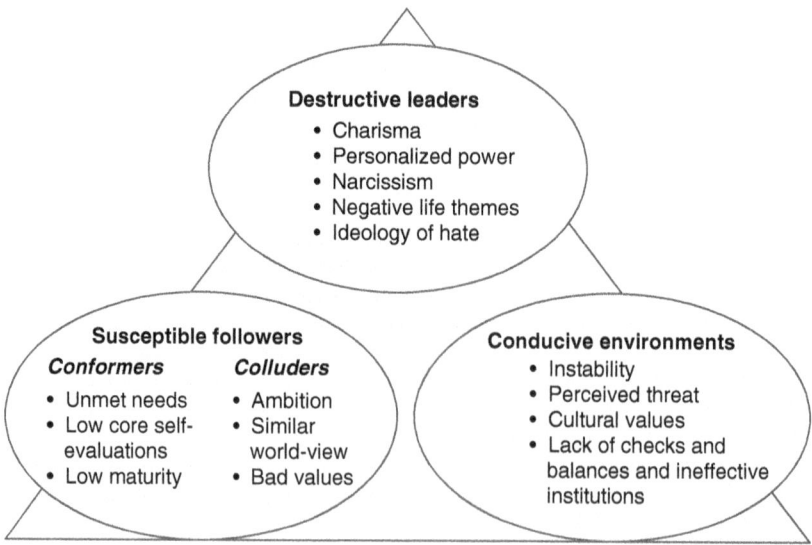

Figure 1.2 **The toxic triangle: elements in three domains related to destructive leadership**

contribute to long-term goals within an environmental or situational context" (p. 178). Leaders unite, direct, coordinate people to achieve a goal.

Toxic, destructive, failed leadership is definable in terms of its (organizational) outcomes. In this sense, leaders alone – however evil, egocentric or insane – do not bring about destruction. Certainly, they tend to be controlling and coercive rather than committed and persuasive. Most of all, they tend to be selfish rather than being interested in developing, empowering or encouraging others. They tend to compromise the quality of life of nearly all of their followers and take their eye off the ball.

So, destructive leaders are dependent on susceptible followers and conducive environments. Padilla and colleagues (2007) have a simple model of their approach.

This model indentifies particular salient features or characteristics of the three parts of the model. They identify five parts to the *individual* part; namely, the characteristics of destructive leaders.

Toxic leaders

- **Charisma**: self-presentation skills, personal energy, limiting the communication of criticism and dissent. Skilled at impression management and apparently indefatigable.
- **Personal need for power**: unethically, continually focused on personal gain and self-promotion. Often involving needs for authority, security and belongingness.
- **Narcissism**: arrogance, dominance, entitlement and grandiosity often are part of aggressive exploitative personal relationship. Selfish and self-absorbed, they are intolerant and autocratic.
- **Negative life themes**: this is a destructive view of the world and his/her role in that world. Due to a deprived, violent, chaotic or abusive childhood these leaders have experienced pain and helplessness. Hence they may believe coercive influence techniques are the only ones which work.
- **Ideology of hate**: this may be self-hatred turned outwards, a generalized hate of authority. Hate is used to legitimize anger and resentment.

Toxic followers

Equally, the model has various facets of the toxic followers. Many have attempted to categorize these into different groups such as bystanders, acolytes, true believers or more simply conformers and colluders. Conformers tend to be immature, with negative self-concept, whilst colluders are more selfish, ambitious, destructive and openly support-ive of toxic tyrants.

- **Negative core self-evaluation**: these followers have low self-esteem which they hope the leader will improve. They also tend to be helpless and fatalistic, hoping the leader will give them power and influence. Toxic leaders reinforce their sense of passivity whilst giving them hope of escape.
- **Low maturity**: this means the super-ego, the sense of right and wrong; conformity to immoral behavior dictated by the leader occurs. Vulnerable, immature, impressionable adults make good followers of strong, but destructive leaders.
- **Ambition**: people with ambitions for status and land make better followers. The more they see there is psychological and material profit to be had in following, the quicker and happier they are to follow.
- **Congruent values and beliefs**: this is the similarity-attraction argu-ment. Simply, followers who share world views with those of the destructive leader are naturally more likely to follow them.
- **Unsocial values**: these are things like greed and selfishness. Under-socialized or morally under-developed people are happy to endorse the violence of toxic leaders.

Toxic environment

The model of Padilla and colleagues (2007) suggests four facets of what they call conducive environments:

1. **Instability**: political, economic and social instability are very fright-ening. Toxic leaders exploit fluidity, advocating radical means to restore peace, harmony and progress. They get granted excessive authority and power that they are reluctant to relinquish.
2. **Perceived threat**: the more people feel personally threatened, the more internal and external enemies they see around, then the happier they are to follow toxic leaders who promise them security.
3. **Cultural values**: cultures that are uncomfortable around ambiguity and uncertainty; those that have elaborate rules and rituals which offer easy solutions to complex problems are easier for toxic leaders to control. Further, there is more disparity between rich and poor, educated and uneducated, high and low status.

4. **Absence of checks and balances**: where power is centralized and those monitoring authority and responsibility are silenced. This is like removing the internal audit from the organization. It means the end of constraint and monitoring.

Conducive environments can lead to the emergence of toxic leaders who, through propaganda and the elimination of rivals, make the environment even more conducive to their approach. There are, according to Padilla and colleagues (2007), three implications for practice. The *first* is sensitive and insightful leader selection and development. This includes looking at past history, moral and ethical standards and dark side personality traits. The *second* is straightening and empowering followers. The *third* is promoting integrity and honesty through policies and procedures.

Most people have experienced a dysfunctional workplace. They are marked by bullying, organizational deviance, lack of trust, absenteeism, inefficiency and many other symptoms of distress.

The questions are what causes and maintains the dysfunctional workplace and how to manage the way out of the situation. They are, of course, enormously complex issues. Inevitably, therefore, different researches have focused on different features or facets of the problem. They can perhaps be divided into different areas.

Some organizations become dysfunctional because certain processes or behavioral patterns are absent. Rate and Sternberg (2007) claim a major cause is *management cowardice*: when good people do nothing. Whole groups (i.e. boards) can and do collude to deny, overlook or "work around" crucial, acute and chronic issues. They are, in short, spineless, gutless or frozen. Courage, they argue, is not the same as boldness or intrepidness because those concepts do not sufficiently pick up themes associated with honor and worthiness. The core components are that people act intentionally and deliberately, despite personal fear, and knowing that there are substantial risks to achieving a "noble good". The idea is that leaders or groups who provide no models of courageously moral leadership can and do cause dysfunctionality in the sense of reduced effectiveness and efficiency.

Kellerman (2004) believes that in modern times it is "more likely now than it was in the past that bad leaders – leaders who are ineffective, unethical or both – will be held to account" (p. 229).

She argues that more and more corporate leaders are being "pushed out" in record numbers. She notes 100 CEOs of the 2500 world's largest companies were "replaced" in 2002, four times the number in 1995.

She believes this speaks to the new "deliver or depart" ethos. She also argues that "*'extreme'* greed is now *likely* to be *considered* a punishable offence" (p. 231) (my italics).

Kellerman (2004) continues: "Convictions, dismissals, recall movements and forced resignations such as these seem to signal a growing intolerance of bad leadership, as well as a trend in which bad leaders and followers are increasingly held to account. But let's not kid ourselves. Change is slow" (p. 231).

Her argument is that bad leadership continues as long as bad followership exists. Followers must take responsibility for rewarding good leaders and punishing bad ones.

Followers sustain and support evil, incompetent, pathological leaders. Kellerman (2004) says they can avoid bad leaders by personal empowerment and being loyal to the whole rather than to individuals. They need to be attentive, courageous and skeptical. They need to take collective action with allies and always ensure the punishment fits the crime. It is, she argues, their role to be a watchdog and to ensure that leaders are held to account.

In this book the focus is on the nature of the leaders themselves. However, it is recognized that the other two components of the toxic triangle have to be in place for total derailment to occur.

Appointment errors

The relatively high incidence of leaders failing is based on three linked factors: poor selection, paradoxical derailers and the idea of "too much of a good thing".

Leaders fail for many reasons of course. They may be "ambushed" and "assassinated" by their followers. The organizations they lead may, for socio-economic and political reasons, be doomed to failure. They may be caught up in an ideological battle they cannot win. A leader's team may themselves be incompetent, callous or malevolent. They may have "problems with authority". They may have a long history of making things difficult for people. Leaders may fail because of corporate governance problems. Checks and balances are not in place. Equally, the leader might inherit a difficult-to-change and patently sick corporate culture.

People promoted within may be severely constrained by issues associated with corporate governance. Leaders promoted from within may have either or both very limited experience of the world or, worse, few if any good role models. Leaders have to deal with significant amounts of stress. This can also easily break them.

Judge and LePine (2009) note that there can be a dark and a bright side to both dark and bright traits. In other words, supposedly desirable, bright, healthy traits like agreeableness can have costs (i.e. conflict aversion, lacking in ambition) whilst dark side traits like hostility can have benefits like higher levels of task performance. Others too have made distinctions between good and bad extraversion or functional and dysfunctional impulsivity. The implication for selection is important: namely, to consider the idea that there may be downsides to apparently positive traits, particularly when they are at extreme levels *and* vice versa.

However, it is contended here that there are three consistent factors which influence derailment.

Selecting in and screening out

Now, more than ever, we are getting used to the idea of screening out people who volunteer or are required to work with children, with highly sensitive information or under conditions where safety is paramount. Police officers in Great Britain who have firearms, those in government security services, even Boy Scouts and Girl Guides leaders are thoroughly "checked out".

Traditionally, the areas of concern (red flags) include alcohol and drug abuse, a criminal record, conflicts with authority, misconduct, chronic financial problems, abnormal sexual interests and habits, poor and inconsistent performance. A particular interest for psychologists has been how people handle anger and frustration. However, it is rare for chief executives, military or political leaders to experience any selecting-out process.

The simple box in Figure 1.3 illustrates the issue. The aim of selection is to accept and select good candidates (A) whilst rejecting the bad, less able or less suitable (D). But selectors make mistakes. Nearly everyone

	GOOD	BAD
SELECT	A	B
REJECT	C	D

Figure 1.3 **A simple selection model**

has made a bad selection decision and lived to regret their error (B). Few know about the other common mistake, which is when they reject a candidate who later turns out to be the ideal candidate (C).

The traditional selection procedure, whether it used structured or unstructured interview, assessment centers, references or tests, nearly always starts, and certainly should start out, with a necessary and sufficient set of abilities, competences or skills deemed appropriate for the job. In short, you specify what you are looking for, and then seek evidence for those factors. So a competence may be team-work or creativity and the process aimed to determine as accurately as possible how much of this trait the person has. If they have enough this is deemed to be a part factor in favour of their successful application.

But what of select out? Most people are not selected because they don't have enough of some skills or competency. It is comparatively rare for selectors to have a set of select-out factors that they actively look for. These may be things like impulsivity or obsessionality, arrogance or volatility. Some people may argue that not having enough of a quality like integrity or honesty implies the presence of a select-out factor. However, if you are not a brilliant scholar this does not mean that you are dim. If you are not strongly creative, it does not mean that you are totally lacking in creativity.

It is centrally important to look for evidence of things you do not want. Few organizations think like this and fewer actually have select-out processes. The consequences are often that leaders with potential derailers sail through. Indeed, as will be noted paradoxically, some of their derailers may actually assist them in the selection process.

Too much of a good thing

Most psychiatrists accept that although the DSM (Diagnostic and Statistical Manual) system (APA, 1994) is categorical and "caseness" oriented (i.e. you are or are not a case), really it is preferable to think of dimensions. So disorders are simply exaggerated styles. Oldham and Morris (2000) called this "too much of a bad thing". They note the distinction between Axis II (personality disorders) and Axis I disorders (like depression), the latter of which are often very biological in nature and treated by medication. Personality disorders are chronic conditions that can make people vulnerable to other clinical conditions ranging from anxiety to drug addiction.

Many people believe there is a linear relationship between a "virtue" and success. The more the merrier. However, it is clearly apparent that leaders can be too vigilant, too tough, too hardworking. Selection errors occur because of linear, rather than cut-off thinking. Too much of a good thing becomes a bad thing.

All leaders have to climb some "greasy pole" in their careers. They need to be chosen and selected. They need to learn the skills of the job. They need to learn corporate culture and corporate politics. They need to read and befriend people. They need courage to take risks. They need to know how to communicate and motivate.

The paradox of many failed leaders is precisely that those factors which help them come to prominence are those that ultimately derail them. The confident good-looking manager may easily turn into the arrogant, narcissistic leader. The bold, mover-and-shaker may easily become the psychopathic chairman. The vigilant managers may later become the corporate paranoid. Beware the articulate, good-looking, confident and fearless (and ambitious) young manager. You may soon have on your hands a narcissistic psychopath.

People succeed in reaching the top through ability, effort and will. Their need to succeed is essentially healthy. It is a driver. But it may not be linked to ability, or indeed be easily satisfied. Need for achievement may lead to pathological ambition. No one succeeds without hard work. But what sort of hard work? And directed at whom for what end?

Retrospective studies of derailment reveal what McCall (1998) names "organizational complicity". The technically innovative, deal-closing, client-attracting senior executives seem worth their weight in gold. They grow the company, stimulate innovation, cut costs. Frequently, the personal history "whiz-kids" with a history of success, may (and usually docs) reveals a slightly less successful side and that is the "soft stuff".

Many derailed leaders are (at least retrospectively) known for their little foibles and peculiarities. It is often about social skills and emotional regulation. They may have temper tantrums or resort to sarcasm or bullying when frustrated. They overreact. They find the blame for everything lies with others.

LISTS AND SPECULATIONS

It is not difficult to come up with a short-list of characteristics which cause derailment. Most people have worked for an over-promoted, haloed high-flyer who simply failed to deliver. Typical factors include:

- Problems with interpersonal relationships; poor social/interpersonal skills, low emotional intelligence. Poor at reading, understanding and inspiring people
- Not achieving goals and targets by not following through, being overly cautious. Not being willing or able to achieve organizational objectives
- Failure to form, build, motivate and lead teams. Being egocentric, isolated or not able to understand and shape group dynamics
- Inability to change or adapt to new circumstances, new technology, new structures or new adversities. Unwilling or unable to understand and respond to new environments
- Being too ambitious, trying to do too much too quickly but more importantly for one's own ends rather than for the benefit of the stakeholders of the whole organization
- Complacent, idle, self-satisfied leaders who are content to let issues drift. This is only really likely to occur in "good times" of peace and prosperity or when the leader's pension pot is secure
- Conflict with all those around them based either on low level paranoia or failure to trust others sufficiently. Equally, the conflict could arise through the dogged pursuit of ideas that no one else believes in.
- Narrow functional orientation usually associated with "letting go" their original specialism, be it in engineering, finance or sales, to take on general management with its emphasis on strategy.

There are many reasons why potential leaders fail:

- Short-termism of greedy but inexperienced, often very smart, managers just out of business school
- Clever, rigid, technical managers who are often analytically very able but unable to persuade others to follow them or adopt their strategies
- Mild-mannered, agreeable types unable to deal with conflict or unable to assert their authority over unruly staff
- Micro-managing "control freaks" who alienate, de-skill and demotivate all those around them
- Rebellious, creative individualists who, for its own sake, enjoy rule breaking and shocking others

- Self-defeating, imposter-syndrome managers who feel they somehow do not deserve the success that they have achieved.

They tend to be categorized by one of a number of different issues. Greed, speed and entitlement; lack of self-awareness; fear of disapproval and disagreement; or masked low self-confidence.

In a review of the dark side leadership derailment literature, Burke (2006) provides lists of factors that he or others have identified as leading to failure. He begins with:

There are some common notions about leadership failure:

- Failing leaders were stupid and incompetent – lacking in talent. Most leaders are very intelligent and have considerable industry-specific knowledge.
- Failing leaders were caught by unforeseen events. The available evidence does not support this as a cause of leadership failure.
- Failing leaders exhibited a failure to execute.
- Failing leaders weren't trying or working hard enough.
- Failing leaders lacked leadership ability. All were unable to get people to follow the course of action that was set.
- The company lacked the necessary resources. Not supported in fact.
- Failing leaders were a bunch of crooks.

(p. 92)

Burke then reviews Kellerman's (2004) list, which has seven types (incompetent, rigid, intemperate, callous, corrupt, insular and evil) that fall under two headings: ineffective and unethical. He also lists five derailers identified by Fulmer and Conger (2004):

1. Failing to deliver results:
   - Fails to hold self and others accountable for results
   - Overpromises and underdelivers
2. Betraying trust:
   - Says one thing and does another
   - Makes excuses or blames others
   - Shades, manages, withholds information to promote his/her personal or functional agenda

3. Resisting change:
   - Has trouble with adapting to new plans, programs or priorities
   - Being exclusive vs inclusive
   - Fails to understand and take into account others' perspectives
   - Devalues the opinions and suggestions of others
   - Fails to engage others with different perspectives or skills than him/herself
4. Failing to take a stand:
   - Is indecisive
   - Stays on the fence on tough issues: won't weigh in until the boss weighs in
5. Over-leading and undermanaging:
   - Lets details fall through the cracks
   - Fails to get involved with the day-to-day workings of the business unit.

Various other lists are mentioned, many heavily influenced by the work of Hogan and Hogan (1997).

Rather than resolve the difference between writers, Burke concludes that there remain many unanswered questions. Do certain deficiencies (e.g. arrogance) matter more later in one's career than earlier? Can a strength become a weakness (strong leadership of subordinates leading to a narrow focus)? Are some patterns of strengths and weaknesses acceptable whilst others are fatal (brilliant but insensitive might derail, whilst organizational savvy but insensitive might not)? Are there some flaws operating in the same way at upper and lower organizational levels (success and derailment). Some flaws (emotional instability, arrogance, abrasiveness) may be more critical at upper levels because the jobs are larger and more complex, the stakes higher and the costs of failure greater.

CONCLUSION

The time has come to see the Elephant in the Board Room; the fact that the emperor has no clothes. The taboo of admitting selection and appointment errors has for too long meant bad, mad and sad leaders have continued *in situ* often wreaking short- and long-term damage on organizations.

Some leadership positions are incredibly difficult to perform in. People are handed a poisoned chalice and they expectedly, often deliberately, fail. Leadership is a great skill and art. It can test people to the limits of their abilities, endurance and stamina. There are indeed cases of exceptionally brave, skilful and wise leaders. Often they are mavericks who triumphed in unusual circumstances. Yet there are lessons to be learnt from those whose stars rose high in the firmament but exploded unexpectedly.

The assumptions of this book are as follows: it is possible to differentiate between bad, mad and sad leaders. This book is primarily about the first two. Often, leaders have a surfeit of particular abilities and preferences that at once make them very desirable but potentially weak. The real danger lies in the arrogant, anti-social, Machiavellian who is often easily able to "cover up" his or her real self. Yet derailment is as much a function of followers as it is of leaders, of "conducive" environments and poor governance mechanisms as it is about sad and mad individuals. Finally, by always selecting in and never selecting out, organizations continue to make themselves vulnerable to appointing yet another elephant in the board room.

2

EARLY RESEARCH AND SPECULATIONS

INTRODUCTION

This chapter will look at, first, the early research and management failure. It will also look at more recent popular writings and provide a very quick overview concerning the extensive literature on leadership. Historians have always been interested in evil, despotic and destructive leaders. Psychoanalysts have also been happily exploring the dark side of leaders. But, as noted earlier, popular interest in leadership failure remains a modern concern. This is not necessarily because modern senior management jobs are more complex, or that through media attention we are becoming much more aware of the whole issue of derailment. It may be that followers want to believe in heroic leaders, and books about success outsell books on failure.

THE HISTORY OF INCOMPETENT LEADER RESEARCH

The work on derailed leaders is comparatively new. There seem to be four identifiable, but linked, strands in the literature:

- Early longitudinal research which followed "normal and ordinary" business leaders and executives over time and documented various incidents of derailment. The best-known person to do this research was Bentz (1967; 1990).
- The US Center for Creative Leadership, which is still celebrated for its imaginative studies of the difference between successful and derailed executives. The most important studies in order of appearance are: McCall and Lombardo (1983), Lombardo and colleagues (1988), McCauley and Lombardo (1990), McCall (1998), and Lombardo and Eichinger (1999; 2006). These studies focused not on having too few of the desirable characteristics but rather on having too many undesirable characteristics.

- Historical surveys of famous failures. This is best epitomized in Dixon's (1972) book on military failure.
- Studies inspired by the personality disorders research, often called "the dark side". This has been rigorously and imaginatively pursued by Hogan for many years (Hogan and Hogan, 1997, 2001; Hogan *et al.*, 2009).

One of the most celebrated early studies on leadership derailment was published over 40 years ago and was an in-depth study of a particular company – Sears, Roebuck & Company. Bentz (1967) showed the typical profile of the then executive population based on various psychometric tests used at the time. It showed executives to be bright, sociable, self-confident and objective but not very reflective, agreeable or interested in aesthetics. He noted that executives' primary goals appeared to be setting up and maintaining a long-term career strategy. They were quite prepared to put up with many adverse conditions as long as it did not threaten these long-term goals. Advancement, compensation, status and recognition were clearly their personal major goals.

Bentz (1967) reported on the unique, predictive studies that attempted to identify talent among new entry managers. Using ability and personality tests they distinguished between a promoted and non-promoted group. More interestingly and uniquely, however, they contrasted 102 successes and 68 failures in the young executives noted for their outstanding merit. One significant and distinguishing factor was that the *failures were less bright*. They were also different in temperament. The less successful/failed executives were more sociable but prone to depression and scored lower on general activity, social leadership and dominance. They were less political and less interested in persuasive and artistic pursuits:

> Here it is especially interesting to note the strength of those variables representing emotional stability as well as social skills and leadership ability. Apparently these variables contribute heavily to the prediction of executive failure. I should also say that when these kinds of studies have been repeated in other situations, the results have generally been corroborative.
>
> (p. 172)

They showed a table with multiple correlations between job success/failure and six areas: emotional stability (0.66); social skills and leadership (0.56); vocational interests (0.31); mental ability (0.29); administrative skills (0.20); and personal drive and competitiveness (0.17).

They then turned their attention to which manager characteristics best predicted store morale as they were working in a retail environment. Personal contact and social distance were crucial to good morale: "Thus, the finding of this research clearly indicates that psychological characteristics of leaders are important determinants of employee morale; the generalization appears to hold that the behavior of the executive in charge of the unit is a crucial determinant of employee morale" (p. 177).

Next, this remarkable study looked at how the psychological profiles of managers predicted their success or failure on specialized executive assignments. Taking into account the complexity of the assignment, they found clear correlates of success including linguistic ability, sociability, optimism, social leadership, dominance and self-confidence. Another in-house study looked at the characteristics of those executives rated as highly mobile within the company. The same pattern emerged: *bright, sociable, dominant mangers were most successful.*

In summary, Bentz (1967) did a mini-meta-analysis of the seven studies on executives. The results were clear. Problem solving and linguistic ability (i.e. fluid and crystallized intelligence) were consistent predictors of success and failure. Of the personality variables, it was social leadership, sociability, general activity, dominance, self-confidence and tolerance that also consistently predicted successful performance. His conclusion was thus:

> Aside from this overriding generalization, it seems to me our work at Sears has pertinence in terms of the following:
>
> 1. Occupational self-realization is a paramount value of executives. Their outlook embraces a long-term career orientation and, since the executive takes for himself the responsibility of co-acting with his peers and superiors in pursuits that are goal-oriented, it can be assumed that he will take a large part of the initiative for his own self-development. Perhaps it is obvious, but developmental programmes are likely to stand a better chance of being effective if they are perceived as vehicles toward enhancement of the executives' long-term career expectations.
>
> 2. A major personality characteristic of executives is a competitive drive for positions of eminence and authority: the need to be recognized as men of influence and status, the ambition to govern, and the desire to excel – these provide a strong impetus toward personal fulfilment and self-realisation. It is logical

to assume that these qualities of motivation underlie much of the executive's long-term career orientation. As a consequence, developmental experiences are likely to be positively initiated or undertaken with enthusiasm if they are set within this mobility-oriented, highly competitive, status-related value system.

3. Executives are problem solvers of a reasonably high order. This intellectual superiority is a necessary factor in their make-up: it makes for ready absorption of complex material, along with the possibility of becoming the kind of continuous learners that long-term mobility and career progress demand.

4. The executive assignment is one that is basically social in nature. Social competence is as necessary to the executive as is typing skill to the secretary. He who lacks social skills has to dig deep into this cache of psychic energies if he is to make his way in an assignment whose basic nature involves getting things done with and through people.

5. The executive life is one that is filled with ambiguities; it is emotionally rigorous. Thus, emotional strength and stamina are mandatory prerequisites for coping with an ever-shifting, ever changing environment.

6. A close association with reality, the ability to review situations in the objective light of their occurrence, the capacity to relate to people and situations without emotional involvement is a measurable quality of being that might well be viewed as a necessary prerequisite for executive effectiveness.

7. Finally, our work indicates that the characteristics predictive of executive success in specialized assignments are nearly identical to those predicting success in more general executive positions. This generality in the prediction of executive effectiveness has significant implications for executive selection, development and mobility.

(pp. 185–8)

In the final section of this most interesting of chapters, Bentz (1967) noted the challenges for the company in a period of considerable growth and expansion. He believed this called for even more successful managers and noted the following: finding intelligent people was crucial. Next, they needed to find good robust measures of administrative decision-making. Third, they needed measures of openness to change, flexibility and creativity. Fourth, they recognized the importance of stability – which they called emotional strength, as part of the "competitive personality".

Inevitably, the language and explanations differ between different writers from different empirical traditions. However, as Hogan and colleagues (2009) note in their excellent review, there are clear themes. They also note: "Derailment can almost always be traced to relationship problems. When relationships are strong, people will forgive mistakes. But when relationships erode, tolerance disappears and mistakes will get a manager fired" (p. 16).

In one of the first studies on upper-level derailment, Lombardo, Rinderman and McCauley (1988) started out defining derailment as being "involuntarily plateaued, demoted or fired below the level of anticipated achievement or reaching that level only to fail unexpectedly" (p. 199).

They note various previous studies that highlight different factors:

- poor at agenda setting and networking
- trouble establishing good relationships with key people
- not realizing that early strengths (technical prowess) can become weaknesses because of over-reliance
- inability to work well with peers
- bad luck, such as taking over in a down-turn.

In their study of executives within the same organizations they found eight factors that differentiated the successful from the derailed. They were:

- ability to handle business complexity – learn quickly, think strategically, absorb technical knowledge
- ability to direct, develop and motivate subordinates and build a good relationship with them
- integrity, loyalty, ethics
- drive for excellence, outstanding achievement rather than personal success
- political awareness and savvy
- stability, composure and coolness under fire
- interpersonal sensitivity and skilfulness
- ability to recruit and select those with talent.

They argued that derailed leaders appear to lack crucial management skills, have personality issues and self-evidently are not good at leading others. They noted that knowledge of derailment can help a lot of businesses both to select better managers and to give help, support and coaching to those showing early signs of derailment.

Rather interestingly, they conclude by asking some salient questions for future research, only a few of which have been answered:

Future research should look for patterns in derailment: Do certain deficiencies (like arrogance) matter later in a career, but not earlier (when it might be seen as decisive or results-orientation)? Can a strength become a weakness (e.g. could strong leadership of subordinates lead to a narrow focus)? Are certain patterns of strengths and weaknesses acceptable and others fatal (e.g. brilliant but insensitive might derail, insensitive but organizationally savvy and loyal might not)? Is there a pattern behind bad luck (are there wrong places at the wrong time)? Are there fatal flaws that override any combination of strengths (e.g. someone who isn't trusted)?

(p. 214).

McCauley and Lombardo (1990) produced an instrument called "Benchmarks" which they noted was a tool for diagnosing managerial strengths and weaknesses. They noted that it was based on studies of how executives learn, change and grow over their careers. A content analysis of interviews yielded 16 categories of critical development events and 34 categories of lessons learnt. The result was a questionnaire with 22 sections. Most are concerned with positive or "bright-side" behaviors but six were about the dark side. These are:

1. **Problems with interpersonal relationships**	Difficulties in developing comfortable working relationships with others	• Adopts a bullying style under stress • Isolates him-/herself from others
2. **Difficulty in molding a staff**	Difficulties in selecting and building a team	• Chooses an overly narrow subordinate group • Is not good at building a team
3. **Difficulty in making strategic decisions**	Difficulties in moving from the technical/tactical level to the general/strategic level	• Cannot handle a job requiring the formulation of complex organizational strategies • Can't make the mental transition from technical manager to general manager
4. **Lack of follow-through**	Difficulties in following up on promises, rarely completing a job, and attention to detail	• Makes a splash and moves on without really completing a job • Has left a trail of little problems
5. **Overdependence**	Relies too much on a boss, powerful advocate, or own natural talent	• Has chosen to stay with the same boss too long • Might burn out, run out of steam
6. **Strategic differences with management**	Disagrees with higher management about business strategy	• Disagrees with higher management about how the business should be run

In their work the respondents demonstrate the reliability and validity of their measuring, showing, for instance, that five out of six negative scales were negatively correlated with the bosses' assessment of their promotability.

They believe their instrument essentially picks up three dimensions that are really important for managerial success and failure: respect for self and others; adaptability; and molding a team.

Their instrument was one of the first in the area and has been used and updated. However, it has been overtaken by now widely used and validated measures like the Hogan Development Survey (Hogan and Hogan, 1997).

MODERN POPULAR WRITINGS

Since the millennium the idea of derailed, failed and toxic leaders has fuelled the popular imagination. Hence there is a large number of popular publications (Charan and Colvin, 1999) and non-specialist publications (Reed, 2004; Capretta, Clark and Dai, 2008) that cover the topic.

Studies on management derailment done in different times and in different countries have suggested a very similar catalogue of themes. Derailed managers fail to meet business objectives or build/lead functioning teams. They seem to have problems with interpersonal relationships and they cope poorly with adaptation and change. Van Velsor and Leslie (1995) asked how culture and time specific derailment is. In doing so they compared American and European studies.

They found that authoritarianism derailed more European than American managers. Problems with interpersonal relations do appear to be exaggerated or modified by organizational culture either to prevent or cause derailment.

They found relatively few noticeable cultural differences, though they did find evidence of temporal differences. *First*, the issue of adaptation to change seemed to be growing as an issue surrounding derailment. *Second*, the issue of teams changed from getting the right people to controlling team dynamics. They argue that derailment is a developmental issue rather than a values issue and that it is therefore pan-cultural.

Van Velsor and Leslie conclude that derailment can be prevented only if managers are prepared to face issues around self-efficacy, and need for control. Most importantly, they need to relate honestly and comfortably to others, learn in the face of change and let go of personal ambition in favour of team-building and functioning.

Perhaps the most simple but crucial question is: What is the base rate of incompetent leaders? Much depends on definition: but what is surprising is the gap between different estimates. Some put it between 3% and 5%; others between 30% and 50%. Certainly, we are getting to know more about the topic. But the number of people filing grievances is going up alarmingly. Asked if they have ever worked for a "seriously incompetent" manager, nearly all say yes. The business press is also brimming with mind-boggling reports of serious senior management incompetence.

In *Fortune* magazine, Charan and Colvin (1999) pinpoint indecisiveness as the cardinal derailment sin:

> Here's what we aren't saying: That failed CEOs are dumb or evil. In fact they tend to be highly intelligent, articulate, dedicated and accomplished. They worked hard, made sacrifices and may have performed terrifically for years ... revenues, profits and market values, a remarkable achievement. And failure as a CEO is never final. These are strong people who can come back successfully in other roles.
>
> Nor are we saying execution is the only reason CEOs falter. Sometimes they adopt a strategy so flawed that it's doomed, or they refuse to confront reality in their markets or they antagonize their board. And when a CEO really goes down in flames, there's almost always more than one reason. But business people learn to focus on the main thing, the explanation that accounts for most of what they're worried about, and in the realm of CEO failures that explanation is clear.
>
> (pp. 77–8)

They continue to come up with various memorable lines.

Before it really happened, and before the turn of the millennium, Luthans and colleagues (1998) speculated on the potential for "Dark Side" leadership in *post communist countries*. Their starting point is that a nation's history and culture directly affects the leaders' style of behavior. Culture dictates how leaders present themselves, how much they want teams around, and how charismatic leaders are required to appear.

The issue is what happens during times of crisis and change: when economies are being transformed from central planning to market forces and when many institutions are failing or seriously readjusting.

This argument is that often there is a fit between a particular culture and the characteristics of dark leadership. They note five characteristics of leaders from communist countries, such as Stalin, Honecker, Ceausescu, Hoxha, etc., and the situation they found themselves in:

1. demanding unconditional loyalty from followers
2. a powerful desire for heroic recognition, high visibility and no blame
3. ignoring negative feedback and failure and a tendency to continue with failing courses of action regardlessly
4. followers providing a halo effect which blinds them to bad leadership
5. the destruction of any potential rivals; a liquidation of all independent thinkers even possible successors.

They argue that cultural factors provide explanation for the continuance of dark leadership. Collectivism rather than individualism, and uncertainty avoidance rather than tolerance of ambiguity may do much for the ascendance of dark authoritarian leaders. Luthans and colleagues (1998) believe communism has left a legacy which means they provide a poor cultural and psychological fit with western-style transformational leadership. They conclude:

> We have argued here that the transforming countries in the post-communist era have been deeply affected by their history, traditional cultural values and the current political, economic, and social crises. Today, more than ever, these nations are in desperate need of strong [but hopefully not "dark"] leadership to help establish new social, economic, and political institutions to facilitate their way into the world market economy and decent quality of life.
>
> (p. 190)

Reed (2004) writing from a *military perspective* noted the toxic leader as a backbiting, belittling bully as well as a maladjusted, malcontent, malevolent or malicious boss. He notes three criteria:

1. an apparent lack of concern for the well-being of subordinates
2. a personality or interpersonal technique that negatively affects organizational climate
3. a conviction among subordinates that the leader is motivated primarily by self-interest.

He notes how the military inculcates an attitude that one must respect rank even if one does not respect the person but that it has its share of inflexible, disrespectful, unethical, intimidating leaders who seek personal above shared gain. He believes that many achieve short-term success even if profoundly disliked by subordinates. Indeed, many rationalize their behavior as necessary to complete tasks efficiently.

However, executive derailment is different only because it is unexpected. It happens to high-flyers. Capretta, Clark and Dai (2008) believe the primary cause is poor interpersonal relationships and poor adaptation to change. They identify a list of factors that lead to failure:

- insufficient diversity of experience
- lack of emotional stability and composure
- defensiveness about failure and poor at handling mistakes
- poor interpersonal skills marked by abrasiveness and intimidation
- poor integrity manifest in trust betrayal and breaking promises.

Overconfidence and arrogance based on limited cognitive and technical skills are deeply problematic. They quote other work on "stallers and stoppers" that help.

Those who prefer to take either an "incompetency" or "unethicalness" perspective on the dark side of leadership develop their own taxonomy often illustrated by case studies.

Some of these taxonomies are based more on evidence than others. Thus Scott's (2005) popular self-help book is aimed for people who have to deal with bad bosses of various types "not fit for command". These include the no-boss boss; the pass-the-buck boss; the clueless but connected boss; the scatter boss; the critically clueless boss; and the dishonest "genius". The book's scheme centers around eight behaviors which are bad at extremes and six other behaviors characteristic of bad bosses, from which a random selection is:

- Incompetent leadership: the leader and at least some followers lack the will or skill (or both) to sustain effective actions. With regard to at least one important leadership challenge, they do not creative positive change. (p. 40)
- Rigid leadership: the leader and at least some followers are stiff and unyielding. Although they may be competent, they are unable or unwilling to adapt to new ideas, new information, or changing times. (p. 41)

- Intemperate leadership: the leader lacks self-control and is aided and abetted by followers who are unwilling or unable effectively to intervene. (p. 42)
- Callous leadership: the leader and at least some followers are uncaring or unkind. Ignored or discounted are the needs, wants, and wishes of most members of the group or organisation, especially subordinates. (p. 43)
- Corrupt leadership: the leader and at least some followers lie, cheat or steal. To a degree that exceeds the norm, they put self-interest ahead of the public interest. (p. 44)
- Insular leadership: the leader and at least some followers minimise or disregard the health and welfare of "the other" – that is those outside the group or organisation for which they are directly responsible. (p. 45)
- Evil leadership: the leader and at least some followers commit atrocities. They use pain as an instrument of power. The harm done to men, women and children is severe rather than slight. The harm can be physical, psychological or both. (p. 46)

Another more scholarly approach is the case study approach epitomized by Kellerman (2004), who sees bad leadership as *ubiquitous and insidious* rather than *aberrant and rare*. She argues that the 'leadership industry' has made leadership look a heroic, selfless, exciting activity. She maintains that limiting stories or research to "bright-side" or good leadership confuses and misleads people and does a disservice.

She notes that leaders can be, and often are, ineffective and authoritarian, and names American presidents who have been ignoble, maladroit, sleazy and stupid. More interestingly, she mentions the roles of followers and crimes of obedience. She asks why some leaders behave badly, and does not favour a trait or disorder approach. She also asks why people follow bad leaders, and there she is happy with a more psychological needs approach.

She distinguishes ineffective vs unethical leadership. Ineffective leaders lack skills, make bad decisions and don't effect change. They are lacking. Unethical leaders put their needs ahead of their followers and are egocentric. They possess neither courage nor temperance.

Kellerman seeks to define, describe and illustrate seven types of leaders. However, she is self-critical in various important ways. She is concerned with the multiple meaning in the "bad". She accepts that generally good, competent leaders are sometimes bad and incompetent; also that corrupt leaders can often be very effective. Most obviously she is concerned about the dangers of her history-based typologies. She notes that none of her types are purer than others and that people differ within each type. She accepts that opinions change and views differ, not only about whether someone was a bad leader but also to which group he or she belonged. More importantly, she notes that her types are not traits or personality types; rather, they are descriptions about sets of behaviors.

However, quoting Weber for support, she defends typologies on three grounds:

> First, the ability to distinguish among the ways of being bad leaders is an untidy world, where the idea of bad leadership is as confusing at it is ubiquitous. Second the seven types serve a practical purpose. They make it easier to detect inflection points – points at which an intervention might have stopped bad leadership or at least cut it short. Finally the types make meaning of being bad. They enable us to know better and more clearly what bad leadership consists of.
>
> (p. 39)

In a rather well-informed but essentially self-help book, Lubit (2004) has five types of toxic managers, each with subcategories: Narcissism (Grandiose, Control Freaks, Paranoid); Unethical (Anti-social, Opportunists); Aggressive (Ruthless, Bullying, Homicidal, Sexual Harassers, Chauvinistic, Volatile); Rigid (Compulsive, Authoritarian, Dictatorial, Passive Aggressive) and Impaired. Any researchers would see this semi-popularized category scheme as a strange mix of serious psychiatry and business speak and thus a little strange.

However, the model is robust enough. The idea is simple. Toxic personality traits make one vulnerable to toxic behavior under stress, which may be encouraged by the organizational culture and business processes. Lubit's strategy is simple but useful. For all the toxic types he provides tables, Table 2.1. They identify the observable symptoms but, more importantly, the underlying factors. He notes their impact on the organization and gives advice to those below and above them.

This book clearly sees the elephant in the board room, though its classification system is far from coherent, or is parsimonious, leading to a strange mix of manager types and too much overlap between conclusions. Nevertheless, the central idea of excess, of surface vs underlying factors, and of serious work consequences is correct.

TABLE 2.1 A description of three types of manager

Symptoms	Underlying factors	Impact	Ways for subordinates to cope	Ways for senior management to cope
Overview of antisocial managers				
Manipulative Deceitful Impulsive Irresponsible Inappropriate affect, angry outbursts Sexual inappropriateness Does not accept any responsibility ever Exploits people without hesitancy or remorse	Likes to break rules Lacks normal inhibitions Devalues people Experiences no guilt Lives for pleasure in the now	Puts organization at risk Destroys morale Traumatizes individuals	Avoid provoking them Transfer out before they destroy you Do not get dragged into their unethical/illegal activities Seek allies in co-workers and mentors Record everything Deal with them with others present	Get rid of them immediately Damage control–review their actions and make amends to staff, customers, and legal authorities Be careful in hiring and promoting Support a culture valuing ethical behavior Check on accuracy of resumes Believe nothing they say
Overview of authoritarian managers				
Rigid adherence to social convention and rules Submission to what they see as legitimate authority Tendency to act aggressively, particularly when sanctioned by "legitimate authorities" Prone to scapegoating and bullying	Belief in hierarchies Fear of chaos Fear of criticism Underlying anger Discomfort with ambiguity	Aggression and excess control impair morale, initiative, and innovation Can paradoxically undermine legitimate authority and cause chaos	Avoid surprising them; keep them informed Demonstrate respect for their authority, rank and status Do not go over their head Follow conventions carefully Do things the way they like them Don't debate with them Avoid letting them damage your work (and thereby your reputation)	Limit their contact with people they may see as another authority Assign to positions where their personality traits will do the least harm to everyone Oversee to continually assess treatment of others Provide focused coaching to modify key problems Utilize their respect for authority to help foster change

Overview of compulsive managers

Rigid insistence on having one's own way	Desire for control over all aspects of work	Impairs creativity, productivity, morale and initiative	Understand their fears and limitations	Assignment to positions where their detail focus and rigidity are helpful (quality control) and not destructive (creative endeavors)
Excessive focus on details and rules over big picture	Perceptual style that sees details but never the big picture	Slows things down	Avoid surprising them; keep them informed	Focused coaching to modify key problematic traits
Total perfectionism	Negative view of people, including self		Focus discussions on work	Assess if anxiety or depression are exacerbating their rigidity
Difficulty with spontaneity and warm emotions	Fear of chaos		Demonstrate diligence	Reward positive features of their pathology
Hypercritical of others	Fear of criticism		Do most things the way they like them	
Non-supportive	Difficulty trusting people		Seek emotional support elsewhere	
Exaggerated focus on work/achievement	Procrastinating			
Indecisiveness and dithering				

Source: Adapted from Lubit's (2004) Tables 5.2 (p. 78), 16.1 (p. 227) and 17.1 (238).

Some themes emerge in the writing on leader failure. "First, failure was associated with inability to develop effective interpersonal relationships (arrogant, stubborn, egocentric). Second, some leaders were afraid to take risks and make errors (cautious, avoid responsibility). Third, excitable individuals were found to have difficult relationships (impatient, moody, negative, volatile, emotional instability. Fourth skepticism and distrust will reduce leaders effectiveness in motivating others (cynical, untrustworthy)". (Lubit, 2004, p. 97)

WHAT WE KNOW ABOUT LEADERSHIP

There are tens of thousands of books on leadership, some autobiographical, some historical and others essentially self-help books (Gill, 2002).

The best, however, are still "thin" on derailment. Thus, Adair (2002), sometime Professor of Leadership Studies and prolific author, considers issues like style of leadership, types of leaders (i.e. servant leader, gentleman leader), leadership skills, as well as specific issues like setting directions, making decisions and communication. He examines specific issues like charisma and the eternal question: "Are leaders born or made?" He is well known for his simple "three circles model" which sees leadership at the heart of three intersecting issues: the role of leadership as task-focused, team-focused and individual-focused.

Whilst Adair (2002), being a trained historian and military specialist, has preferred to investigate the issue through the examples of great leaders, he is not afraid to investigate such characters as Machiavelli and Hitler. He sees Machiavellians as offering short-term advantages through cunning and deceit, but long-term losses because of a forfeit of trust. Hitler is recorded as deeply charismatic and insightful: however, he was too self-confident to listen, impudent and irascible.

However, little is written about psychopathology, derailment or evil in many books. It has been estimated that there are nearly 100,000 serious and popular books about leadership. Popular how-to, heroic books by business leaders and writers, as well as consultants, stream off the press. They can be grouped into various categories: studies (autobiographical and biographical) of famous leaders; studies of certain leadership characteristics like charisma or emotional intelligence; books about how to spot, select and develop leaders, as well as the occasional challenge to the whole idea.

There is also no shortage of gurus or experts willing to tell people how to become better leaders – indeed, to become great leaders of any group at any time in any circumstances. They assume that leadership skills can be readily learnt, presumably by putting into practice their advice.

According to the laws of demand and supply, there must be a demand for these books. Curiously, those organizations like the military whose job it is, almost totally, to train leaders, seem not to use them. Equally, when asked, few, if any, actual business leaders ever claim to have read these books let alone attribute any of their success to them. In this sense, are leadership books best placed in the "self-help" section of bookshops?

The lay person defines leadership in terms of who is at the top of an organization. It is all about the characteristics of the boss, though others believe it has as much to with what he or she does, such as team-building or strategic thinking. It could be described as the cult of leadership that is the fascination with what makes people unique, special and supreme.

"Great" leaders

The "prototypical hero" school of leadership picks a historical example of a great leader; selectively describes all their positive acts and traits and then tries to derive "lessons" in leadership for today. A good example of this is a paper by Kets de Vries (2003) on Alexander the Great. Although, unusually, he acknowledges Alexander's hubris, narcissism, megalomania and mood swings, he also emphasizes all the strengths of the "master conqueror". He concludes:

> Alexander also taught the world a number of important lessons on leadership. Through his example, contemporary leaders in business and politics can learn much about what leaders should (and should not) do. The major lessons he taught us should be applied every day in offices and conference rooms throughout the world:

- Have a compelling vision that speaks to the collective imagination
- Develop a creative strategy responsive to enemy strengths
- Create a well-rounded executive role constellation
- Model excellence
- Encourage innovation
- Manage meaning to foster group identification
- Encourage and support followers

- Invest in training and development
- Consolidate gains
- Plan for succession
- Create mechanisms of organizational governance.

(p. 373)

Some writers argue that what makes leaders unique is that others are prepared to follow them. Sometimes their weaknesses are their strengths (and vice versa) but they sense or read situations well. Leadership is certainly a very complex job. Leaders have to manage expectations, social relationships and intimacy, and understand "tough love". They themselves have to be coaches and mentors giving feedback. They have to give and get commitment to tasks. They have to avoid many traps, like being dependent on their followers or believing their own propaganda.

Equally, academics have tried to come to grips with this unwieldy area by attempting to write comprehensive, critical and analytical books on the topic. Thus, for instance, Adair (2002) in his book on inspiring leadership uses numerous case studies to illustrate some simple but fundamental points he believes are true of all leadership:

- People are most willing to follow those who (appear) to know what they are doing
- Leadership involves the consistent and spontaneous arousing of the enthusiasm and willing support of others to the common task at hand
- Leadership is not about position, rank and privilege but rather about meeting the needs of the task, the team and the individual
- The greatest temptation of leaders is arrogance, the only antidote for which is humility
- Great leaders listen more, keep silent often, and put their followers in the foreground more
- Leaders share hardships, risks, privation and dangers of their followers
- Leaders need to be thinkers, good decision-makers as well as intuitive and imaginative. They need to deal in strategy and long-term visions, and most importantly, to communicate those visions
- The real test of leadership is whether people will follow them in defeat and hardship rather than success
- Leadership communication is mainly about stirring up energy, enthusiasm and engagement
- Trust and good communication go hand in hand

- Leadership comes into its own when people are free and equal because they need to feel partners, companions or comrades in a common enterprise
- Humility in leaders is a virtue because it includes seeing the truth about oneself but also being open to more learning.

There also seems to be an unquenchable thirst for typologies of supposedly good leaders. For instance, Rooke and Torbert (2005) in the influential *Harvard Business Review* describe seven ways of leading, the most common of which are called *Expert* (38%), who "rule" by logic and expertise; *Achiever* (30%) who are action and goal oriented; and *Diplomat* (12%) who are conflict-avoidant, supportive, consensus-seeking types. There are fewer *Individualists* (10%), *Opportunists* (5%) or *Alchemists* (3%). This is a reinvention of the old stylistic approach which turned out to be interesting but unhelpful.

Inevitably, any typological approach means there are competing approaches. Thus Bedell-Avers and colleagues (2009) compare *charismatic*, *ideological* and *pragmatic* leaders. Charismatic leaders, they argue, are visionary, future-time oriented, focused on their followers' needs and eloquently emotionally persuasive. On the other hand, ideological leaders are seen to be past oriented, focused on ideals and shared heritage, visionary but come to light because of historical circumstances. Pragmatic leaders are non-visionary, present focused, functional leaders who attempt rational persuasion and negotiation as their communication strategy.

The history of leadership studies

The psychological literature on leadership has focused on six major areas:

1. positional power and leadership roles
2. the characteristics/personality of individual leaders
3. types of groups that are led
4. the leadership influence process
5. contextual, environmental and social factors that favour certain leaders
6. leadership emergence and involvement.

Over the last 100 or so years of psychological research there seem to have been five phases of research into leadership. The *trait approach*, also known as the "great person" approach, stalled because of lack of agreement between those who came up with essential lists. They were not rank ordered and there seemed little idea of their origin or how they related to one another. Were they necessary or sufficient? Did they neglect the role of the followers or the situation? Indeed, were the traits a cause or consequence of the experience of leadership?

This "great man" or charismatic approach to leadership can be traced to the ancient Greeks. This approach can be seen in works of Socrates to Weber and even Freud. However, personality studies linking traits to some measure of leadership have shown only a weak relationship. It is apparent that many other factors are salient other than personality and ability of individual leaders. The same fate befell the backward-looking biographical approach, which looked for individual causal factors (traits, beliefs, values) of recognized leaders. But no pattern emerged from these studies, which often underplayed the historical and social context in which the "special" individuals operated.

Recently this trait approach has even been attacked because of its potential bias and essential incorrectness. First, most people do not, or cannot, become leaders because they do not have the special traits and qualities. Second, it is only those individuals who can do the special job that are leaders – an inspiring, empowering elite.

The argument against the still-popular trait approach is essentially this. Just as leaders shape and transform others, so situations do the same to the leaders. Some leaders are only effective in very particular contexts where they are accepted as leaders. Put simply, the trait approach has too little explanatory power and evidence.

After the Second World War the *behavioral or style approach* came about. It focused on how leaders lead and various attempts were made to come up with models of leadership style like autocratic, democratic, laissez-faire. Today this is seen in those popular tables which attempt to differentiate between managers and leaders. The style approach still focused on the individual preferences of leaders. It seemed in essence very little different from the trait approach.

The 1960s saw the high-point of the *situational approach*, which looked at the fit between leader, the led and the social situation. The idea was that particular circumstances – i.e. crises, wars, economic turbulence – mean certain types and styles of leader become acceptable and desirable. This is why so many famous and exemplary leaders like Churchill seem only "right for the moment". Social psychologists have never linked personality trait descriptions and explanations for behavior.

However, like all the approaches before it, the social psychologists over-played their hand by claiming there was little or no difference between people. The situational approach is essentially 'contrarian': a reaction to the trait approach. People are victims, pawns, puppets of their social and political contexts. This approach quite clearly neglects the obvious point that people choose and change situations: they put themselves up for election to, and selection for, certain jobs and they change the situation once they get them.

However, what situationists and contingency theorists do argue is that there is obviously no one best style or person for leadership. This must be contingent on the situation one is leading.

At the beginning of the 1980s, the concept of charisma returned as well as the "discovery" of different *types* of leader: i.e. the servant leader, the spiritual leader, etc. Perhaps the best known is the *transformational* leader who was seen to be the most desirable. This led, once again, to an explosion of new leadership concepts, and books, particularly those which looked at how heroic figures (i.e. Shackleton, Jesus Christ), achieved their ends. There is an amazing range of "new leadership" models like organic, visionary, servant, even pragmatic leadership. However, to a large extent these simply reinvent the trait approach, using more contemporary terminology.

The turn of the millennium saw the emergence of the fifth theme: the causes of leadership failure. Suddenly it was acknowledged that a large number of leaders actually failed in their task and thus continuing literature attempted to understand that process.

"Modern" themes

Social psychologists have been more influential in recent times, arguing that leadership is a dynamic process concerned with the interaction of leaders and followers. Good leadership is a function of the perception of the followers. It is a relationship business; a social exchange. It is not exclusively an issue of gaining and using power effectively as Machiavelli might have to.

In their review of current theories on leadership, Avolio and colleagues (2009) identified various emerging themes and theories. These include:

1. *Authentic* leadership which is about making balanced decisions, having high moral standards; being transparent in information

sharing and feelings; as well as having self-awareness about strengths and weaknesses

2. *New-genre* (vs traditional) leadership which focuses on charismatic, inspirational, transformational and visionary concepts. However, the question remains as to the factors that moderate or mediate between the leadership style, follower dynamics and situational factors

3. *Complexity* leadership is all about coordinating dynamics and unpredictable agents in a fluid knowledge-driven economy. It sees organizations as complex, adaptive systems and leaders as people embedded in a complex interplay of numerous interactions

4. *Shared* (collective/distributive) leadership, which is leadership by groups or teams. It concerns how mutual and ongoing influence processes in top teams lead to organizational outcomes

5. *Exchange* leadership is about leaders and followers contractually accepting mutual obligations to achieve their ends. It is about how shared interests and goals lead to respect, trust and support

6. *Follower-centered* leadership looks at how followers' identity and self-concept lead them to promote and follow particular leaders

7. *Servant* leadership is the idea that these honest, empathic leaders who build and lead communities achieve high follower commitment, satisfaction and motivation

8. *Spiritual* leadership means for most the idea of focus on non-material, as well as material outcomes, though the term remains vague and controversial

9. *Cross-cultural* leadership is about leading multinational groups and organizations. It is essentially how cultural values dictate leadership styles and outcomes

10. *E-leadership* which is a distributed, electronic, distanced non-face-to-face leadership. It is the issue of how technology has made this possible. It is the leadership of virtual teams.

Born or made?

The old chestnut regarding whether leaders are born or made has lately been the focus of behavioral geneticists. Whilst it is generally accepted that ability and temperament are "born" and "attitudes, values and skills" are made, the question concerns the relative influence of the one over the other. Certainly the data suggest both intelligence and personality are reasonably heritable (40%–70%), so it may be assumed leadership is "substantially" heritable.

Identical twin studies done on different groups in different counties suggest about *a third* of the variability in leadership style and emergence was due to heritability. This leaves two-thirds to "life context" of early childhood and early work experiences. The question then becomes *what* particular family, educational and work experiences promote leadership motivation and style, and *how* does it work?

Do different people, who vary in genetic inheritance (ability and personality), *differ* in how they experience *the same* environment? That is, do inherited factors predict how people choose, change and learn from environments? Further, if we understand these answers, how, when (and indeed, why) can or should we promote interventions that contribute to emergence of leadership in particular individuals?

The born or made issue poses the change and development question, which is: Can leaders change? The answer is yes, but only if they want to. Kets de Vries (2006a) believed that, along with the motivation to change, there are other requirements: the capacity to be open and responsive; be capable to talk about emotions; be able to manage anxiety and vulnerability; psychological mindedness; a capacity for introspection; responsiveness to the observations of others and flexibility.

Leadership development

The simple question: "What interventions (i.e. training, experiential learning) actually work to develop leaders?" has attracted much more opinion than evidence. What literature there is on the topic, however, suggests the following, perhaps not surprising, results. *First*, all *interventions* (i.e. training, role-playing, assignments) work (roughly) equally well, irrespective of how long they endure. *Second*, the effect is relatively short-lived. *Third*, it is not clear what the most/least impactful of the ingredients are. That is, is it best to aim for self-awareness, self-concept, motivation or whatever?

All sorts of questions occur, such as whether leadership development should be offered to groups rather than individuals; who is responsible for it; what methods work best and why; whether it is a good investment; whether it can and should be outsourced; how is it best evaluated?

The cynic and skeptic want a simple issue addressed. Is there good evidence that time and money spent on (any form of) leadership development leads to organizational efficiency/effectiveness/profits improving over the long term? The probable answer is no: that is absence of evidence, rather than evidence of absence.

Evolutionary psychology of leadership

Hogan (2007b) characteristically proposed a simple evolutionary view of leadership. It went thus: all groups have hierarchies and certain individuals vie for more status. Babies inherit status from their mothers. Alpha males get status from building teams but are frequently challenged. For hunter-gatherers the status of the leader who "rules with consent" is based on skill, good judgment and moral identity. They find tyranny and despotism aversive.

In an important review Van Vugt, Hogan and Kaiser (2008) argue that leadership emergence and style, like many other mechanisms such as mate selection, evolved to solve adaptive problems faced by the ancestors. Individual and group survival depends on cooperative effort following wise decisions. People have to be willing to sacrifice various things to ensure survival in competition with other groups. If one group is internally aligned and has a leader with good decision-making ability, they should triumph over less coordinated groups with efficient information processing.

Leaders must understand the need for coordination and how to do it. Next, they need to plan, communicate and facilitate group decision-making. As society developed from hunter-gatherers, through tribes and clans, to modern nation states, so the size and structure of groups changed, which affected the nature of leadership.

Van Vugt and colleagues (2008) point out some of the implications of the evolutionary perspective. Most people are followers, which seems to put them at an evolutionary advantage except under conditions of threat and uncertainty. Under stable, prosperous conditions, leadership is more resented and seemingly less needed. People chosen as leaders need to be fit (strong), wise (old enough), ambitious (to want to become leaders), intelligent (to make good decisions), insightful (with social intelligence), competent and benevolent.

Situational factors play an important role where problems shift from group coordination (socio-emotional) to solving complex problems (tasks) to dealing with crises. A leader's style and profile thus make them better or worse at dealing with specific situations.

Dominance in leadership situations is necessary but has to be exercized subtly. Groups develop 'levelling mechanisms' such as gossip, desertion, and insistence on elections.

The modern organization with leaders being responsible for many functions and being required to perform multiple competing tasks is evolutionarily new. We have evolved from small homogenous hunter-gatherer family groups and feel alienated from and apathetic to big groups. Here, organizations that decentralize and delegate to smaller functional units show followers that have higher moral involvement and commitment.

For Van Vugt and colleagues (2008) we are "designed" to respond to a particular prototype of leaders, but modern organizations "throw-up" and appoint those who are quite different. That is, those ancestral leadership virtues of integrity, persistence, competence, decisiveness and vision seem to be missing from the competency lists of head hunters trying to find our best leaders.

Psychoanalysis and leadership

Relatively few psychoanalytically trained experts have attempted a Freudian analysis of good and bad leadership. Kets de Vries (1999; 2006a; 2006b) is a clear exception. In various books and papers, he lays out the clinical approach and its primary premises:

1. All behavior, even odd or deviant, has a rational explanation. Psychological detectives with proper training can uncover the motives of others like derailed or derailing leaders.
2. The unconscious plays a large role in determining every action, fantasies, fears, hopes and thoughts. The unconscious can make people prisoners of their past. It can and should be explored for self-understanding and mental health.
3. Emotions contribute fundamentally to behavior and identity. Emotions affect thinking. Emotional awareness, expression and regulation are important for mental health and functioning.
4. Development is an inter- and intrapersonal process. We are shaped by our past. Other people influence our inner working.

Kets de Vries talks of the *inner theatre*:

the tragic-comedy of the inner stage that continually and profoundly affects our outer behavior. We tend to transfer patterns of behavior from the past to the present, from one to another group of individuals. We displace the thoughts, ideas and fantasies that originate with certain authority figures. It is a reversal or reliving of issues from the past directed to persons in the present.

Executives need to understand that the phenomenon of transference is natural and ubiquitous, although we are not always capable of noticing and recognizing it.

(2006a, p. 7)

Psychoanalysts are particularly interested in issues like narcissism, charisma and hypomania. They also are particularly concerned with the imposter syndrome where successful leaders feel fakes and frauds and deny their success.

Earlier, Goethals (2005) noted the originality and provocativeness of Freud's ideas about the psychodynamics of leadership. Freud thought people had a "thirst for obedience": a desire (instinctively) to submit to authority. People accord prototypic leaders with (idealized) prestige. Leaders can capture and control (and enslave) a group with repeated, colourful, strident messages. The leader's prototype is the father who imposes his will on the group and is narcissistic and jealous. Followers feared their leaders but, because they had the illusion that the leaders loved them, they loved their leaders in return.

So, like the evolutionary psychologists, Freudians emphasize the archaic heritage, the legacy of the ancestral past. Just as boys identify with and idealize their fathers, so followers seek to satisfy their leaders. Just as fathers appear dangerous and paramount with a strong and imposing will, so we respond to leaders who show the "correct" characteristics.

Freud emphasizes the role of leadership charisma to make followers believe they are capable of great things. They inspire by word and example and give meaning to events. Freud never neglected the idea that leaders need to fit the expectations of followers: they need to be strong, active, and good which are, in some sense, the archetypal schema of the great leader. He argued that leaders must themselves be ideological (held in fascination by a strong faith) in order to inspire the group. It is this that gives them overpowering, irresistible and mysterious power. They need, in modern terminology, to articulate strong stories of identity. Hence the importance of rhetoric, of vision and of making the group feel good about themselves.

Goethals (2005) noted another Freudian leadership theme: the illusion of equal love. That is they are held in equal regard by the leader. This emphasizes commonality and similarity. Followers (especially males in the primal horde) are in love with, but in terror of, the angry father/chief. Equal treatment is critical to compliance. Hence all the work on fairness and justness in leaders. Leaders need to understand the necessity for distributive and procedural justice.

The impact of poor leadership

It is self-evident that abusive, passive and incompetent leaders cause stress in their staff. Staff report alienation and helplessness, distress and depression, physical illnesses as well as reduced job and life satisfaction. Leaders are the custodians and gatekeepers of all organizational rewards and thus have considerable power.

Kelloway and colleagues (2007) argue that leadership style is one of the most ubiquitous potential stressors in any workplace. They believe it is possible to make a broad distinction between two types of poor leaders: first, abusive, aggressive and punitive leaders; and, second, those that lack appropriate skills.

Abusive leaders are stereotypic bullies, harassers and emotional abusers of their staff. It is worse being bullied or abused by a boss than by a colleague or customer because of an employee's sense of control. Next, there are passive, avoidant, laissez-faire leaders. They are the opposite of the classic transformational leader who is inspirational, empathic and proactive.

Poor leaders cause stress because of their high demands on their staff but also because of the lack of control they afford them. Leaders powerfully influence followers' sense of control (perceived control) and actual control (environmental control) that they have over their working lives. Control is about exercising alternatives and having a sense of self-efficacy. The worst combination is having a high-demand, low-control, low social-support job. According to Kelloway and colleagues (2007), poor leaders increase the following types of stress:

- Workload and work pace – setting unrealistic targets and deadlines
- Role stressors like ambiguity and conflict – where expectations are either not clarified or else are mutually incompatible
- Career concerns like job insecurity, job obsolescence, or poor prospects associated with poor effort–reward balance
- Work scheduling – giving people little control or say over their rotations, shifts or night work

- Interpersonal relationships – low social support, inequitable and unjust treatment
- Job content and control – giving people small, unskilled, meaningless tasks that make them work automatically.

They note the importance of social support in the workplace and something that mitigates the effects of stress. It buffers the effects of poor leaders. However, bad leaders fail to provide any support thus increasing stress. This includes instrumental support (task-specific help – emotional support (empathy), informational support (advice, directions) and appraisal support (feedback and encouragement). What good leaders give most, bad leaders give least.

Thus, poor leaders create stressful work environments by acts of omission and commission: passive withdrawal and failing to carry out their responsibilities as well as aggressive, demanding, bullying.

State-of-the-art

Academic reviewers have tried many times to make sense of this fascinating but frustrating literature which is at once partisan and partial, as well as contradictory and inconclusive. Some have argued that the study of management leadership has failed and got us nowhere. There is no agreement; only weak theories and little evidence to support some of the more dramatic ideas.

Some attempt a "new model". Thus Gill (2006) argues there are four dimensions which relate to leadership: intellectual/cognitive, including intuition and imagination; emotional, focusing on emotional intelligence; spiritual; and behavioral. These need to be brought together in four functions: developing a vision and mission; clarifying shared values; developing clear, imaginative and realistic strategy; and empowering others.

The leadership literature moves or at least focuses differently as things change. Thus Gill (2006) notes the big challenge for new leaders given 'big issues' like cultural and gender diversity, globalization, the rise of the knowledge economy, changes in technology, terrorism, etc. The rise of the virtual organization also poses particular problems. As ever, leaders have both to react to and to drive change.

Yet the central question is whether what makes leaders do what they have to do is really different. Every generation appears to believe that in their time things are different, more complex and fluid, more fast-moving and problematic. The question is whether this really calls for different types of leaders with different skills, or simply better leaders.

DYSFUNCTIONAL ORGANIZATIONAL CULTURES

Most people have had some experience of dysfunctional organizations. They have been called toxic, sick and deviant. They are characterized by backstabbing, dishonesty and aggression. But a central question for those interested in derailment is whether failed leaders help create or maintain dysfunctional cultures, or whether they are a function of them.

Social psychologists and sociologists stress the importance of group level, situational and organizational forces in shaping behavior. Thus, they are interested in structure and cohesiveness, group norms and patterns of communication. Norms pre- and proscribe behaviors: they can endorse violence or workaholism, dishonesty or social support for colleagues.

Organizational culture definitely shapes organizational behavior. It is a function of its history: the values, vision and vicissitudes of founders and powerful leaders. It is kept alive by rituals and stories. It is reflected in the explicit and implicit reward and incentive systems. It promotes social conditions that promote certain behaviors and it lowers restraints that inhibit others. It dictates what is and what is not really important; how people should respond emotionally and how they should behave.

Organizational cultures inevitably constrain and limit individual behavior. In this sense, they can encourage or discourage individual behaviors.

Van Fleet and Griffin (2006) have a simple 2×2 model which considers the extent to which both individuals and cultures have "propensities" to show or elicit dysfunctional behaviors. They note:

> For example, if a top manager is commonly known to be untruthful, if a leader does not respect the rights of others, or if the leader puts profits before all else, others in the organization will likely recognize the signals. As the signals get institutionalized throughout the firm, its culture will become increasingly dysfunctional. In this way, the leader's values are "taught" to others and shape their behaviour in the organization.
>
> What leaders pay attention to sends powerful messages throughout the organization. What do leaders seem to notice, what comments do they make, what do they seem to reward and punish?

What agendas do they set for meetings? How do they react to problems and/or change? Is there a code of ethics and is it actually followed? How is budgeting handled – top down or bottom up? Who gets promoted or receives special privileges? These are all important actions by which leaders influence an organization's culture and the behaviour of those in the organization.

(p. 704)

Bad leaders create and sustain dysfunctional cultures. They model, consciously or not, what they want. The bully makes harassment acceptable. But strong cultures can prevent or resist those behaviors.

Harvey, Martinko and Douglas (2006) focused on the leader–subordinate relationship as a cause of dysfunctional leadership and culture. They provided an attribution process model which focuses on the typical attribution style of the leader. Their argument was that leadership style and biases, with respect to followers' behavior, leads to a particular emotional and behavioral response. Thus, if they tend to blame staff for all errors but discount their contribution to success, they are likely to have a style that discourages and demoralizes staff.

Balthazard, Cooke and Potter (2006) chose a particular questionnaire – the Organizational Culture Inventory – to describe dysfunctional cultures. The questionnaire can be used to describe a culture at two levels. At the higher level there are three styles: Constructive, Passive Aggressive and Aggressive Defensive. These can also be described at a more detailed level where there are four styles within each of the three higher-order styles. Thus passive/defensive includes avoidant, dependent, conventional and approval.

Their model suggests that the two "negative" cultures have essentially both individual and organizational outcomes. At an individual level, they maintain a negative, dysfunctional culture impact on five factors:

1. Role clarity: the extent to which organizational members know what is expected of them
2. Communication quality: the extent to which organizational members exchange clear and consistent messages regarding what is expected
3. Fit with organization: the extent organizational members comfortably "fit in" the organization
4. Behavioral conformity: the extent to which organizational members are required to think and behave differently than otherwise would be the case (person/norm conflict)

5. Job satisfaction: the extent to which organizational members report positive appraisals of their work situation.

Similarly, at an organizational level a dysfunctional culture impacts on five organizational outcomes which Balthazard *et al.* (2006) list as:

1. Quality of products/services: the extent to which members evaluate as positive the quality of their organization's products or services
2. Commitment to customer service: the extent to which members make sure customers feel good about the service provided by the organization
3. Adaptability: the extent to which the organization responds effectively to the changing needs of its customers
4. Turnover: the extent to which members expect to leave the organization within two years
5. Quality of workplace: the extent to which members appraise their organization as a good place to work.

They used data from over 60,000 employees and different departments to support their hypotheses. They concluded thus:

> Political and social realities shape all forms of human conduct within and between organisations and their partners. Regardless of professionalism and professed or assumed goal sharing or congruency, organisational members may not behave in ways that promote efficiency and effectiveness if doing so is inconsistent with their reference prevailing culture. Within any organisation there may be a variety of cultures, shaped by characteristic differences in professional orientation, status, history, power visibility or other factors. In this paper we have shown that understanding these cultures in terms of expected behaviours and norms can explain why some organisational units (or the entire organisation) exhibit dysfunctional behaviours that are counter to the organisation's expressed values or mission, and which hamper efficiency and effectiveness. We have also presented a validated technology for cultural assessment that can be used at many levels, from individual to enterprise, which identified these underlying cultural components. Clearly, fixing dysfunctional organisations requires first and foremost insights into the relatively tangible aspects of their culture that is reflected in the behaviours that members believe are expected of them.
>
> (p. 727)

TOXIC LEADERS AND NEEDY FOLLOWERS

Some researchers have lumped all corrupt, destructive, evil bosses under the title of toxic leaders, but they go on to explain why followers accept and even cause leaders who are toxic. They seem co-dependent: locked in together in a very unhealthy partnership. Lipman-Blumen (2005) attempted to explain their *allure*: why we elect and then follow them. She lists nine very familiar qualities or characteristics: lack of integrity; "insatiable" ambition; enormous egos; arrogance; amorality; avarice; "recklessness"; cowardice; and incompetence. In many ways this is a description of the dark triad. Her central thesis is this:

> The major attraction of toxic leaders stems from their readiness to promise us simultaneously the possible and the impossible. That is, they assure us they can both calm our fears *and* keep us safe. Toxic leaders offer us this grand illusion of security to quell two stubborn types of anxiety: *our existential angst*, sparked by our awareness of death's inevitability; and our *situational fears*, instilled by a world marked by economic meltdowns, downsizing, illness, accidents, blackouts, earthquakes, wars, and terrorist attacks that erupt with no advance notice. Further, because these leaders frequently manage to soothe our anxiety, we begin to believe they probably can, indeed, keep us safe, as well.
>
> The illusionary promises of toxic leaders fit, tongue-in-groove, with the complex existential, psychological, and social forces their followers confront. That is, they jibe with the challenges we followers face in an unfinished world. In that world, we try to quiet our fears through successful competition, through heroic action, measured against the society's achievement ethic. The outcome of our daily strivings can enhance or diminish our self-esteem. Leaders' promises also suit our complex personal needs, coloured by our yearning for immortality or at least a small slice of heroism. Buffeted by the powerful interaction of these personal and social forces, we followers become supremely vulnerable to authority figures – good, bad, and middling.
>
> (p. 236)

She notes 14 destructive behaviors including violating and subverting processes; stifling criticism; feeding illusions; identifying scapegoats; setting people against one another; and feeding their followers untruths that exploit their most fundamental fears. They abuse their people by "deliberately undermining, demeaning, seducing, marginalizing, intimidating, demoralizing, disenfranchising, encapsulating, imprisoning, torturing, terrorizing or killing" (p.19) their own followers.

Even exemplary leaders have "toxic chinks" and we often have media myopia about our living leaders but Lipman-Blumen's central and intriguing question is: "what are the forces that propel followers, again and again, to accept, often favour and sometimes create toxic leaders [?]" (p. 24). In answering this, she lists five factors that lead us to follow all – including toxic – leaders, and three explaining why we actually create them.

Using a mixture of psychoanalytic and social psychological ideas, Lipman-Blumen (2005) identifies six simple but powerful factors as to why we need leaders. Three are psychological – need for reassuring parental figures; to feel chosen/special, because we need security and certainty; and because we fear personal powerlessness. Social factors include simultaneously our need for acceptance and community, and our fear of social isolation and ostracism. Thus at times we are prepared to exchange freedom for security. Our sense of weaknesses and powerlessness helps us, including toxic leaders, keep control. But toxic leaders play on our fears of exclusion, uncertainty, helplessness. "The disproportionate authority and power of our parents, as well as teachers and clergy, set us up to respond almost robotically to other authority figures" (p. 48).

(Toxic) leaders offer us visions that are illusory: if insight and knowledge, even noble. Yet the journey or trip is a trap. The leader is neither omniscient nor omnipotent but eager to take credit for any success. Most of us yearn for certainty, security and stability in a world of flux and change. Toxic leaders can exploit instability and the anxiety it brings. Lipman-Blumen (2005) argues that although we may yearn for independence, if and when we achieve it, we feel only isolated and adrift.

She believes we, the followers, create "godlike" leaders because they offer us illusions (visions) of safety and strength that we crave. Being a real, dedicated follower puts us at the center of knowledge and power but can drag us under. Toxic leaders exploit our fear of change and ambiguity. People surrender to leaders who offer a new and demanding ideology with a clear rational and schedule of events for a new order and a continuing and reassuring relationship. We have a need for cultural myths and social norms.

Yet ceding personal responsibility for our fate to clearly imperfect humans who inevitably fail: "We risk either blindly manacling ourselves to toxic leaders or, by our neediness, pushing otherwise non-toxic leaders over the line into toxicity. We invite authoritarianism to visit as a temporary guest, who, once ensconced in the back bedroom, may be nearly impossible to evict" (p. 89).

In this sense, Lipman-Blumen (2005) suggests that followers may cause toxicity in their otherwise non-toxic leaders. She argues that crises make us, as followers, particularly vulnerable to the deceit of charismatic potentially toxic leaders. We create control myths ("the all-knowing" leader has our interests at heart and can handle the "crises") that function to make us feel both inferior and safe; that instil fear of repercussion; that protect the status quo; and that promise ennoblement and immortality.

She divides followers into three groups. First, there are the *benign* followers who may be either anxious or pragmatic, some of whom are impatient for a lead; they don't evaluate closely or critically. Next, are the *leaders' entourage* of trusted protectors who got power, perks and patronage from the leaders; and, finally, there are *malevolent* followers who are there to topple the leader and usurp his place.

However, Lipman-Blumen (2005) does suggest how one might deal with toxic leaders. This involves speaking out and having policy safeguards against toxic leadership. More interestingly she notes how to detect the "first symptoms of toxicity in a nontoxic leader". They are the usual signs: arrogance, evasiveness, secretiveness, cruelty, self-interestedness. It is all about confronting anxiety, uncertainty and ambiguity as followers. She advocates strengthening democratic organizations and demanding leaders who disillusion us with inconvenient truths and who "kick the vision habit". She says it is better to have less we/they talk and more compassion and humility in our leaders. It is advisable to redefine leadership as a responsibility rather than a privilege and select those with authenticity and social consciousness more than ambition.

For Lipman-Blumen, we followers are the *cause of toxic leaders* of all kinds. We ask too much of them; "invest" in their superhuman powers; have unrealistic expectations of them. She concludes:

Developing a complex understating of our self and our world moves us further along this essential path to constructive, Other-oriented leadership. Less driven by endless anxieties, overweening competitiveness, insatiable egos, endless needs for self-esteem, a pernicious achievement ethic, and calls to false heroics, we finally can assert our autonomy, and set ourselves free. Then, through autonomy and freedom, we can find the inner strength not simply to escape, but to reject – resolutely and repeatedly – the allure of the toxic leader.

(p. 250)

Management and leadership are "contact sports". Leaders influence, and are influenced by, their followers. It is a social exchange. Ideally both are united to the pursuit of similar goals. Followers never play a passive role even in the most extreme conditions. Followers temper and shape leaders.

The leadership literature tends to focus too much on intrapsychic forces in leaders rather than interpersonal behaviors of leaders. In this sense, derailing leaders are as much a function of their followers as their unique personality.

Clements and Washbush (1999) have isolated factors associated with both leaders and followers that *together* lead to failure. They list five negative failures of leaders:

1. a failure to "look inside" or introspect on their needs, values and motives
2. mirroring or a tendency to see themselves as others see them. This projected self can lead to fantasies
3. narcissism and with it intolerance of criticism; unwillingness to compromise and a taste for sycophantic followers
4. emotional illiteracy or low emotional intelligence
5. an inability to let go, hanging on to power because of too strong an ego identity with the leadership position.

However, they also list the follower's negative face, arguing that inspired and empowered followers can provoke leadership derailment. This may be both purposeful and deliberate as well as simply inadvertent. Followers influence leaders by their abilities, attitudes and traits and also through the synergy that results from typical interactions. Followers can be active or passive, independent or dependent. They can be critical and independent or uncritically dependent. Both leaders and followers can feel vulnerable in the face of the other.

Leaders can derail followers if they have various syndromes. Those who favour control seek all leadership actions on a superior–inferior, dominant–submissive dimension and resist following. Histrionic followers are task-avoiding attention seekers. Passive aggressive followers are apparently compliant but always resentful. Dependent followers can sacrifice reality to have their needs met. Masochists unusually seek out blame and eschew praise, leading to very odd interaction patterns.

Thus, just as you can have Machiavellian leaders, so you can have Machiavellian followers. Deluded, dim and disordered leaders and followers can have shared packs and shared madness. The issue is this: the needs of followers can very often shape the behavior of leaders. Derailment is a joint consequence of the interaction of leaders and followers. In this sense, derailed followers can cause leadership derailment in those leaders otherwise effective in their job.

DESTRUCTIVE LEADERSHIP

Another related concept is that of *destructive* leadership. This has been defined by Einarsen and colleagues (2007) as "the systematic and repeated behavior by a leader, supervisor or manager that violates the legitimate interest of the organization by undermining and/or sabotaging the organization's goals, tasks, resources, and effectiveness and/or motivation, well-being or job satisfaction of subordinates" (p. 208). They do not believe that the definition should include "intent". That is, that destructive leaders may not intend harm but due to their thoughtlessness, insensitivity or lack of confidence they effectively do so.

In their paper, Einarsen and colleagues (2007) provide a model (see Figure 2.1) based on two dimensions that yield four types of leaders, two of which are destructive.

- *Tyrannical* leaders belittle, humiliate and manipulate subordinates. Also known as abusive or intolerable bosses and petty tyrants, they destroy all interpersonal relationships in the organization. Often this style of leadership can produce impressive short-term results. They use propaganda, scapegoats, have insider groups and diffuse distrust right through the organization.
- *Derailed* leaders are, according to this model, the worst because they are destructive towards both subordinates and the organization as a whole. Aloof, ambitious and arrogant, these scheming leaders fail to adapt or learn from their mistakes.
- *Supportive-disloyal* leaders steal organizational resources often to support the misconduct of their staff. They are often involved

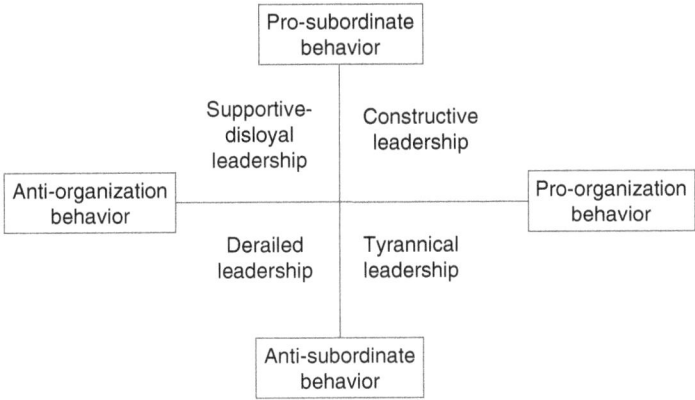

Figure 2.1 **A typology of leadership**

in embezzlement, fraud and theft, which some share with their staff.

Thus, for Einarsen and colleagues, destructive leadership is an over-arching concept. Indeed, others have picked up on this concept. Schaubroeck and colleagues (2007) believe that the core issue is the effect of these leaders on follower distress. The traits that they iden-tify are primarily hostility (anger, cynicism, distrust) and neuroticism (moodiness, vigilance). They argue:

> it may be expected that persons prone to various expressive and neurotic forms of negative emotionality are likely to be callous, antagonistic, fearful of subordinate initiative, and prone to exhibit frustration. Such supervisors may be unwilling to communicate effectively with subordinates and are likely to limit subordinates' abilities to cope with day-to-day problems.
>
> (p. 231)

They tested and confirmed ideas that the more hostile and neurotic the boss is, the more staff manifest "somatic complaints, depres-sion, experienced anxiety on the job, and turnover intentions and negative overall satisfaction, workload satisfaction and organizational commitment" (p. 235).

Using the same concept, Mumford and colleagues (2007) differenti-ated between ideological, charismatic and pragmatic, non-charismatic leaders. Their central question was whether this leads to different kinds of leader violence. As part of their analysis they categorized leaders by three criteria: Violent, Ideological and Western (e.g. Franco, Lenin); Violent, Ideological and Non-western (e.g. Arafat, Pol Pot, Mao Zedong); Violent, Non-ideological, Western (Hitler, Mussolini) and Violent, Non-ideological, Non-western (Ceausescu). Equally, among the Non-violent leaders there are those categorized as Ideological and Western (Bonhoffe, Reagan), Ideological and Non-western (Ghandi, Nehru) and finally Non-ideological, Western (Kennedy, Thatcher) and Non-ideological, Non-western (Nasser, Mandela).

Whilst some would be highly surprised by these categorizations, the authors do try to point out why organizations led by ideologues may be particularly prone to violence.

> *First*, because ideological leaders formulate visions through reflection on failed case models (articulating a value-based vision as a way of avoiding similar problems in the future), ideological leaders may be prone to expression of the outcome uncertainty and negative life found to promote destructive acts in prior studies. *Second*, a focus on shared, presumably superior values, may promote denigration of others who reject those values. Such denigration and dehumanization of others, has been shown to promote social violence. *Third*, the values advocated by ideological leaders may provide a basis for development of the sense of moral superiority found to both promote and justify violence. *Fourth*, a sense of superiority combined with perceptions of injustice may lead ideologues to engage in violence against unjust and "unclean" others.
>
> (p. 220)

Their argument was that four sets of factors – individual, group, organizational and environmental – together lead to violence. In their highly important content analysis they looked for makers of these particular types. These are shown in Table 2.2.

They conclude thus:

> Traditionally, studies of destructive, or personalized, leadership have sought to understand the sources of leader violence in terms of individual characteristics such as narcissism and negative life themes. In fact, the present study provides some further support for this proposition in that variables such as entitlement (related to narcissism), low openness (related to authoritarianism), and information distrust (related to fear and outcome uncertainty) were found to differentiate violent from non-violent leaders.

TABLE 2.2 **Examples of markers for individual, group, organizational, and environmental predictors**

Individual	Group	Organizational	Environmental
Sensitivity to injustice	*Victimization*	*Violence as control*	*Social conflict*
• Contacts government officials regarding unjust events • Boycotts organizations for unjust acts • Speaks of what is "right" and "wrong" • Gives resources to those who have been treated unfairly • Avoid business dealings with people who are viewed as unjust or improper	• Ridiculed by public • Members killed/beaten by other groups • Forced to meet in hiding • Petitions to government about unfair treatment • Talks about unfair treatment at rallies	• Members who disobey organizational rules are beaten or killed • Members who attempt to leave the organization threatened with violence • Culture includes stories of past violence • Leaders carry weapons • Violent acts are committed against families of disobedient members	• Competing religious groups in region • Rival ethnic groups in region • Groups make claims for same objects • Discontentment over large differences in socio-economic status • Reign of unpopular leader
Low openness	*Group feelings of superiority*	*Sense-breaking*	*Economic exploitation*
• Sudden break in communication with others who have different views • Owns very specific and narrow collection of books or literature • Avoids debate about beliefs and values • Members of individual's social circle are similar in nationality or culture • Performs actions for groups without asking for reasons	• Advocates extreme policies • Rallies reference a need for radical change • Propaganda uses terms like "density" or "ordained" • Identifies specific targets necessary for change to occur • Propaganda states that group will change the world	• Propaganda uses explicit examples of "inequalities" • Members are told they are not respected by society • Members are required to think of, or meditate on, unfulfilled aspects of life • Repeatedly blames the same organization for problems • Members are forbidden to associate with others outside the organization	• Infrequent changes in dominant group leadership • Dominant group withholds resources • Few laws protecting workers' rights • Few educational opportunities for lower class • Extremely low wages for lower class

Continued on next page

Table 2.2 (Continued)

Individual	Group	Organizational	Environmental
Sense of asceticism	*Strong group culture*	*Rituals*	*Strong traditional culture*
• Practices self-disciplined religious activities (e.g. fasting) • Mentions importance of purity of lifestyle • Home and office are simple and non-extravagant • Only purchases simple and necessary foods • Leisure activities require self-discipline (e.g. martial arts)	• Performs rituals/ceremonies that emphasize beliefs and values • Distributes materials that articulate beliefs and values • Attire reflects belief system • Recites oaths at meetings • Refers to values/principles when making group policy decisions	• Rituals and ceremonies are considered "sacred" or "holy" • Rituals are kept secret from outsiders • Use of symbolic items at organizational meetings • Ceremonies or rituals for successful completion of missions • High degree of affect during rituals	• Region has multiple monuments to historical leaders • Majority of region participates in same rituals for number of years • Common hierarchy is evident in non-work venues (e.g. churches) • Members of population engage in customs of past • Current problems in legal system are interpreted using past framework

In this regard, however, it should be borne in mind that entitlement, low openness, and information distrust were subsumed under a broader dimension that included selective interpretation of information and reality distortion. This broader dimension, labelled selective information processing, suggests that biased self-serving appraisals of others and their intention, especially the projection of negative intentions, may play an important, albeit often overlooked, role in violent behavior on the part of outstanding leaders, and, perhaps destructive behavior by leaders in general.

However important individual characteristics may be, this is clear given the results obtained in the present study, attempts to understand the origins of violence should not focus solely on characteristics of the leader are warranted. Group insularity, institutional sanctioning of violence, and environmental corruption were all also found to distinguish violent and non-violent leaders. In fact, group insularity and corruption were found to be stronger predictors of violence than reality distortion in the regression analyses. This finding is of some importance because it suggests that group, organizational, and environmental conditions may give rise to the emergence of violent leaders and may make possible the expression of violent tendencies on the part of leaders. Thus, a key question to be addressed in future research is identification of the specific mechanisms by which group insularity, institutional sanctioning, and corruption, among other group, organizational, and environmental influences, operate to shape the emergence and expression of violent tendencies on the part of leaders.

(p. 233)

MALIGNANT CHARISMA

Many researchers have noted the potential dark side to charisma, defined as the use of various impression management processes (i.e. rhetoric) to inspire followers in pursuit of a vision. They clearly inspire, persuade and mobilize.

Charismatic leaders with high self-esteem, need for power and self-monitoring skills portray themselves as credible, morally worthy, innovative, powerful and trustworthy. They can, and do, elevate their followers' sense of self-efficacy and self-esteem. They script, stage and perform a role (Gardner and Avolio, 1998). Their audience, the followers, particularly those who believe in the romance of leadership, attribute charisma to them. Followers who spread the charismatic message often identify strongly with, and direct high levels of positive effect towards, these charismatic leaders (Gardner and Avolio, 1998).

Few researchers see charisma as a trait but rather as a style and even more as a relationship. Charismatic leaders articulate and repeat messages about ambitions, aims and values that are deeply attractive to followers. This convergence between leaders and followers enhances the self-esteem and self-efficacy of the latter which lead them to attribute charisma to their leader (Weierter, 1999).

One essential feature of the charismatic leaders is the ability to inspire a vision. Strange and Mumford (2002) made an important distinction between two highly related types of leadership: charismatic vs ideological. Both inspire visions, but ideological leaders (like Thatcher, Gandhi, Lenin) stress personal values and standards whilst charismatic leaders (like Kennedy, Churchill, Mussolini) stress social needs and change requirements. They question when one style (ideological) is likely to prove more attractive to followers.

> First, when an organization, or society, is based on a shared set of values, or beliefs, as opposed to mutual production dependence, ideological leadership is likely to prove particularly compelling. Second, when crises in the organization, or society, centre around culture rather than performance, ideological leadership may prove particularly attractive to followers, especially when there is a strong culture and a core of widely shared values. Third, when periods of change have proven unsuccessful and consensus cannot be built around an envisioned future, then an ideological style may prove more compelling than a charismatic style.
>
> (p. 374)

The issue, however, is the charismatic leader with narcissistic tendencies. This is the dark side of charisma. Sankowsky (1995) argues quite correctly that it is the collusion of the followers of dark side charismatic leaders that causes the problem. He argues the pattern in the thinking of followers goes like this: we idolize our leader and therefore his or her vision. We comply with conviction and bolster the leader's strength. We do not always succeed in our goals and let him or her down. We are to blame and we listen only to the leader.

A lot of the work on the charisma of tyrants and dictators has been done by historians. Thus Glad (2002), in a paper subtitled 'Malignant Narcissism and Absolute Power', notes the fundamental paradox in the behavior of tyrants. Their skills of deception, intimidation and manipulation help them secure power but they become vulnerable as they cross moral boundaries to get absolute power. Thus they engage in behaviors that undermine their position and invite challenges to their rule. The hypothesis is that attempts to consolidate absolute power lead a narcissist into a vicious cycle. First, the orchestrated adulation and dysfunctional friendships feel false. Next, grandiose plans lead to rash and ruthless behavior, so inspiring tyrants. Third, "project over-reach and creation of new enemies leads to increasing vulnerability, a deepening paranoiac defence and volatility in behaviour" (p. 6).

Glad (2002) clearly sees negative charisma on a scale from benign to malignant. She notes the self-destructive cycle of many tyrants starts because of the narcissistic nature of power. She notes that power brings deference and feelings of omnipotence. It can be used to eradicate criticism, enemies, even the past. Third, it can overcome loneliness because the tyrants can command company and "friendship".

Yet adulation cannot compensate for low self-esteem. Power allows tyrants to act out, with shocking impurity, grandiose fantasies which others constrain.

O'Connor and colleagues (1995), in a historiometric study of destructive charismatic leaders, also makes the distinction between good/bad or socialized vs personalized charismatic leaders. The socialized charismatic leader empowers others and maximizes gains for the whole organization irrespective of personal needs, whilst the personalized charismatic leader is exploitative, self-aggrandizing and discriminatory. Destructive, personalized leaders' greed, dishonesty and amorality destroy organizations. Yet the personalized leaders' charisma can act as a very positive force:

> The personalized leader articulates a vision of an unsocialized world which is the product of beliefs and motives and which is driven by attempts to defend a weak self-system. The high fear and narcissism experienced by personalized leaders contributed to a view of the world where personal safety is achieved through domination and deindividuation of others. In the absence of self-regulatory mechanisms such as guilt, moral standards, and controlled inhibitors of impulses, destructive actions are carried out. The socialized leader, on the other hand, is not acting in a defensive manner and the vision of an effective leader is to use power not as a method of domination but as a method of empowering others.
>
> (p. 530)

CONCLUSION

There are, reassuringly, some very detectable themes all the way through this literature. Derailed leaders, whether labelled toxic or destructive, do have difficulty with many interpersonal relationships and therefore difficulty in building and leading teams. They seem too inflexible and unable to adapt to new conditions. Often they have too narrow a functional orientation and therefore fail to meet business objectives.

The literature of leadership is less coherent than that on derailment. It poses many, seldom answered, questions. Derailed leaders are often alluring to dependent followers and together they cause dysfunction in organizational cultures: i.e. the toxic triangle.

Hogan, Hogan and Kaiser (2009) have summarized the extant literature by arguing that derailed leaders are essentially lacking in one of four skill areas: *intrapersonal* (emotional maturity, self-awareness), *interpersonal* (social skills and emotional intelligence), *leadership* (team-building, role modelling) and *business skills* (planning, organizing, monitoring). Thus, those low on intrapersonal skills tend to be too ambitious and not adaptable. Those low on interpersonal skills conflict with management and also have poor political skills. Those low on leadership skills are likely to be over- or under-managers. Those low on business skills are poor at strategy, communication and task performance. These skills are interrelated: failure or inadequacy in one can affect the overall performance of the individual.

Derailed leaders tend to be intimidating or manipulative or ingratiating. Hogan and colleagues (2009) list five early warning signs under five domains: poor results (missed objectives, cover-ups, dodgy finances, customer complaints); narrow perspectives (too detail-oriented, out-of-date, reliant on technical skills); poor team-building (autocratic, micro-management, high turnover); poor working relationships (insensitive, abrasive and abusive); and, finally, showing inappropriate or immature behavior (poor at coping, gossiping, refusing to accept responsibility).

3

PERSONALITY STYLES, TRAITS AND DISORDERS

INTRODUCTION

There are many reasons why workplaces are dysfunctional (Farson, 1997; Finkelstein, 2003). One lies in the pathology of senior managers who create and maintain a toxic culture epitomized by mistrust, dishonesty, and lack of equity (Furnham, 2004; Kets de Vries, 1999). Pathology refers to something more than incompetence, being a bully, inefficient or corrupt. It is to assert that some bosses have certain disorders and that it is these that account for their behavior which results in a dysfunctional workplace for others. This chapter will concentrate on an intra- and interpersonal psychological perspective whilst acknowledging that, inevitably, situational and organizational factors play a role in precipitating derailment. Thus, whilst a manager may be perfectly effective and competent under certain conditions, his or her "pathology" may cause specific problems when work pressures rise or unusual conditions occur.

As noted in Chapter 1, although lay people (and psychiatrists) think in *categorical* terms (i.e. "he is or is not a psychopath"), psychologists think in *dimensional* terms. Thus there are degrees to which one can be accurately described as an extravert, a neurotic and, indeed, a psychopath. This chapter will consider those with personality disorders in type-terminology. This is partly because most people talk and think in typological rather than dimensional terms (she is tall, he is extraverted, they are neurotic). Further, the way psychiatrists think about, and measure, disorders is essentially in typological terminology: where individuals have manifest a certain number of behaviors associated with a disorder (i.e. 8 out of 12), they fulfil the criteria of caseness or labelling. However, these cut-off points are always fairly arbitrary and an individual who has 12 out of 12 critical behaviors is a rather different person than one who manifests the required 8 alone. Furthermore, and there appears to be no research on this topic, although the criteria behaviors are given equal weight, it is likely that some are much more deleterious to psychological functioning at work than others. This will be discussed appropriately later in the chapter.

Further psychological researchers try to be parsimonious in their trait descriptions. Thus, all individuals can be "profiled" on a set number of dimensions. It is these profiles which may be used to identify individuals who may be particularly prone to derailment, failure or dysfunctional management techniques. That is to say there is often evidence of *co-morbidity* with the personality disorders. It is not unusual for a person to be a "case" on more than one dimension at the same time. Thus, one could be labelled both as a narcissistic and histrionic personality at the same time. This is not unusual and, indeed, may be expected from the way these disorders lie on different axes. The central point, however, is that we all have a fairly unique psychopathology profile and it is important to attempt to describe and explain an individual's psychological function and dysfunctioning in terms of the total profile.

Again, as noted in Chapter 1, three categories or types are most commonly implicated in management derailment and they are, in order of frequency: anti-social (psychopath), narcissistic and histrionic. Machiavellianism (which is not strictly a personality disorder) is often considered as a third dimension (see Toxic Triangle) (Jakobwitz and Egan, 2006). These have been variously described as the *dark triad* of personality (Paulhus and Williams, 2002) though there is some disagreement about all dimensions. In lay terms, psychopaths are selfish, callous, superficially charming, lacking in empathy, and remorseless; narcissists are attention seeking, vain, self-focused and exploitative, whilst Machiavellians are deceptive, manipulative and deeply self-interested.

Paradoxically, it is often these disorders that prove to be an asset in acquiring and temporarily holding down senior management positions. The charm of the psychopath, the self-confidence of the narcissist, the clever deceptiveness of the Machiavellian and the emotional openness of the histrionic may, in many instances, be useful business traits. When candidates are physically attractive, well-educated, intelligent and with a dark triad profile, it is not difficult to see why they are selected for senior positions in management. In this sense, assessors and selectors must bear part of the blame for not *selecting out* those who so often derail so spectacularly. They do not notice, in the biography of the individual all the crucial indicators of the disorder. Alternatively, the biography as portrayed in the CV may easily be a work of fiction.

This chapter asserts that, paradoxically, personality disorders may serve certain individuals in certain businesses well in climbing the ladder of success. If they are bright and intelligent, their disorder profile may, at least for a time, seem beneficial, even attractive, in the business environment. However, it is likely over time to be discovered and to lead to manifold types of business failure.

When thinking of a psychopath, the lay person often conceives of a dangerous mass murderer or perhaps the amazingly successful confidence trickster. Similarly, many would admire the self-confidence of the person with narcissistic personality disorder. Further, the emotional liability and showiness of the histrionic personality-disordered manager in a creative job may result in their being rated as creative rather than disturbed. The clever deviousness of the Machiavellian may also be admired as an indication of toughness. In this sense "mild" forms of these pathologies could appear generally, or at specific times, which could be very advantageous.

Two recent developments in the research on personality disorders has alerted psychiatrists and psychologists to the real possibility of some senior (and junior) managers having personality disorders. The *first* is the increasing literature on what is called the 'successful psychopath' (Hall and Benning, 2005). Researchers have found that psychopaths in senior management jobs are often quite successful. Indeed, their abnormal behaviors appear to be advantageous in certain settings, hence the emergence of the classification, almost oxymoronic, of the "successful psychopath". Studies have been made of groups of individuals who have not been incarcerated or had many problems with the law despite their amoral and immoral behavior (see Chapter 4).

The *second* development comes more from psychology than psychiatry and has involved the development of measures of the personality disorder (Furnham and Crump, 2005). Whereas psychiatrists often favour typological classifications (one is, or is not, a _____ according to a 'cut-off' score), psychologists prefer the dimensional approach. Thus, there are degrees of disorders, which are logically related to "normal" traits. Indeed, the *spectrum hypothesis* suggests that many personality disorders occur simply in these individuals with very high or very low personality trait scores. For example, the very Conscientious may manifest symptoms of obsessionality, or Neurotics forms of hysteria. Thus, it is quite possible to understand how an individual with a particular profile might be able to function very successfully in the business environment. Indeed, in particular environments (business sectors) at certain times (bull/bear markets) it may be particularly advantageous to have various personality disorder inclinations.

It is possible to conceive of certain unusual working environments that may almost require some of the beliefs and behaviors associated with certain of the disorders. Thus, military special forces may find the callousness associated with a psychopath advantageous. Equally, those in quality control or health and safety may feel that various obsessional checking behaviors are beneficial to the job. However, it should be pointed out that these are more likely to be an exception rather than the rule.

Trait psychologists have also tried to examine the links between traits and disorders to make for a more parsimonious description of individuals (De Clercq and De Fruyt, 2003; Durrett and Trull, 2005; Hogan and Hogan, 1997; Millon, 1981; Rolland and De Fruyt, 2003; Saulsman and Page, 2004; Widiger *et al.*, 2000, 2001, 2002). This also helps to give some psychosocial and biological explanations as the theorizing on the origins, mechanisms and processes associated with traits probably exceeds that of the personality disorders. A great deal of the psychiatric work on disorders is about classification. There is considerably less research on both the aetiology (and prognosis) of these disorders as well as the behavioral mechanisms and processes that describe and explain how they function. The rapprochement between (clinical and personality) psychology and psychiatry is to be welcomed.

PERSONALITY DISORDERS

Psychiatrists and psychologists share various common assumptions with respect to personality. Both argue for the stability of personality over time. The DSM criteria (APA, 1994) talk of "enduring pattern", "inflexible and pervasive", "stable and of long duration". The pattern of behavior is not a function of drug use or some other temporary medical condition. Furthermore, the personality pattern is not a manifestation or consequence of another mental disorder. Personality traits and personality disorders are stable over time and consistent across situations. They change relatively little over time. In this sense, there should be obvious biographical clues to an individual's make-up. This, perhaps, explains the popularity of bio-data in selection (Gunter, Furnham and Drakeley, 1993).

Both psychologists and psychiatrists believe that personality factors relate to cognitive, affective and social aspects of functioning. Both disorders and traits affect how people think, feel *and* act. It is where a person's behavior "deviates, markedly" from the expectations of an individual's culture that personality disorders are manifest. "Odd behavior" is not simply an expression of habits, customs, or religious or political values professed or shown by a people of particular cultural origin. In other words, it is odd to all people within a cultural context and that includes the curious and often bizarre world of business!

The DSM manuals (APA, 1994) note that personality disorders all have a long history and have an onset no later than early adulthood. There are some gender differences: thus, the anti-social disorder is more likely to be diagnosed in men, whereas the borderline, histrionic and dependent personality is more likely to be found in women. Some personality disorders have symptoms similar to other disorders – anxiety, mood, psychotic, substance-related, and so on – but they have unique features. The essence of the difference between normal traits and disorders is: "Personality Disorders must be distinguished from personality traits that do not reach the threshold for a Personality Disorder. Personality traits are diagnosed as a Personality Disorder only when they are inflexible, maladaptive and persisting and cause significant functional impairment or subjective distress" (APA, 1994: 633). In this sense, disorders can partly be seen as extreme traits. Indeed, there is a hypothesis called the *spectrum* hypothesis, which believes that disorders are extreme traits, between one and two standard deviations away from the norm (Furnham, 2006). Thus, psychopaths/anti-social individuals are extremely low on Agreeableness (or psychoticism in Eysenck's terminology), whilst Histrionic types are extremely Neurotic, and Obsessive Compulsive extremely Conscientious. The question, of course, is where the line is drawn that distinguishes an "extreme" trait from a personality disorder. Furthermore, the range of personality disorders seems wider than that of traits and it is clear that some disorders do not seem clearly related to personality traits, at least as defined by the five-factor model (Furnham and Crump, 2005). The DSM-IV provides a clear summary:

General diagnostic criteria for a Personality Disorder

A. An enduring pattern of inner experience and behavior that deviates markedly from the expectations of the individual's culture.

This pattern is manifested in two (or more) of the following areas:

1. cognition (i.e. ways of perceiving and interpreting self, other people, and events)
2. affectivity (i.e. the range, intensity, liability, and appropriateness of emotional response)
3. interpersonal functioning
4. impulse control

B. The enduring pattern is inflexible and pervasive across a broad range of personal and social situations.
C. The enduring pattern leads to clinically significant distress or impairment in social, occupational or other important areas of functioning.
D. The pattern is stable and of long duration and its onset can be traced back at least to adolescence or early childhood.
E. The enduring pattern is not better accounted for as a manifestation or consequence of another mental disorder.
F. The enduring pattern is not due to the direct physiological effects of a substance (e.g. a drug of abuse, a medication) or a general medical condition (e.g. head trauma).

(APA, 1994, p. 633)

There are 10 or more defined and distinguishable personality disorders, some of which will be considered in due course: *Paranoid Personality Disorder* is a pattern of distrust and suspiciousness such that others' motives are interpreted as malevolent. *Schizoid Personality Disorder* is a pattern of detachment from social relationships and a restricted range of emotional expression. *Schizotypal Personality Disorder* is a pattern of acute discomfort in close relationships, cognitive or perceptual distortions, and eccentricities of behavior. *Antisocial Personality Disorder* is a pattern of disregard for, and violation of, the rights of others. *Borderline Personality Disorder* is a pattern of instability in interpersonal relationships, self-image, and affects, and marked impulsivity. *Histrionic Personality Disorder* is a pattern of excessive emotionality and attention seeking. *Narcissistic Personality Disorder* is a pattern of grandiosity, need for admiration, and lack of empathy. *Avoidant Personality Disorder* is a pattern of social inhibition, feelings of inadequacy, and hypersensitivity to negative evaluation. *Dependent Personality Disorder* is a pattern of submissive and clinging behaviour related to an excessive need to be taken care of. *Obsessive-Compulsive Personality Disorder* is a pattern of preoccupation with orderliness, perfectionism, and control. *Personality Disorder Not Otherwise Specified* is a category provided for two situations: 1) the individual's personality pattern meets the general criteria for Personality Disorder and traits of several different Personality Disorders are present, but the criteria for any specific Personality Disorder are not met; or 2) the individual's personality pattern meets the general criteria for a Personality Disorder; but the individual is considered to have a Personality Disorder that is not included in the classification (e.g., passive aggressive personality disorder).

(APA, 1994, p. 629; emphasis in original)

It should be noted that these personality disorders are grouped along different axes or different clusters. When clustering, *three* are usually made: A (paranoid, schizoid, schizotypal); B (Anti-social, Borderline, Histrionic, Narcissistic) and C (Avoidant, Dependent and Obsessive-Compulsive). It is those disorders in Cluster B associated with low Conscientiousness and Agreeableness that are being considered in this chapter. These appear to be those most related to management dysfunction.

It should also be noted that with each different edition of the manual there are noticeable changes. Some disorders get dropped and others emerge. This is of interest and concern to all taxonomic specialists, but need not concern us here unduly.

One of the most important ways to differentiate a particular personal *style* from personality *disorder* is flexibility. There are lots of difficult people at work but relatively few whose rigid, maladaptive behaviors mean they continually have disruptive lives, troubled lives. It is their inflexible, repetitive, poor stress-coping responses that are the marks of many disorders (Furnham, 2004).

Personality disorders influence the sense of self – the way people think and feel about themselves and how other people see them. The disorders often powerfully influence interpersonal relations at work. They reveal themselves in how people "complete tasks, take and/or give orders, make decisions, plan, handle external and internal demands, take or give criticism, obey rules, take and delegate responsibility, and co-operate with people" (Oldham and Morris, 1991, p. 24). The anti-social, narcissistic, histrionic, obsessive compulsive, passive-aggressive and dependent types are particularly problematic in the workplace.

People with some personality disorders have difficulty expressing and understanding emotions. It is the intensity with which they express them and their variability that makes them odd, difficult and prone to derailment. More importantly, they often have serious problems with self-control.

There are various ways in which experts have tried to classify the disorders themselves. But of most relevance to this chapter is the work of researchers who have understood the impact of personality disorders of those at work. Without doubt it goes as far back as Hogan's work. Hogan and Hogan (1997) note that a "view from the dark side", as they call the personality disorders, gives an excellent understanding of the causes of management derailment. They argue that there are obviously many "mad" managers in organizations and that helping people to identify potentially bad or derailed managers can help to alleviate a great deal of suffering. They see the usefulness of a measure of the disorders as a useful risk audit that might reveal how managers behave under stress and their particular and peculiar vulnerabilities.

There have now been various semi-popular books that have translated and relabelled the personality disorders.

They also note from their reading of the literature that derailment is more about *having* undesirable qualities rather than *not having* desirable ones. This results from people at work being more concerned with select-in, rather than select-out, criteria. That is, they really look for what they do not want as opposed to what they do want. There is frequently no mechanism for, interest in, or ability to look for potential signs of derailment, including the personality disorders. The business of selection can be seen in a simple 2×2 matrix: Select/Reject and Good/Bad. The aim is to select the good candidates and reject the bad (inappropriate, less able, etc.). However, most selection involves the "Select Good" box by specifying what abilities, competences, experiences and motivations managers *should* have. They are rejected if they do not have "enough" of these or fail to reach a standard. The flaw in this very common approach is not to look specifically for characteristics that should lead to rejection, that is, to seek for evidence of traits that one does not want. In this sense, it may be important to specify both select-in and select-out criteria, and among the select-out criteria may be evidence of the personality disorders.

The research of Hogan and Hogan in the area has led them to seven specific conclusions: there is substantial (between-study) agreement regarding the dysfunctional dispositions/traits associated with management incompetence and derailment. Many derailed managers

TABLE 3.1 **Different labels for similar disorders**

DSM-IV Personality Disorder		Hogan and Hogan (1997) HDS Themes		Oldham and Morris (2000)	Miller (2008)	Dottlick and Cairo (2003)
Borderline	Inappropriate anger; unstable and intense relationships alternating between idealization and devaluation.	Excitable	Moody and hard to please; intense but short-lived enthusiasm for people, projects or things.	Mercurial	Reactors	Volatility
Paranoid	Distrustful and suspicious of others; motives are interpreted as malevolent.	Sceptical	Cynical, distrustful and doubting others' true intensions.	Vigilant	Vigilantes	Habitual
Avoidant	Social inhibition; feelings of inadequacy and hypersensitivity to criticism or rejection.	Cautious	Reluctant to take risks for fear of being rejected or negative evaluation.	Sensitive	Shrinkers	Excessive caution
Schizoid	Emotional coldness and detachment from social relationships; indifferent to praise and criticism.	Reserved	Aloof, detached and uncommunicative; lacking interest in or awareness of the feelings of others.	Solitary	Oddballs	Aloof
Passive-aggressive	Passive resistance to adequate social and occupational performance; irritated when asked to do something he/she does not want to.	Leisurely	Independent; ignoring people's requests and becoming irritated or argumentative if they persist.	Leisurely	Spoilers	Passive resistance
Narcissistic	Arrogant and haughty behaviors or attitudes, grandiose sense of self-importance and entitlement.	Bold	Unusually self-confident; feelings of grandiosity and entitlement; over-valuation of one's capabilities.	Self-confidence	Preeners	Arrogance
Antisocial	Disregard for the truth; impulsivity and failure to plan ahead; failure to conform.	Mischievous	Enjoying risk-taking and testing the limits; needing excitement; manipulative, deceitful, cunning and exploitative.	Adventurous	Predators	Mischievous

Continued on next page

85

TABLE 3.1 **(Continued)**

DSM-IV Personality Disorder		Hogan and Hogan (1997) HDS Themes	Oldham and Morris (2000)	Miller (2008)	Dotlick and Cairo (2003)
Histrionic	Excessive emotionality and attention seeking; self-dramatizing, theatrical and exaggerated emotional expression.	Colorful	Dramatic	Emoters	Melodramatic
Schizotypal	Odd beliefs or magical thinking; behavior or speech that is odd, eccentric or peculiar.	Imaginative	Idiosyncratic	Creativity and vision	Eccentric
Obsessive-compulsive	Preoccupations with orderliness; rules, perfectionism and control; over-conscientiousness and inflexibility.	Diligent	Conscientious	Detailers	Perfectionistic
Dependent	Difficulty making everyday decisions without excessive advice and reassurance; difficulty expressing disagreement out of fear of loss of support or approval.	Dutiful	Devoted	Clingers	Eager to please

(especially those with narcissistic personality disorders) have impressive skills, which is why their disorders are not spotted at selection but only later by their subordinates. Bad managers are a major cause of misbehavior (theft, absenteeism, turnover) by staff: it is poor treatment that often makes them resentful, vengeful and disruptive.

They have always argued that it is important to take the *observer's* view of personality – that is the descriptions of the personality disorders from those that deal with them. In this sense it is less wise to rely on self-report in interview or by questionnaire as opposed to observer reports by colleagues, subordinates and clients. The problem for much research is that it can describe what derailed and derailing managers do rather than why they do it. Although the origin (in terms of learning or biology) is not clear for the personality disorders/derailment factors, their consequences are very apparent. The most obvious one is, quite simply, the inability to learn from experience. A second crucial consequence of the disorders is that they erode trust. That is, dysfunctional managers lose the trust of all those that they deal with.

Kets de Vries (2006a), who was a very early exponent of the personality disorders framework for understanding leader derailment, has noted the importance of understating both the pathology of leaders and followers. He noted also that: "Anyone trying to analyse their own or a leader's style, then, should remember that 'pure' prototypes are fairly rare. Because of the blending of styles, diagnoses are very difficult to make" (p. 131).

However, he also speculates about the probability of a derailing leader and followers' pathology (see Table 3.2).

TABLE 3.2 **An overview of the spectrum of personalities**

Disposition	Leadership tendencies	Follower tendencies
Narcissistic	Very high	Low
Dramatic	Medium	High
Controlling	High	High
Dependent	Very low	High
Self-defeating	Very low	High
Detached	Medium	Medium
Depressive	Low	Low
Abrasive	Medium	Low
Paranoid	High	Medium
Negativistic	Very low	Medium
Antisocial	High	Low

Source: Manfred Kets de Vries, *The Leader on the Couch* (Jossey-Bass, 2006).

Note that four personality disorders are thought to be common in derailed leaders: narcissistic, anti-social, controlling and paranoid, and four in pathological followers: controlling, dependent, dramatic and self-defeating.

Others have picked up on the personality disorder literature. Goldman (2006a; 2006b) provides two interesting case studies of people with narcissistic and anti-social personality disorder to illustrate the difference as he sees it between toxic and personality-disordered leaders. He is a cautious advocate of the DSM nomenclature and concludes thus:

Troublesome is the growing incidence in pop leadership publications of pseudo-diagnoses and references to personality disorders, but without meeting the DSM criteria for same. As social scientists we are more than capable of describing and interpreting narcissistic and borderline executives or we describe entire companies as narcissistic, then we are making sweeping personality assessments and potentially stigmatizing individuals with an unwarranted, flippant, unofficial personality disorder diagnosis. Without a working knowledge and application of the DSM we are constantly confusing and blurring the lines between 'narcissistic behaviours' or 'narcissistic traits' and 'abnormal narcissistic personality disorders'. Considering the possible consequences for our words for leaders and organizations, I find there is little margin for error. Any error is egregious. Are we merely borrowing, shaping and moulding the DSM-IV-TR in order to extend our management arsenal into the exotic and topical arena of toxicity? Are we not concerned with the precision of DSM language and diagnoses designed by our neighbours over in counselling and industrial psychology and psychiatry?

Since it only takes one sick leader to bring down an organization are we satisfied with a repertoire of leadership assessment tools that fall short of recognizing the prevalence and inevitability of narcissistic personality disorder among our leaders? Trivializing pathologies and perceiving them as normal disturbances in the workplace is potentially quite detrimental in a volatile workplace already embroiled in bullying, toxic behaviors, aggression, violence and what has recently been identified as organizational terrorism. Surely undiagnosed or misdiagnosed pathologies in our leaders are a precursor to ever escalating organizational dysfunction. Just one failure to timely assess may yield dramatic interpersonal and systemic repercussions including sabotage, plunging motivation and productivity, increased turnover and a high incidence of internal grievances, formal complaints and litigation.

(p. 410)

SUBCLINICAL DISORDERS

It is possible that the particular characteristics of other disordered individuals can make them attractive, or at least seem competent, in certain other jobs. Thus, people with mild paranoid personality disorder may be quite successful in the security business. Obsessive compulsives may succeed in many health and safety jobs.

It is important to bear in mind three factors with regard to personality-disordered people at work. First, it is crucial to take into consideration other factors such as physical appearance, level of cognitive ability and social skills. The brighter and more physically attractive people are the more they are likely to be "forgiven" various shortcomings. There is a vast literature in social psychology on the halo (and horns) effect which shows that attractive people are always judged more attractive than less attractive people.

Second, it is indeed rare for an individual to have one "clean and clear" personality disorder. Individuals have a profile which means, from a categorical perspective, that they reach "caseness" scores in more than one disorder at the same time. Similarly, if one takes the psychological or dimensional approach it is apparent that people have rich and complex profiles. Thus, an anti-social personality may have a similar score on another dimension: that is, one has to explain particular pathological behavior at work by understanding the full profile of the individual.

Third, biographical details remain important. The middle-class, anti-social personality will, no doubt, manifest very different traits from the working-class personality. Education and early work experiences can influence significantly how the disorders are manifest.

Equally, there are other concepts not technically defined as personality disorders but which are relevant. One is Machiavellianism. Machiavellianism may lead to destruction. Machiavellianism refers to people who are cynical, egocentric, controlling, distrustful and manipulative. They are deeply low on Agreeableness and empathy. They are supposed to epitomize the philosophy of the Italian writer, who advised: never show humility; morality and ethics are for the weak; it is better to be feared than loved. They are expedient. Rather than rewarding loyalty and friendship and caring about decency, fair play and honour, they concentrate only on winning.

In the world of business, they employ tactics aimed at disarming or humiliating their enemies (Greenberg and Baron, 2003). These include neglecting/"forgetting" to share important information; always striving to make others look bad and incompetent to their seniors; failing to meet their contractual obligations and spreading false rumours.

However, technically, Machiavellianism is considered an attitudinal, belief or stylistic variable, not a personality trait or disorder. Nevertheless, it is very apparent from the aforementioned that there is considerable overlap with personality disorders, particularly the anti-social personality.

MANAGING THE DISORDERS AND EXTREME TRAITS

What assessors and selectors must do, however, is look for signs of these behaviors before employment commences. Given the propensity of certain personality types to lying, exaggeration and attribution errors, this has to be done through others/observers rather than the individual themselves. In other words, the interview will not suffice to gather data though it may give certain clues.

It is a strong recommendation and requirement for certain jobs that due diligence is taken. This may mean fairly extensive background searches to ensure that the work-history of the individual is fully explored. This means contacting the bosses, colleagues and report staff at the various places where the candidate claimed to work. It means certainly interviewing many more people than the candidate gave as referees. It also means probing very carefully the veracity of many clauses.

It has been asserted that, using psychiatric criteria for the diagnosis of the personality disorders, it is possible to partly explain management derailment in terms of these disorders. It seems that many of these managers are on the borderline for diagnosis but may be easily "pushed over" the brink by a set of particular circumstances. Thus, an acute business problem or chronic issue may cause a number of crises and great stresses such that these individuals' "dark side" emerges. In this sense, the disorders mentioned above as long as they are not extreme (on the linear side) could be considered "potential risks for derailment".

There are two important practical issues. The *first* is how to identify such individuals. The *second* is how to prevent such individuals getting into positions in organizations that can cause great damage. It seems unlikely that individuals will diagnose themselves or seek help. Whilst this may occur for some Narcissists and Hysterics, it is very unlikely to be the case with Psychopaths. It is, however, quite probable that peers, subordinates and clients of psychopaths come to recognize their particular behaviors.

In this sense, 360-degree ratings may prove particularly useful for picking up signs of pathology. Most 360-degree questionnaires concentrate on particular competency behaviors with regard to such things as teamwork, communication and innovation. Some of these could easily be rewritten to try to take cognizance of the manifestations of the disorders. Thus, four or five items from each of the three personality disorders highlighted above may be included in a 360-degree feedback form. If there is both great disparity between the target manager (self-report) and his or her observers, be they boss, peers or customers, and if the observer ratings agree on the negative behaviors then the person may warrant further attention.

The sort of behaviors to look for refer to various things such as management style (haughty, insincere, manipulative), interpersonal relations (shallow, backstabbing, unskilled), job focus (impatient, erratic, unreliable) and other general "dark side" behaviors like lying, cheating and bullying.

De Fruyt and colleagues (2009) noted the importance of assessing personalities "at risk" in selection and developing settings. Again, they showed how certain "normal" personality traits at high vs low levels are good indicators of risk.

It is important to try to distinguish between "normal" and "abnormal" times and situations. Thus, if the negative, risky or dangerous behaviors manifest themselves only when the manager is under great stress (not of his or her making) and these stress episodes are not overly frequent, then it may be that with some help the situation may be recovered.

The question remains at the organizational level: what should the organization do to prevent managers from potentially derailing other managers. An obvious start is to attempt to assess these issues at recruitment and selection. Thus, one may use a "select-out" set of criteria. Data on these could come from standard questionnaires (Hogan and Hogan, 1997), various checklists (Saulsman and Page, 2004), but equally useful reference checks. Clearly, not enough organizations actively look for behaviors and traits that they don't want, as opposed to competences that they do.

A second series of issues relates to the situation where a manager is already in place in an organization and appears to be derailing because of evidence of one or more personality disorders. One obvious possibility is to try some sort of counselling or therapy. There remains some debate as to how amenable the personality disorders are to treatment (Babiak and Hare, 2006; Kets de Vries, 1999). It is likely that some are more amenable to treatment than others (i.e. Obsession vs Psychopath) and that much depends on the nature of the treatment.

Another issue may be to try to limit or control the situations where the "risk-prone" manager is less likely to manifest problems or where they are less "tempted" or provoked into inappropriate behavior. This may mean trying to reduce their stress or moving them to jobs where they have fewer problems. Inevitably, this does suggest a ceiling beyond which they probably should not rise.

Yet another approach, which appears to be advocated by Oldham and Morris (2000), is to educate those around these (correctly diagnosed) individuals to ensure that they understand and control rather than provoke and exacerbate this condition. This could also mean looking out for classic behaviors.

CONCLUSION

This chapter has concentrated on the three personality disorders and how "successful" psychopaths, narcissists and histrionics, etc., behave at work. Many people assume that these pathological disorders will easily be diagnosed and that it is virtually impossible for such individuals to rise to important positions in business. That is simply not true and there is increasing evidence that well-known and initially respected politicians, religious leaders, lawyers and business people turn out to be clearly diagnosable as having a disorder.

Further, this chapter asserts that, paradoxically perhaps, one of the three personality disorders discussed above may indeed help people in many business settings. The willingness to take risks on the part of the psychopath, the confidence of the narcissist; the emotional maverickness of the histrionic may make them particularly attractive for certain people in certain businesses.

The data on the prognosis for the personality disorders is not hopeful. They are unlikely to be changed much, though they can be managed. There is no very clear cut-off point on the continua that make up these three disorders. People may be on the borderline and in the "dangerous area" which clearly makes them less of a risk than if they were more extreme on the continua.

The intelligent, educated, middle-class individual with one (or more) of these disorders no doubt fares better. They can even be seen as an asset at certain times in the business cycle. But over the long term they are likely to reap problems for themselves, their direct reporting staff, their colleagues and their company. They can, as a single individual, turn the happy, efficient and functional workplace into one where people distrust each other, sabotage work and underperform. As powerful individuals, they can often be seen as the root cause of the shift from functional to dysfunctional workplaces.

PART II

4

THE SUCCESSFUL PSYCHOPATH

INTRODUCTION

There is an extensive, compulsive and fascinating literature on the psychopaths among us. Films have made people think psychopaths are all deranged axe-murderers and serial killers. But they are also convicts and mercenaries; con-artists and corporate executives. This chapter will look at what Hare (1999) called "White Collar" psychopaths and what are now often referred to as *successful psychopaths*.

The term "psychopath" or "sociopath" was used to describe anti-social personality types whose behavior is amoral or asocial, impulsive and lacking in remorse and shame. Once called "moral insanity", it is found more commonly among lower socio-economic groups, no doubt because of the "downward drift" of these types.

In his famous book called *The Mask of Insanity*, Cleckley (1941) first set out 10 criteria: superficial charm and intelligence; absence of anxiety in stressful situations; insincerity and lack of truthfulness; lack of remorse and shame; inability to experience love or genuine emotion; unreliability and irresponsibility; impulsivity and disregard for socially acceptable behavior; clear-headedness with an absence of delusions or irrational thinking; inability to profit from experience; and lack of insight. The book is, indeed, a classic in psychology and psychiatry because of its insight. Cleckley noted the slick but callous business person, the smooth-talking and manipulative lawyer, and the arrogant and deceptive politicians as psychopaths.

Cleckley identified 16 personality traits that, through his work with such individuals, he believed captured the essence of the psychopathic personality. The following are Cleckley's 16 traits:

1. superficial charm and good "intelligence"
2. absence of delusions and other signs of irrational thinking

3. absence of "nervousness" or psychoneurotic manifestations
4. unreliability
5. untruthfulness and insincerity
6. lack of remorse or shame
7. inadequately motivated anti-social behavior
8. poor judgment and failure to learn by experience
9. pathologic egocentricity and incapacity for love
10. general poverty in major affective reactions
11. specific loss of insight
12. unresponsiveness in general interpersonal relations
13. fantastic and uninviting behavior with drink and sometimes without
14. suicide rarely carried out
15. sex life impersonal, trivial, and poorly integrated
16. failure to follow any life plan.

Cleckley stressed the personality dimensions of this disorder, and clearly believed that most psychopaths are not violent. Whilst he acknowledged that a substantial proportion of incarcerated individuals exhibit psychopathic traits, he asserted that the majority of psychopaths are not incarcerated. According to Cleckley, the psychopath:

> is not likely to commit major crimes that result in long prison terms. He is also distinguished by his ability to escape ordinary legal punishments and restraints. Though he regularly makes trouble for society, as well as for himself, and frequently is handled by the police, his characteristic behaviour does not usually include committing felonies which would bring about permanent or adequate restrictions of his activities. He is often arrested, perhaps one hundred times or more. But he nearly always regains his freedom and returns to his old patterns of maladjustment.
>
> (p. 19)

DEFINITION

As with all psychiatric illnesses, there have been discussions and debates about definitions and terms. Babiak and Hare (2006) clarified the distinction between three overlapping terms:

> Psychopathy is a personality disorder described by the personality traits and behaviours. Psychopaths are without conscience

and incapable of empathy, guilt, or loyalty to anyone but them-selves. Sociopathy is not a formal psychiatric condition. It refers to patterns of attitudes and behaviours that are considered anti-social and criminal by society at large, but are seen as normal or necessary by the subculture or social environment in which they developed. Sociopaths may have a well-developed conscience and a normal capacity for empathy, guilt and loyalty, but their sense of right and wrong is based on the norms and expectations of their subculture or group. Many criminals might be described as sociopaths.

Anti-social personality disorder (APD) is a broad diagnostic cat-egory found in the American Psychiatric Association's (APA, 1994) Diagnostic and Statistic Manual of Mental Disorders, 4th edition (DSM-IV). Antisocial and criminal behaviours play a major role in its definition and, in this sense, APD is similar to sociopathy. Some of those with APD are psychopaths but many are not. The difference between psychopathy and antisocial personality disorder is that the former includes personality traits such as lack of empathy, grandios-ity and shallow emotion that are not necessary for a diagnosis of APD. APD is three or four times more common than psychopathy in the general population and in prisons. The prevalence of those we would describe as sociopathic is unknown but likely is considerably higher than that of APD.

(p. 19)

The defining characteristics of psychopathy tend to fall on two dimen-sions. The *first* is socio-emotional, where the psychopath is superficial and lacking in empathy, guilt or remorse. They are also deceitful and manipulative whilst being prone to egocentricity and grandiosity. The *second* is their social deviance associated with boredom susceptibility, impulsivity and lack of self-control. In children, they show evidence of behavior problems and in adulthood anti-social behavior. This has led to the development of a checklist.

POPULAR DESCRIPTIONS

Oldham and Morris (2000) call these types '*Adventurous*'. They describe the psychopath in popular terminology which makes it easier for non-specialists to spot. First, *Nonconformity*, where they live by their own internal code of values; second, *Love of challenge* and the thrill of risk; third, *Little mutual dependence*; and fourth, *Persuasiveness*, which is being silver-tongued, and influential. Next they have a *Strong sex drive* with different partners and, sixth, a consistent *Wanderlust*, that is, they love to keep moving on, settling neither on place nor people nor jobs. Seventh, they favor a *Freelance lifestyle* not worrying about finding work, preferring to exist by their talents, skills, ingenuity and wits. Eighth, they are *Easy and generous with money* and ninth high-spirited *Hell-raisers and mischief-makers*. Tenth, they show *Courage*, physical boldness, and toughess. Last, they always *Live in the present*. In short, they are inconsistent, aggressive, immoral, anti-conformists. They are also impulsive, reckless, egocentric and totally lacking in remorse.

Hogan and Hogan (2001) call the anti-social person *Mischievous*. They note that these types expect that others will like them and find them charming, and they expect to be able to extract favors, promises, money and other resources from other people with relative ease. However, they see others as merely to be exploited, and, therefore, have problems maintaining commitments and are unconcerned about social, moral and economic expectations. They are self-confident to the point of feeling invulnerable, and have an air of daring and sang-froid that others can find attractive and even irresistible. In industries where bold risk-taking is expected, they can seem a very desirable person for senior management positions.

Miller (2008) calls psychopathic bosses "predators". He claims they think "It's a dog-eat-dog world. Look out for number one. Rules are for losers. I'm smarter than all these suckers … My needs come first. I can get over anyone" (p. 58). Miller (2008) notes that psychopathic bosses are prototype cut-throat, chainsaw-type entrepreneurs. The interpersonal inquisitiveness is more about getting to know how to manipulate people than befriend them. They joy in outsmarting "suckers", which reinforces their personal sense of cleverness and powerfulness. They can easily become experts, cheats, embezzlers or harassers. Curiously, they often risk a lot for a little because of their love of thrill and excitement.

Miller (2008) notes two types of psychopathic bosses: first, the bright, devious, cunning, conning, natural manipulator. This is the plotting, smooth operator. The less bright psychopathic boss is more likely to use bullying and intimidation.

The psychopathic boss is not loyal or grateful but will humor staff that fulfil his or her needs and purposes. They will disregard people once they have served their purpose. They steal credit but hand out blame. The personality disorders website suggests the mnemonic CORRUPT

C: conformity to law lacking
O: obligations ignored
R: reckless disregard for safety of self or others
R: remorse lacking
U: underhanded (deceitful, lies, cons others)
P: planning insufficient (impulsive)
T: temper (irritable and aggressive).

The psychopathic boss's self-deception, self-confidence and reckless-ness lead to lots of conflicts, but they have almost no ability to learn from experience. According to Hogan and Hogan (1997):

> They tend to be underachievers, relative to their talent and capa-bilities; this is due to their impulsivity, their recklessness, and their inability to learn from experience. These people handle stress and heavy work loads with great aplomb. They are easily bored, and find stress, danger and risk to be invigorating – they actively seek it. As a result, many of these people become heroes – they intervene in robberies, they rush into burning buildings, they take apart live bombs, they volunteer for dangerous assignments, and they flour-ish in times of war and chaos. Conversely, they adapt poorly to the requirements of structured bureaucracies.
>
> (p. 49)

POSSIBLE CAUSE

Babiak and Hare (2000) summarize the issue neatly:

> Are psychopathic features the product of nature or nurture? As with most other things human, the answer is that both are involved. A better question is "To what extent do nature and nurture influ-ence the development of the traits and behaviours that define psychopathy?"
>
> (p. 107)

The answer to this question is becoming much clearer with the application of behavioral genetics to the study of personality traits and behavioral dispositions.

Several recent twin studies provide convincing evidence that genetic factors play at least as important a role in the development of the core features of psychopathy as do environmental factors and forces. Researchers Blonigen, Carlson, Krueger and Patrick (2003) stated that the results of their study of 271 twin pairs provided "substantial evidence of genetic contributions to variance in the personality construct of psychopathy". Subsequently, researchers Larrson, Andershed and Lichtenstein (2006) arrived at a similar conclusion in their study of 1090 adolescent twin pairs: "A genetic factor explains most of the variation in the psychopathic personality." Viding, Blair, Moffitt and Plomin (2005) studied 3687 seven-year-old twin pairs and also concluded that "the core symptoms of psychopathy are strongly genetically determined". Babiak and Hare (2000) reported that the genetic contribution was highest when callous unemotional traits were combined with anti-social behaviors:

> Evidence of this sort does not mean that the pathways to adult psychopathy are fixed and immutable, but it does indicate that the social environment will have a tough time in overcoming what nature has provided. As noted in *Without Conscience*, the elements needed for the development of psychopathy – such as a profound inability to experience empathy and the complete range of emotions, including fear – are provided in part by nature and possibly by some unknown biological influences on the developing foetus and neonate. As a result the capacity for developing internal controls and conscience and for making emotional 'connections' with others is greatly reduced.
>
> To use a simple analogy, the potter is instrumental in moulding pottery from clay (nurture) but the characteristics of the pottery also depend on the sort of clay available (nature).

(pp. 24–5)

One obvious question is how common psychopathic traits are in the average population. One recent big study found these affect less than 1% of the population but are more common among prisoners, homeless people and psychiatric patients. Psychopaths tend to be violent, young males (Cold *et al.*, 2009a). It is argued that of the prison population around 8% of males and 2% of females are psychopaths (Cold *et al.*, 2009a).

PSYCHOPATHS AT WORK

Hare (1999), in a chapter on white-collar psychopaths, noted how many were "trust-mongers" who, through charm and gall, obtained, then very callously betrayed, the trust of others. He notes how they make excellent imposters and how they frequently target the vulnerable. They target and exploit people's gullibility, naivety and Rousseauian view of the goodness of man.

He calls them *subcriminal psychopaths* who can thrive as academics, cult-leaders, doctors, police officers and writers. They violate rules, conventions and ethical standards, always just crossing legal boundaries. He also gives a rich case study description of what he calls a *corporate psychopath*. He notes that there is certainly no shortage of opportunities for psychopaths who think big. It is lucrative: "They are fast talking, charming, self-assured, at ease in social situations, cool under pressure, unfazed by the possibility of being found out, and totally ruthless" (p. 121).

Babiak and Hare (2006) believe most of us will interact with a psychopath every day. But their skills and abilities make them difficult to spot. Often, they tend to be charming, emotionally literate and socially skilled. Next, they are often highly articulate. Third, they are brilliantly chameleon-like in their impression management. They note:

> This is not to say that most people can't be charming, effective, socially facile communicators and still be honest – of course they can. Many people use impression management and manipulation techniques to influence others to like and trust them or to get what they want from people – very often subconsciously, but sometimes as the result of training, practice and planning. However, wanting people to like and respect you (and doing what it takes to achieve this) is not necessarily dishonest or insincere – the need for approval and validation from others is normal. Social manipulation begins to be insincere if you really don't care about the feelings of others or you try to take unfair advantage of others. The difference between the psychopathic approach and the non-psychopathic approach lies in motivation to take unfair and callous advantage of people. Psychopaths simply do not care if what they say and do hurts people as long as they get what they want, and they are very good at hiding this fact. Given his or her powerful manipulation skills, it is little wonder why seeing a "psychopathic" personality beneath someone's charming, engaging surface is so difficult.

Not all psychopaths are smooth operators, though. Some do not have enough social or communicative skill or education to interact successfully with others, relying instead on threats, coercion, intimidation and violence to dominate others and to get what they want. Typically such individuals are manifestly aggressive and rather nasty, and unlikely to charm victims into submission, relying on the bullying approach instead.

(p. 19)

The successful psychopath has, essentially, a manipulative approach to life. Their sole aim is to get what they want with effort, emotion or fear and whether they deserve it or not. Hence the importance of various groups that may be called "the organizational police", auditors, human resources, quality controllers whose job it is to ensure compliance with standards.

There is a small but growing literature on the successful, that is, non-institutionalized psychopath (Ishikawa *et al.*, 2001; Widom, 1978; Widom and Newman, 1985). They are described as carefree, aggressive, charming and impulsively irresponsible. They have the essential personality characteristics of the psychopath but seem to refrain from really serious antisocial behavior, though their behavior is often illegal and almost always immoral. Researchers have identified many politicians and business leaders as non-criminal psychopaths. They are duplicitous, but not illegally so. They show many patterns of misconduct but seem not to get caught. They seem brilliant at tactical impression management and are drawn to unstable, chaotic, rapidly changing situations where they can more easily operate. Successful, non-incarcerated psychopaths seem to have compensatory factors that buffer them against criminal behavior, like higher social class and intelligence. In this sense, the successful psychopath has a wider set of coping mechanisms than less privileged and able psychopaths who soon get caught. It is the articulate, good-looking, educated psychopath that is most dangerous at work.

Self-report measures of the psychopathic personality give a clear indication of the sort of behaviors that are relevant (Benning *et al.*, 2005). Impulsive non-conformity (reckless, rebellious, unconventional); Blame externalization (blames others, rationalizes own transgressions); Machiavellian egocentricity (interpersonally aggressive and self-centered); Carefree non-planfulness (excessive present-orientation with lack of forethought or planning); Stress immunity (experiencing minimal anxiety); Fearlessness (willing to take risks, having little concern with potentially harmful consequences) and general Cold-heartedness (unsentimental, unreactive to others' distress, lacking in imagination). These seem to factor into *two* dimensions: one related to high negative emotionality and the other low behavioral constraint. Further research by Benning and colleagues (2005) led these authors to think about two distinct facets of the psychopath: *fearless dominance* (glib, grandiose, deceitful, low stress) and *impulsive antisociality* (aggressive, antisocial, low control). This suggests that within the psychopath population one may be able to distinguish between these two groups.

Anti-social (psychopathic) managers show a blatant and consistent disregard for, and violation of, the rights of others. They often have a history of being difficult, delinquent or dangerous. They show a failure to conform to most social norms and frequently, if not bright or privileged, get into trouble with the law for lying, stealing and cheating. They are always deceitful, as indicated by repeated use of aliases and "conning others" for personal profit or pleasure. They can be, in short, nasty, aggressive, con-artists – the sort who often get profiled on business crime programmes. They are also massively impulsive and fail to plan ahead. They live only in, and for, the present. They show irritability and aggressiveness, as indicated by repeated physical fights or assaults. They manifest a surprising reckless disregard for the physical and psychological safety of self and others – or the business in general. In an environment that values risk-taking they are clearly in their element. They are famous for being consistently irresponsible. Repeated failure to sustain consistent work behavior or to honor financial obligations is their hallmark. Most frustrating of all, they show lack of remorse. They are indifferent to, or cleverly rationalize, having hurt, mistreated or stolen from another. They never learn from their mistakes. It can seem as if labelling them as antisocial is a serious understatement.

Anti-social, adventurous managers are not frightened by risk: they thrive on it. They love the thrill of adventure and are happy to put others' lives at risk as well as their own. They tend to be self-confident and not overly concerned with the approval of others. They live for the moment: they are neither guilty about the past nor worried about the future. They can be seriously reckless and tend not to tolerate frustration well. They resist discipline and ignore rules. They have poor self-control and think little about the consequences of their actions. They need excitement all the time and are very easily bored. They can be successful entrepreneurs, journalists, bouncers, lifeguards.

It is an interesting question to try to understand in what sorts of jobs psychopathic traits might be, at least for a time, advantageous. This may refer both to the type of job but also a particular situation, such as when an organization is changing rapidly, in decline, or under investigation. They like outwitting the system – opportunistically exploiting who and what they can. They usually hate routine and administration, which are seen as drudgery. No wonder people who work for them feel so demoralized.

They make bad bosses and bad partners because they are egocentric and only continue on in a relationship as long as it is good for them. They rarely have long-lasting, meaningful relationships. They have two human ingredients missing which are pretty crucial to a fully-functioning person: *conscience and compassion*. They score very low on Agreeableness and Conscientiousness. Hence they can be cruel, destructive, malicious and criminal. They are unscrupulous, and are exploitatively self-interested with little capacity for remorse. They act before they think and are famous for their extreme impulsivity.

Dotlich and Cairo (2003) note that the Mischievous psychopath knows that the rules are really "only suggestions". They are rebels without a cause; rule breakers who believe rules, laws and other restrictions are tedious and unecessary. They clearly have destructive impulses and a preference for making impulsive decisions without considering any consequences. They can, and do, speak their mind, use their charms and creativity but for no clear business goal.

They document five signs and symptoms. Staff question the mischievous leaders' commitments and projects they have initiated but subsequently neglected; they frequently never take time or effort to win people over; everything rates as a challenge to them. Also they are easily bored and they have to spend a lot of effort covering up cock-ups and mistakes.

DEALING WITH PSYCHOPATHS

How to deal with the psychopath? Easier said than done; however, Dotlich and Cairo (2003) offer four pieces of advice for what is no doubt a successful psychopath. Encourage them to take ownership for their action and interrogate their rule-breaking, consequence-ignoring behaviors. *Second*, encourage them to think clearly about which rules they will really follow as opposed to break. *Third*, they may benefit from being on the receiving end of the sort of mischief they dish out. Finally, they might benefit from confiding in a coach.

Oldham and Morris (2000) offer "tips on dealing with the adventurous person in your life". They note one needs to be very vigilant about what they are up to and not to be hopeful of easily (or ever) changing them much. They warn partners (in business or love) to be cautious and careful and not get drawn into their world, and also not to expect help and support, which they are very unlikely to receive.

Babiak and Hare (2006) offer lots of advice to people dealing with psychopaths. The following is their advice if the psychopath is the client:

1. Get paid up front. If you lose the case, you will be blamed and unpaid. If you win the case, the client will take the credit and you *still* be unpaid.
2. Be very careful about boundaries. The client is not your friend, and will collect and use against you whatever information is obtained. (This includes information related to the case *and* related to you personally.)
3. Remain in charge. A psychopathic client will attempt to run the show and to manipulate you and the system, making your job much harder.
4. Don't take at face value the client's description of events or interactions with others. Check everything out.
5. Be aware that the client will distort and minimize his or her criminal history. When confronted with the inaccuracies, the client will offer excuses that place the blame on defence attorney, a corrupt system, or others.
6. The client will flatter you as long as things are going smoothly. If the case goes sideways, often because of the client's tendency to take charge and to ignore advice, you will become the enemy.
7. Keep copious notes on *everything*.

(p. 314)

WORKING WITH PSYCHOPATHS

Babiak (1995) found five characteristics in the many studies of industrial psychopathy and various case studies. He has reported case studies of individuals and begun to describe how they succeed despite their predisposition. He has noted from a series of case studies:

Comparison of the behaviour of the three subjects observed to date revealed some similarities: each a) began by building a *network of one-to-one relationships* with powerful and useful individuals,

b) *avoided virtually all group meetings* where maintaining multiple facades may have been too difficult, and c) *created conflicts* which kept co-workers from sharing information about him. Once their power bases were established, d) *co-workers who were no longer useful* were abandoned and e) *detractors were neutralized* by systematically raising doubts about their competence and loyalty. In addition, unstable cultural factors, inadequate measurement systems, and general lack of trust typical of organizations undergoing rapid, chaotic change may have provided an acceptable cover for psychopathic behaviour.

(pp. 184–5, emphases added).

It is difficult to estimate the number of successful "industrial" psychopaths. It is also sometimes difficult to explain why they "get away with it" for so long. However, it is no mystery when enquiring from those who work or have worked with a successful psychopath how much misery or dysfunctionality they can bring to the workplace. The idea is that psychopaths easily get hired using charm and blatant lies. Next, they soon identify, befriend, woo and "sweet-talk" all the powerful "key-players" in the organization. They build these people into a support network aimed both to establish their own reputation and, more importantly, undermine their potential opponents. Next, they abandon those who have been useful to them.

Babiak and Hare (2006) believe that psychopaths are, indeed, attracted to today's business climate. They devised a questionnaire to help people at work spot them. There are, according to the authors, 10 markers of the problem. The successful, industrial psychopath is characterized by the following. He or she:

1. comes across as smooth, polished and charming
2. turns most conversations around to a discussion of him- or herself
3. discredits and puts down others in order to build up own image and reputation
4. lies to co-workers, customers, or business associates with a straight face
5. considers people he or she has outsmarted or manipulated as dumb or stupid
6. opportunistic; hates to lose, plays ruthlessly to win
7. comes across as cold and calculating
8. acts in an unethical or dishonest manner
9. has created a power network in the organization and uses it for personal gain

10. shows no regret for making decisions that negatively affect the company, shareholders, or employees.

Psychopaths can easily look like ideal leaders: smooth, polished, charming. They can quite easily mesh their dark side – bullying, amoral, manipulative. In the past it may be politics, policing, law, media and religion that attracted psychopaths but, more and more, it is the fast-paced, exciting, glamorous world of business.

The issue with the psychopathic boss is whether they are subclinical vs clinical psychopaths and what in fact "pushes" them over the limits. Hare (1999) in his clinical study of psychopaths asks: "can anything be done?" He says nothing seems to work, precisely because psychopaths see no reason to change. Further, therapy can make them worse because it teaches them more effectively how to deceive, manipulate and use people. They learn therapy language (getting in touch with their feelings) without ever actually changing.

However, he does offer a survival guide that comes under two headings: Protect Yourself and Damage Control. The former is a warning to be on your guard; disregard their clever acting; beware their flattery, feigned kindness and tall stories; and know yourself, because psychopaths are skilled at detecting vulnerability. He also warns those who deal with psychopaths to be very aware of who the victim is: that is, psychopaths like to portray themselves as victims, yet it is more likely to be you.

Hare (1999) warns those who associate with psychopaths to be aware of their power struggles and to set firm ground rules to prevent manipulation. He also advises to cut your losses: the psychopath's appetite for power and control knows no bounds and such a person is best left to their own devices.

In their practical, popular and work-oriented book on successful psychopaths, Babiak and Hare (2006) note how psychopaths attempt to ruin others' reputations, in terms of their competence and loyalty. They operate as brilliant manipulators and puppeteers to destroy your reputation. Because they try to create conflict in work teams through "divide and conquer", it is important to build and maintain relationships at work. They offer seven pieces of advice if your boss is a psychopath:

1. Build, nurture and maintain your (true) reputation as a good performer
2. Keep records of everything and put it in writing

3. Make use of, and be very wary of, the performance appraisal process
4. Avoid confrontation by minimizing contact and never responding to bait
5. Be very wary about making a formal complaint, as anonymity is not always assured and retribution very likely to follow
6. If you have to leave (by transfer, resignation), do so on good terms
7. Move on, remembering the lesson.

They offer similar advice for the psychopathic co-worker, subordinate or client.

Babiak and Hare (2000) suggest that there is a common pattern when psychopaths join a company. They charm at assessment and through their honeymoon period. Soon, they become manipulative and disparaging to others, and indulge in flagrant image-enhancement. Then they confront by trying to neutralize enemies and abandoning those of little use to them. Finally, if successful, they tend to abandon their patrons as they move ever upward and onward. To be alerted to the possibility of this pattern may help identify psychopaths before it is too late.

CONCLUSION

The term "psychopath" is much used but more misunderstood. Psychopathy lies on a continuum from low to high. Successful, subclinical, industrial psychopaths can be very successful at work. If they are clever and presentable, their superficial charm and boldness may suit them well, particularly in business situations that are rapidly changing. Further, it is stress that may push people "over the line" from people with "weak conscience" and taste for excitement into subclinical and even psychopathic behavior.

One test of whether a person is a subclinical psychopath lies in their biography. From the age of adolescence onwards it may be possible to detect early signs of delinquency, brushes with the law and a string of people lining up to testify, quite happily, about the way they were lied to, cheated and "conned" by a particular individual they trusted. Hence the importance of thorough biographical checks when selecting senior managers.

5

NARCISSISM AT WORK

INTRODUCTION

This chapter is predicated on four fundamental axioms. The *first* is that self-esteem at both the global (facet) and specific (domain) levels is normally distributed in the population. Like nearly all human characteristics and traits, from creativity to conscientiousness and integrity to intelligence, there is, in the general population, a bell curve (normal) distribution with a few people with very high self-esteem and a few with very low self-esteem. Further, it has trait-like qualities, being stable over time and relatively consistent across social situations.

The *second* is that the relationship between self-esteem and social adjustment is possibly more curvilinear than linear. That is, too much is as bad as too little self-esteem. Optimal self-esteem, combined with optimal self-insight, is related to healthy, productive and stable social relationships at, and outside, work. Having little self-esteem and self-confidence can inhibit the development of relationships, whilst too much self-esteem (narcissism) can equally impair social relationships. It should be noted that Sedikides and colleagues (2004) argued, and demonstrated, that "normal" narcissists are psychologically healthy, but admitted that extreme levels may be associated with psychological disturbance and illness.

The *third* is that self-esteem has a powerful influence on the success individuals have in their ability to initiate, maintain and benefit from social relationships in and out of the workplace. Many factors determine the quality and quantity of their social relationships, but self-esteem plays an important part.

Fourth, the causal relationship between self-esteem and overall success at work, in both the social and output sense, is bi-directional leading to *virtuous* and *vicious* cycles. It is misleading to believe that the direction of causality is from self-esteem to work success, therefore implying that enhancing self-esteem has a simple causal relationship to work-related behavior. Indeed, there may well be circumstances when the primary causal relationship is the other way around. That is, teach people to become successful at work and their self-esteem goes up. Successful people feel good about themselves: that is, it is not that teaching self-esteem leads to success, but rather success at work enhances self-esteem.

There is a vast literature on "self" words in psychology such as self-esteem, self-confidence, self-worth and self-awareness. The idea is that people make assessments and evaluations about themselves, particularly their abilities and personality, but also about their motives, their physical attractiveness and their "potential". Whilst these self-assessments are inevitably subjective, they can be measured at least against the judgment of others. Further, it is assumed that the more accurate these assessments against objective, observatory or even reputational criteria, the more healthy and adapted the individual. On the other hand, low accuracy implies the possibility of delusions. Self-awareness is thus seen as a crucial index of mental health and adaptation.

It is common to see talented, attractive and conscientious people at work underachieve or underperform because of their low self-esteem. Through their primary or secondary socialization, as well as the simple lack of opportunity or accurate feedback, certain individuals hold views about themselves which inhibit their behavior. They seem never to explore or exploit their potential. Some seek help and can benefit from attempts to bolster their self-esteem appropriately.

One definition of narcissism is where a person's assessment of some aspect of their self (ability, appearance, motives, personality) is different from, (i.e. greater than) the subjective but aggregated rating of others or by valid, objective test results. In this sense, narcissists are simply not self-aware. Further, this lack of self-awareness can have considerable effect on a narcissist's relationship with others who clearly do not share their perceptions.

There is a great deal of research on self-awareness, starting from early work in multi-source now called 360-degree feedback (Furnham and Stringfield, 1994; Furnham, 2007). Thus, one way to possibly detect narcissism in the workplace is to seek out managers who show large discrepancies in their 360-degree, multi-source feedback, with self-ratings being consistently and significantly higher than ratings of peers, superiors or subordinates. In other words, those who show a self-enhancement bias (Paunonen *et al.*, 2006).

This hypothesis was tested by Judge and colleagues (2006) who looked at narcissist self-ratings and other ratings of leadership, workplace deviance, contextual and task performance. They found evidence to support all their ideas; namely, that narcissism is positively related to enhanced self-ratings, but negatively related to ratings of the other. They also predicted, and found, that the narcissism score of an individual is more strongly and negatively related to other ratings of contextual rather than task performance. Thus, narcissists see themselves as particularly altruistic, courteous and virtuous, as well as being seriously job-outcome focused. Further, they found narcissism had incremental validity over the "Big Five" in predicting ratings, particularly in other ratings. The more Open and Conscientious the person, the higher their self-ratings but narcissism contributed unique variance. In other words, "normal" personality measures do not pick up on narcissism.

All self–other rating differences are, of course, interesting and predictive, but where they originate and how they are maintained is the most interesting. Judge and colleagues (2006) argue that self-aggrandizing typically denigrates others and deprives them of *their* self-esteem. Further, self-aggrandizers may make bad decisions and have distorted views of the world because of their brittle ego, which also punishes those giving negative or threatening feedback.

This chapter will focus on those with too much self-esteem: those, effectively, with narcissistic personality disorder. Whilst many people, adolescents in particular, may appear too full of arrogance and hubris at times, one "qualifies" for the diagnosis of the disorder only if various criteria are met.

There is a potential paradox with this personality disorder which, indeed, distinguishes it from other personality disorders like the antisocial personality disorder. That is, narcissists may at first be beneficial at work or in social relationships. People are attracted to those with self-confidence, no doubt because they believe they have something to be self-confident about. Narcissists assume their experience has taught them that they have been successful in the past (at many things) and will no doubt, therefore, be successful in the future. *Indeed, self-confidence in others may be particularly attractive to those who struggle with it in themselves.*

Highly self-confident people do well at job interviews and can inspire considerable trust in others. The problem arises when self-confidence "spills over" into arrogance and narcissism. Further, there may be a very thin line between healthy self-confidence and unhealthy narcissism. However, it should always be borne in mind that for high self-confidence to be healthy it should be based on actual criteria. It may not reach the "criteria" of full-blown narcissism, but may still be maladaptive. At the core of the problem is a keen and accurate self-awareness of one's abilities, attributes and preferences.

DEFINITIONS

Rosenthal and Pittinsky (2006) attempted a definition of narcissistic leadership:

> Accordingly we propose the following definition: Narcissistic leaders' actions are principally motivated by their own egomaniacal needs and beliefs, superseding the needs and interests of the constituents and institutions they lead.
>
> We define egomaniacal needs and beliefs to include many of the patterns pervasive in narcissistic personality – grandiose sense of self-importance, preoccupation with fantasies of unlimited success and power, excessive need for admiration, entitlement, lack of empathy, envy, inferiority, and hypersensitivity.
>
> What is critical about this definition, and what differentiates it from simply describing narcissistic leaders, is that it is sensitive to the context in which the leadership takes place – as with theories of power, motivation, narcissistic leadership considers leaders' psychological motivations; and as with charismatic leaders, narcissistic leadership takes situational factors and follower perception into account. Unlike the study of narcissistic leaders, it is not directly linked to leader personality traits, including their narcissism – non-narcissists can engage in narcissistic leadership, whereas narcissists are capable of leading non-narcissistically.
>
> The central reason for adopting a perspective focused on narcissistic leadership rather than on narcissistic leaders is that it is difficult to characterize the relationship between leader personality characteristics and their actions.
>
> (p. 629)

They note the overlap in definitions and conclude:

> In a similar vein, whilst narcissistic leadership is not (and should not) be incompatible with power motivation and charismatic

leadership, it is easier to clarify how it differs from those theories than it is to state empathically whether a particular narcissistic leader fits within those categories. For instance, both narcissistic leadership and power motivation may involve aggressive and exploitative leader behaviour. However, the motivations for that behaviour are easier to distinguish – as self-enhancing, expansive quest for superiority versus a desire to pursue power in order to have a positive impact on others. Likewise, narcissistic and charismatic leadership may both entail using charm and magnetism to win over devoted followers. Such behaviour would be characterized as charismatic leadership if it involves a genuinely dynamic relationship between leader and followers. However, if the followers simply function as "audience members" through whose admiration the leader bolsters his or her own self-image, it would be defined as narcissistic leadership.

(p. 630)

Brown (1997) identifies six major sets of "traits" that characterize narcissism, which can be located at individual, group and organizational levels:

1. *Denial*: the denial of facts about oneself, the realities of the constraints around one's work, and about the details of past occurrences in order for their ego ideal not to be challenged.
2. *Rationalization*: the development of plausible justifications for explaining behavior that does not support the belief in the ego ideal. This can come in the form of rationalizing failures, and justifying self-serving policies and decisions as if they were done in the interest of the group.
3. *Self-aggrandizement*: engaging in behavior that serves to convince both oneself and others of one's fantasy of power, control and greatness. This includes over-stating one's virtues, merits and achievements.
4. *Attributional egoism*: attributing positive organizational outcomes to one's own efforts, and unfavourable outcomes to external factors or other people, regardless of one's own role. Such false attributions seek to defend the ego ideal of the narcissist.
5. *Sense of entitlement*: a feeling that one is entitled to organizational privileges such as success, power and admirations, whilst at the same time lacking empathy for others and exploiting people in the pursuit of self-interest.

6. *Anxiety*: the experience of an ongoing difficulty in maintaining self-esteem accompanied by hypersensitivity to criticism, and persistent feelings of insecurity.

THE NARCISSISM MYTH AND LEGEND

Several versions of the myth of narcissism survive. They are warnings about hubris and pride. Most rely on the Ovid version of the myth:

> Narcissus was the son of Cephissus, the river god, and the nymph Leiriope. By the time he was sixteen everyone recognized his ravishing beauty, but he scorned all lovers – of both sexes – because of his pride. The nymph Echo was hopelessly in love with Narcissus but she was hindered by her inability to initiate a conversation. Eventually Narcissus rejected her. She wasted away in her grief to a mere voice. A young man, similarly spurned, prayed that he would love himself unremittingly. The goddess Nemesis answered this prayer by arranging that Narcissus would stop to drink at a spring on the heights of Mount Helicon. As he looked in the water he saw his own reflection and instantly fell in love with the image. He could not embrace his reflection in the pool. Unable to tear himself away he remained until he died of starvation. But no body remained – in its place was a flower.

An earlier version has been more recently discovered; a similar but subtly different version. In this story Ameinias, a young man, loved Narcissus but was scorned by him. To tell off Ameinias, Narcissus gave him a sword as a present. Ameinias used the sword to kill himself on Narcissus' doorstep and prayed to Nemesis that Narcissus would one day know the pain of unrequited love. This curse was fulfilled when Narcissus became entranced by his reflection in the pool and tried to seduce the beautiful boy, not realizing it was himself he was looking at. He only realized it was his reflection after trying to kiss it. Completing the symmetry of the tale, Narcissus took his sword and killed himself from sorrow. His corpse then turned into a flower. Thus, Narcissus died because he could love his image only at the expense of himself.

Poets, painters and moralists have been intrigued with the myth, seeking to interpret its meaning. The Freudians found the myth beguiling and sought intrapsychic and psychopathological interpretations. There have also been various illuminating psychological accounts of famous plays like Miller's (1949) *Death of a Salesman* as being a prototypic story of narcissism (Tracy and Robins, 2007). Freudians argue that we develop an "ego-ideal" when defending ourselves from feelings of fear, helplessness and isolation. This is an image of what it could be if we could be at the center of our world. Adult narcissists reinvent this self-centeredness with love reserved entirely for the self.

At the heart of the myth is the caution against misperception and self-love: the idea that inaccurate self-perceptions can lead to tragic and self-defeating consequences. There appears to be a moral, social and clinical debate about Narcissism. The moral issues concern the evils of hubris; the social issue is about the benefits, or otherwise, of modesty; the clinical debate is about the consequences of misperceptions. This chapter focuses on how narcissism "plays out" in the workplace.

Psychologists have also attempted to measure narcissism and to distinguish it from simply being a form of "high self esteem". The most established measure is probably the Narcissistic Personality Inventory, which appears to have four identifiable factors (Emmons, 1984; Raskin and Hall, 1981):

1. Exploitativeness and Entitlement: the complete belief that one is very good at and entitled to manipulate people for one's own end
2. Leadership and Authority: the belief that one is extremely talented at leadership and all authority roles
3. Superiority and Arrogance: the belief that one is a "born leader" and quite simply better than others
4. Self-Absorption and Self-Admiration: a belief that one is special and worth adoration and respect.

It is important to bear these in mind when examining individual studies in the area.

Pullen and Rhodes (2008) made an interesting distinction between "thick-skinned" masculine narcissism and "thin-skinned" feminine narcissism. The feminine version also shows problems of self-esteem and ability to love themselves in a healthy and natural way. The former are destructive, the latter defensive. They argue with case studies that the inflated ego-ideal of the feminine narcissist may be managed by performing services to others and echoing back their expectations.

NARCISSISTIC CULTURE

Is it possible that narcissism is sanctioned, or indeed encouraged, by an organizational or national culture? Can whole cultures endorse or encourage narcissism to make it appear normal, even desirable? Observers have noted a change in the puritan, service-above-self value system to the "me-culture" that appears almost narcissistic.

Many commentators on contemporary culture have attempted to discern trends and patterns that trace the waxing and waning of movements, ethics or cults. One influential analysis of American culture has been that of Lasch (1979), who argues that the dominant American culture of competitive individualism has changed into the pursuit of happiness and a narcissistic preoccupation with self. Central to Lasch's (1979) thesis is the decline of the Protestant Work Ethic (PWE) and what he calls "changing modes of making it". In doing so, he very succinctly describes the PWE as it underpinned American culture:

> Until recently the Protestant work ethic stood as one of the most important underpinnings of American culture. According to the myth of capitalist enterprise, thrift and industry held the key to material success and spiritual fulfilment. America's reputation as a land of opportunity rested on its claim that the destruction of hereditary obstacles to advancement had created conditions in which social mobility depended on individual initiative alone. The self-made man, archetypical embodiment of the American dream, owed his advancement to habits of industry, sobriety, moderation, self-discipline and avoidance of debt. He lived for the future, shunning self-indulgence in favour of patient, painstaking accumulation; and as long as the collective prospect looked on the whole so bright, he found in the deferral of gratification not only his principal satisfaction but an abundant source of profits. In an expanding economy, the value to investments could be expected to multiply with time as the spokesmen for self-help, for all their celebration of work as its own reward, seldom neglected to point out.

(pp. 52–3)

For Lasch (1979), the *Puritan* gave way to the *Yankee*, who secularized the work ethic and stressed self-improvement (instead of socially useful work) that consisted of the cultivation of reason, wisdom and insight as well as money. Wealth was valued because it allowed for a programme of moral self-improvement and was one of the necessary preconditions of moral and intellectual advancement.

The spirit of *self-improvement*, according to Lasch (1979), was debased into *self-culture* – the care and training of the mind and body through reading great books and healthy living. Self-help books taught self-confidence, initiative and other qualities of success. The

118

management of interpersonal relations came to be seen as the essence of self-advancement. People were told that they had to sell themselves in order to succeed. The new prophets of positive thinking discarded the moral overtones of Protestantism. The pursuit of economic success was now accepted along with the need to exploit and intimidate others and to ostentatiously show the winning image of success.

The new mind-set meant that people preferred admiration, envy and the excitement of celebration to being respected and esteemed. People were less interested in how people acquired success – defined by riches, fame and power – than that they had "made it". Success had to be ratified and verified by publicity. The quest for a good public image led to a confusion of successful completion of the task with rhetoric that is aimed to impress or persuade others. Thus, impressions overshadowed achievements, and the images and symbols of success were more important than the actual achievements.

It became important, according to Lasch's historical analysis, to get on with others; to organize one's life in accordance with the requirements of large organizations; to sell one's own personality; to receive affection and reassurance. The dominant perception was that success was dependent on the psychological manipulation of one's own and others' positive and negative emotions and social behaviors.

The pursuit of self-interest, formerly identified with the accumulation of wealth, has become a search for pleasure and psychic survival. Social conditions approximate the vision of republican society conceived by the Marquis de Sade at the very outset of the republican epoch (Lasch, 1979, p. 69).

For Lasch (1979), the cult or ethic of narcissism has a number of quite distinct features:

- *The waning of the sense of historical time.* The idea that things are coming to an end means that people have a very limited time perspective, neither confidently forward nor romantically backward. The narcissist lives only in, and for, the present.
- *The therapeutic sensibility.* Narcissists seek therapy for personal well-being, health and psychic security. The rise in the human potential movement and the decline in self-help tradition have made people dependent on experts and organizations to validate self-esteem and develop competence. Therapists are used excessively to help develop composure, meaning and health.
- *From politics to self-examination.* Political theories, issues, and conflicts have been trivialized. The debate has moved from

the veridical nature of political propositions to the personal and autobiographical factors that lead proponents to make such suppositions.

- *Confession and anticonfession.* Writers and others attempt simple self-disclosure, rather than critical reflection, to gain insight into the psycho-historical forces that lead to personal development. But these confessions are paradoxical and do not lead to greater, but rather to lesser, insights into the inner life. People disclose, not to provide an objective account of reality, but to seduce others to give attention, acclaim, or sympathy and, by doing so, foster the perpetual, faltering sense of self.
- *The void within.* Without psychological peace, meaning, or com-mitment people experience an inner emptiness which they try to avoid by living vicariously through the lives of others, or seeking spiritual masters.
- *The progressive critique of privatism.* Self-absorption with dreams of fame, avoidance of failure, and quests for spiritual panacea means that people define social problems as personal ones. The cult sug-gests a limited investment in love and friendship, avoidance of dependence and living for the moment.

Lasch (1979) argues that psychological insights into the narcissistic personality of our time fails to miss the social dimension of this behav-ior pattern, such as pseudo-self-insight, calculating seductiveness, and nervous self-deprecating humour.

Narcissism, or the ethic of self-preservation, appears to many peo-ple to be the best way of coping with the tensions, vicissitudes, and anxieties of modern life. The traits associated with this ethic – charm, pseudo-awareness, promiscuous pan-sexuality, hypochondria, protective shallowness, avoidance of dependence, inability to mourn, dread of old age and death – are, according to Lasch who does not provide evidence, learnt in the family and reinforced in soci-ety but are corruptible and changeable. Ultimately, the paradox of narcissism is that it is the faith of those without faith; the cult of personal relations for those who are disenchanted with personal relations.

This cynical view of the change of the work ethic into the narcissism ethic is an analysis from a socio-historical view of current America. To what extent it is generally or specifically true is uncertain as, indeed, is whether it applies to other countries with similar political and economic climates. Perhaps because profundity is always associated with pessimism, Lasch's (1979) analysis has failed to reveal much good about this ethic. It could be argued that Lasch's analysis understates the problem as it appeared in the decade of the last century (and millennium) where me-values and narcissism thrived in the west. In other words, Lasch's analysis is fundamentally correct but out-of-date.

It may also be that norms and values in the workplace condone and promote narcissism. It is therefore possible that many organizational cultures take on board narcissistic values which are trumpeted. Organizations may therefore have selected, sought and praised those with self-esteem bordering on narcissistic personality disorder. In this sense, narcissism can be seen as the property of culture as well as individuals.

THE SOCIAL PSYCHOLOGY OF MODESTY AND SELF-ENHANCEMENT

Judeo-Christian teachings advocate the virtue of modesty, of being moderate, unassuming or even reticent in estimating and describing one's abilities. Modesty is freedom from such things as boastfulness, vanity or self-assertion. Modesty is valued for being unpretentious and non-deceptive. It can be seen in people's attitudes, dress and social conduct.

However, at the core of the definition is the idea of perceptual accuracy. Modest people do not underestimate their achievements, abilities or merits, but neither do they overestimate them. They are quietly, unpretentiously aware of what they can or cannot do.

The problem of an accurate portrayal of one's abilities is particularly problematic with those outside the normal range. For those, say, within one standard deviation of the mean, there should be no particular problems with accurate disclosure about abilities. The problem lies for those over two standard deviations above or below the norm. The question becomes: Is it healthy, or indeed acceptable, to present oneself as very inadequate, well below average with few abilities or desirable characteristics? Equally, can it be acceptable to "show off" when one believes one's self to be in the top 2% of the population. Can humility and hubris be acceptable because they are accurate reflections of ability?

If being honest about one's abilities is desirable then self-enhancement should be thought of as undesirable. Yet there remains an interesting paradox. Self-enhancement is both pervasive and often thought of as socially and clinically desirable. Sedikides, Gregg and Hart (2007) list various related psychological constructs which all attest to the same issue:

- *the better than average effect*: people think they are all better than average at most things
- *self-serving bias*: people are happy to claim credit for their success of any type but reject taking responsibility for their failures
- *Amnesic neglect*: people actively and selectively forget feedback that shows their shortcomings
- *over-optimism*: people see their own, but not their peers', future as unrealistically bright and positive
- *moral hypocrisy*: consistent and conspicuous attempts to appear highly moral without actually being so.

They argue that self-enhancement is pervasive and potent, and pose the question: "Can it be curtailed or at least modestly induced?" They suggest that this is possible because self-enhancement is partly malleable and controllable. This can be achieved by modifying moods by close relationship and by introspection. Social psychologists, in contrast to personality theorists, always stress situational, rather than stable trait, predictors of behavior. Thus they strive to demonstrate that such things as narcissism are simply reactions to particular social forces. Equally, they argue that situations can be contrived or manipulated either to increase or decrease incidence of narcissistic behavior. Sedikides and colleagues (2007) conclude thus: modesty may bestow minimal mental health gains in the short run, but intrapersonal and interpersonal benefits in the long run. Alternatively, modesty and self-enhancement may be associated with different types of mental health gains. For example, self-enhancement may be linked most strongly with resilience, and modesty with life satisfaction. Likewise, modesty and self-enhancement may be associated with different types of social benefits. Thus, self-enhancement may promote advancement to glamorous and high-status social positions (e.g. actor, politician), whereas modesty may promote advancement to useful and moderate-status positions (e.g. civil servant, nurse). Future research would do well to focus on untangling this complex interplay of factors. Both modesty and self-enhancement may be critical to attaining different aspects of optimal human functioning.

HARMFUL EFFECTS OF HIGH SELF-ESTEEM

For nearly 30 years, it has been an accepted fact in psychology that low self-esteem was the root cause of many social problems, particularly among young people. Thus, everything from teenage pregnancy to suicide and delinquency to school failure was due to low self-esteem. Hence the development and proliferation of the self-esteem movement, which attempted through a variety of crypto-clinical and educational interventions to raise the esteem of various targeted groups. The assumption was that because self-esteem has such powerful causal power it was the most efficient way to improve the lot of various groups that experienced a variety of social problems.

Millions were poured into this industry, which was sanctioned by many different groups. Studies in many of the social, medical and clinical sciences seemed to suggest the link was clearly established. Well over 1000 popular books in the self-help tradition endorsed the message. A few, often moral, voices were raised about the issue of the disconnect between praise and achievement and the possible implications of the pervasive discourse of constant affirmation. Indeed, Twenge (2006) argued that individuals born between 1970 and 1990 were the 'Generation Me' cohort, with elevated feelings of egotism, entitlement and self-centeredness. It is an argument for the consistent secular increase in narcissism. These findings have been empirically challenged (Trzesniewski, Donnellan and Robbins, 2008a; 2008b; 2008c).

However, over the last few years social psychologists have challenged many of these assumptions and found them wanting. One challenge came from Emler (2005) who did a careful, critical evaluation of the literature. His conclusion was, essentially, that there is little evidence for the *causal power* of low self-esteem creating social problems or, for that matter, of the efficacy of programmes that attempted to raise it. The research drew a number of specific conclusions:

- Relatively low self-esteem is *not* a risk factor for delinquency, violence towards others (including child and partner abuse), drug use, alcohol abuse, educational under-attainment or racism.
- Relatively low self-esteem is a risk factor for suicide, suicide attempts, depression, teenage pregnancy and victimization by bullies. However, in each case it is only one among several related risk factors.
- Although the causal mechanisms remain unclear, relatively low childhood self-esteem also appears to be associated with adolescent

eating disorders and, among males only, with low earnings and employment problems in young adulthood.

- Young people with very high self-esteem are more likely than others to hold racist attitudes, reject social pressures from adults and peers, and engage in physically risky pursuits such as drink-driving or driving too fast.
- The most important influences on young people's levels of self-esteem are their parents – partly as a result of genetic inheritance and partly through the degree of love, concern, acceptance and interest that they show their children. Physical and sexual abuse are especially damaging for children's feelings of self-worth.
- Personal successes and failures also influence self-esteem. But despite the attention given to the effects on high or low achievement in school, the degree of influence of self-esteem is relatively small.
- Children's self-esteem can be raised by parenting programmes and other planned interventions, but knowledge of why particular interventions are effective is limited.

Emler, in fact, argued that low self-esteem could have beneficial motivational characteristics whilst high self-esteem could lead to arrogant, conceited, self-satisfied behavior rather than provide specific benefits.

In addition to reviews, experimental studies began to show the negative effects of high self-esteem. That is, they appeared to show that people with high self-esteem pose a greater threat to themselves and others than those with low self-esteem.

Baumeister's (Baumeister et al., 2003; Bushman and Baumeister, 1998) imaginative studies have probably provided the best empirical evidence that there is no causal relationship between low self-esteem and life success, though this conclusion has been disputed. Some recent longitudinal studies suggest otherwise (Trzesniewski et al., 2008c). In fact, if anything, the opposite is true. Still others have shown that self-esteem can have both positive and negative consequences. If people derive their self-esteem from external factors like physical appearance, they may be prone to eating disorders (Crocker and Wolfe, 2001).

The essence of the argument is that we need to be accurate in self-evaluation, which is about our competences, with both a spirit of acceptance and realism. To be self-accepting, we need to take responsibility for our actions. Hence, there is a difference between authentic or genuine self-esteem and external or false self-esteem. The former is internal and under our control, the latter external and under the control of others who may be insecure and fickle.

Similarly, it is important to try to distinguish between unhealthy narcissism, with all its ego-inflatedness and self-absorbed vanity, and genuine, correct and appropriate high self-esteem. Those with narcissism are dependent on others to affirm them. In this sense, they are highly vulnerable and addicted to their positive affirmations. Thus the genuine narcissist keeps seeking personal validation but this is never enough to convince them of their own adequacy. Because they do not have genuine high self-esteem, they strive to fake it.

As will be noted, there have been various attempts to make differentiations in the narcissism literature which spans psychiatry and psychology. It has been conceived as a type and a trait, even a psychological process. There have been studies on overt (more exhibitionistic and aggressive) vs covert (anxious, defensive, vulnerable) narcissists (Otway and Vignoles, 2006) and many attempts to differentiate "healthy", "productive" narcissism from "unhealthy", "destructive" narcissism. Indeed, there appear to be some differences when there is a "clinical" vs "non-clinical" account of narcissism (Campbell, 2001). This problem may be resolved by the trait concept whereby it is possible to locate everybody on the self-esteem–narcissistic trait. Clinicians may see only extreme cases who are recommended for therapy, whilst personality and organizational psychologists see less "extreme cases" who appear "relatively" well-adjusted. However, there is a considerable and fascinating psychiatry on the Narcissistic Personality Disorder (NPD).

NARCISSISTIC PERSONALITY DISORDER

Dotlich and Cairo (2003) list narcissism-arrogance, in their terms, as the first (probably major cause) of why CEOs fail. It is a case of you're right but everybody else is wrong; a blinding belief in your own opinions. They note four common symptoms:

1. a diminished capacity to learn from others or previous experience
2. an off-putting (inferiority) outright refusal (ever) to be accountable and hence responsible
3. resistance to change because they know "my way" is best
4. an inability to recognize their (manifold) limitations.

Oldham and Morris (2000) have noted that narcissists never seem defensive or embarrassed about their ambition, and are supremely confident in their ambitions. However, because they are so aware of, comfortable with, and grateful for, their strengths, they are easily and profoundly wounded by any suggestion that they have serious weaknesses or shortcomings.

At work, they tend to be high-energy, outgoing and competitive. They seem instinctively drawn to office politics, and how to find and use power. They will charm those in authority or those from whom they believe they have something to gain.

This disorder apparently occurs in only 1% of the population. It is also called a disorder of arrogance or self-confidence. The website www.personalityresearch.org/pd.html suggests that the word SPECIAL is a helpful way to diagnose the narcissistic personality disorder:

- **S:** special (believes he or she is special and unique)
- **P:** preoccupied with fantasies (of unlimited success, power, brilliance, beauty, or ideal love)
- **E:** entitlement
- **C:** conceited (grandiose sense of self-importance)
- **I:** interpersonal exploitation
- **A:** arrogant (haughty)
- **L:** lacks empathy.

Oldham and Morris (2000) summarize the psychiatric diagnostic criteria by phrases like grandiosity, hypersensitivity, attention-seeking, ego-centrism, and a deep and abiding sense of entitlement.

The DSM-IV manual (APA, 1994) has nine diagnostic features. Narcissists are boastful, pretentious and self-aggrandizing, overestimating their own abilities and accomplishments whilst simultaneously deflating others. They compare themselves favorably to famous, privileged people, believing their own discovery as one of them is long overdue. They are surprisingly secure in their beliefs that they are gifted and unique and have special needs beyond the comprehension of ordinary people. Paradoxically, their self-esteem is fragile, needing to be bolstered up by constant attention and admiration from others. They expect their demands to be met by special favorable treatment. In doing so, they often exploit others because they form relationships specifically designed to enhance their self-esteem. They lack empathy, being totally self-absorbed. They are also envious of others and begrudge them their success. They are well-known for their arrogance and their disdainful, patronizing attitude. As managers, their difficult-to-fulfil needs can lead them to have problematic social relationships and to make poor decisions.

The manual points out that they are exceptionally sensitive to set-backs, feeling both degraded and humiliated. They mask this with defiant counter-attacks and rage. They may withdraw from situations that led to failure or try to mask their grandiosity with an appearance of humility. Those diagnosed with Narcissistic Personality Disorder tend to be male.

There are also many issues with differential diagnosis, that is, distinguishing what is unique about the disorder. The most useful features in discriminating Narcissistic Personality Disorder from Histrionic, Antisocial and Borderline Personality Disorders (which are characterized by interactive styles, respectively coquettish, callous, and needy) are the *grandiosity* characteristics of Narcissistic Personality Disorder. The relative stability of self-image, as well as the relative lack of self-destructiveness, impulsivity, and abandonment concerns, also help distinguish Narcissistic Personality Disorder from Borderline Personality Disorder. Excessive pride in achievements, a relative lack of emotional display and disdain for other's sensitivities help distinguish Narcissistic Personality Disorder from Histrionic Personality Disorder. Although individuals with Borderline, Histrionic, and Narcissistic Personality Disorders may require much attention, those with Narcissistic Personality Disorder specifically need that attention to be admiring. Individuals with Antisocial and Narcissistic Personality Disorder will share a tendency to be tough-minded, glib, superficial, exploitative and unempathetic. However, Narcissistic Personality Disorder does not necessarily include characteristics of impulsivity, aggression and deceit. In addition, individuals with Antisocial Personality Disorder may not be as needy of the admiration and envy of others, as persons with Narcissistic Personality Disorder (APA, 1994, p. 661).

At work, narcissistic individuals have a grandiose sense of self-importance (for example, they exaggerate their achievements and talents, expect to be recognized as superior without commensurate achievements). Inevitably they believe they rightly deserve all sorts of markers of their specialness: bigger offices and salary; inflated job titles, a bigger budget dedicated to their needs; more support staff; and greater liberty to do as they wish.

Most individuals with NPD are preoccupied with fantasies of unlimited success, power, brilliance and money. They believe that they are "special" and unique and can therefore only be properly understood by, or should associate with, other special or high-status people (or institutions). They may try to "buy" themselves into exclusive circles. They often require excessive admiration and respect from people at work for everything they do. This is their most abiding characteristic. They usually have a sense of entitlement – that is, unreasonable expectations of especially favourable treatment or automatic compliance with their manifest needs. Worse, they take advantage of others to achieve their own ends, which makes them inefficient and disliked as managers. They are unsupportive but demand support for themselves. All are unwilling to recognize or identify with the feelings and needs of others in and out of work. They have desperately low Emotional Intelligence, though are apparently unaware of this. Indeed, they may assume they have superior emotional intelligence. Curiously they are often envious of others and believe that others are envious of them. In this sense, they are deluded. They show arrogant, haughty behaviors or attitudes all the time and everywhere at work (and home) (Hogan, 2007a).

Narcissists are super-self-confident: they express considerable self-certainty. They are "self-people" – self-asserting, self-possessed, self-aggrandizing, self-preoccupied, self-loving – and ultimately self-destructive. They seem to really believe in themselves: they are sure that they have been born lucky. At work they are out-going, high-energy, competitive and very "political" depending, of course, on their normal (big five) trait profile. Thus the extraverted, conscientious narcissist may be rather different from those more neurotic and open. They can make reasonable short-term leaders, as long as they are not criticized or made to share glory. They seem to have an insatiable need to be admired, loved and needed. This can appear amusing or pathetic to outside observers. They are often a model of the ambitious, driven, self-disciplined, successful leader or manager. The world, they believe and demand, is their stage.

But narcissism is a *disorder* of self-esteem: it is essentially a cover-up. People with NPD self-destruct because their self-aggrandizement blinds their personal and business judgment, and managerial behavior. At work they exploit others to get ahead, and yet they demand special treatment. Worse, their reaction to any sort of criticism is extreme, including shame, rage and tantrums. They aim to destroy that criticism, however well-intentioned and useful. They are poor empathizers and thus have low emotional intelligence. They can be consumed with envy and disdain of others, and are prone to depression as well as manipulative, demanding and self-centered behaviors; even therapists don't like them.

Many researchers have tried to "unpick" the essence of the paradoxical, fragile self-esteem of the narcissist. The narcissist's self-esteem is at once unstable and defensive. It seems their self-esteem is utterly contingent on others' feedback. Further, it is dissociated between explicit (overt) and implicit (covert) views (Tracy and Robins, 2007).

Hogan and Hogan (2001) call these types "Arrogant", "the lord of the high chair" – a two-year-old, sitting in a high chair demanding food and attention, and squealing in fury when his or her needs are not met. Narcissists expect to be liked, admired, respected, attended to, praised, complimented and indulged. Their most important and obvious characteristic is a sense of entitlement, excessive self-esteem and, quite often, an expectation of success that often leads to real success. They expect to be successful at everything they undertake; they believe that people are so interested in them that books will be written about them, and when their needs and expectations are frustrated, they explode with "narcissistic rage".

What is most distinctive about the narcissists is their self-assurance, which often gives them charisma. Hogan and Hogan (1997) note that they are the first to speak in a group and they hold forth with great confidence, even when they are wrong. They so completely expect to succeed, and take more credit for success than is warranted or fair, that they refuse to acknowledge failure, errors or mistakes. When things go right it is because of their efforts; when things go wrong, it is someone else's fault. This is a classic attribution error and leads to problems with truth-telling because they always rationalize, and reinterpret their failures and mistakes, usually by blaming them on others.

Narcissists can be energetic, charismatic, leader-like, and willing to take the initiative to get projects moving. They can be relatively successful in management, sales and entrepreneurship, but usually only for short periods. However, they are arrogant, vain, overbearing, demanding, self-deceived and pompous; yet, they are so colourful and engaging that they often attract followers. Their self-confidence is attractive. Naïvely, people believe they have to have something to be so confident about.

Narcissists handle stress and heavy workloads badly but seemingly with ease; they are also quite persistent under pressure and they refuse to acknowledge failure. As a result of their inability to acknowledge failure, or even mistakes, and the way they resist coaching and ignore negative feedback, they are unable to learn from experience. In a more accessible, almost self-help book, written as a collaboration between psychiatrist and journalist, Oldham and Morris (2000) chose the more neutral term 'self-confidence'.

Oldham and Morris (2000: 80) note nine characteristics of these types they call 'Self-Confident'. First is *High Self-regard*, having no doubts about their uniqueness and specialness. Second, they expect others to *Treat them well at all times*. Third, they are *Deeply ambitious* and achievement-oriented, selling themselves, their goals, their projects and their ideas. Fourth, they are very *Political*, being very shrewd in their dealings with others. Next, they are always *Competitive*, trying always to get to the top and stay there. Sixth, their *Self-impression is one of hero*, the star, top dog. Seventh, they seem very *Aware of their own thoughts and feelings*. Eighth, they naturally accept compliments, praise, and admiration "gracefully". Finally, they are deeply *Sensitive to criticism*.

More importantly, they note four tips for working with narcissists. First, don't criticize or compete with narcissists. Next, because narcissists are not directive, they do not manage well or set directions for their staff. They also provide precious little support of any kind, which one simply has to accept. To get anywhere with a Narcissist boss, it seems important constantly to flatter and compliment them. This is advice for those working with narcissists. It clearly has taken an optimistic perspective, never considering that a narcissistic boss could be both abusive and deeply incompetent.

Miller (2008), in another popular book about personality disorders, describes narcissistic bosses and employers as "preeners" and gives advice to those who may be either. For bosses, he suggests documenting your credentials, being realistic about what you can be proud of and treating all employers with respect. He suggests that the potentially narcissistic employee take an honest self-inventory (to gain insight); emulate the successful and present their ideas appropriately. Similarly, Dotlich and Cairo (2003) offer three pieces of advice for this leadership type. Determine if you fit the arrogance profile (i.e. try a little self-awareness), find the truth-tellers in the organization and ask them to level with you (i.e. get real feedback); use setbacks as an opportunity to cross back over the line before big failure hits.

There remains considerable debate about the treatment of, and prognosis for, each of the personality disorders. Until relatively recently it was argued that they were particularly difficult to treat and that prognosis was therefore poor.

The business world often calls for, and rewards, arrogant, self-confident, self-important people. They seek out power and abuse it. They thrive in selling jobs and those where they have to do media work. But, as anyone who works with and for them knows, they can destabilize and destroy working groups by their deeply inconsiderate behavior. Management and self-help books stress how to cope with clinical or subclinical narcissism. Few take a very negative view or report case studies where narcissists personally destroy whole organizations.

THE TWO SIDES OF NARCISSISM

Paunonen and colleagues (2006) have identified two strands in the narcissistic leadership literature. The first is that although many narcissists are described as charismatic, their egotistical Machiavellianism derails them in the end. But in contrast to this *dark* view, there is a *bright* view. This suggests that narcissists have low depression and anxiety, and high subjective well-being. Further, their obviously strong needs for achievement, control, power and status serve them well to obtain leadership positions, but their inward focus usually leads in the long term to self-destruction.

Clearly, the exploitative, entitlement-obsessed narcissist who manipulates those around him or her for own ends is unlikely to be successful in the long run. However, Paunonen and colleagues (2006) are happy to distinguish between the benign and pathological narcissist. Further, they are happy to think of narcissism as a trait (not a type) which consists of a constellation of distinct intercorrelated traits on a continuum.

In their study of narcissism and leadership, Paunonen and colleagues (2006) measured egotism, which they took to represent the bright side of narcissism, and Machiavellianism, the dark side. They also measured two aspects of impression management: the conscious version and the less conscious delusional version. Their study was a peer-rating study of military cadets who rated five factors: leadership, popularity, benevolence, aggression and honesty. Their results supported their theory; notably, that the highest-rated leaders had the bright-side narcissism profile, high in egoism and self-esteem but low in manipulativeness and impression management. Indeed, they concluded by arguing that they were "hard pressed" to think of any situation where narcissism would not threaten the leader–followership relationship, leading it to quick collapse.

Many writers on leadership narcissists contrast the upside-bright or downside-dark traits of narcissistic leaders. This helps resolve the apparent conflict of ideas that narcissistic managers can (perhaps only in the short term) be good managers. Rosenthal (2007) notes a number of the problematic intercorrelated dark-side traits and the leaders with whom they are most associated:

- Feelings of inferiority – the need to be surrounded by flattering sycophants (Mao Tse-Tung, Krushchev)
- An insatiable need for recognition and superiority – unrelenting quest to gain power to show potency (Saddam Hussein)
- Hypersensitivity and anger – intense, vengeful, hostile rage when crossed (Kennedy, Castro)
- Lack of empathy – idiosyncratic, self-centered, hubristical behavior (Bush)
- Amorality – cruel acts justified to others (Saddam Hussein)
- Irrationality and inflexibility – over confident, fantasy thinking and decision making
- Paranoia – seeing enemies everywhere.

It may well be that certain organizations at certain points in their history attract narcissists who do well: those who consistently court attention through PR, those in crisis or those who crave "strong leadership" may seek out those who are dangerously narcissistic.

On the other hand, Rosenthal (2007) sees narcissism as being crucial in a crisis. Narcissists can have great vision and take dramatic action. They not only appear to be, but also are, larger-than-life figures described as "productive narcissists". These are the PR-hungry CEOs driven to gain power, glory and the admiration of others. They can be visionaries and risk-takers seeing the big picture whilst downplaying rules, laws and conventions which handicap them. When they have some insight and self-awareness into their preferences and abilities, and which organizational forces are in place to restrain them, they can act as great forces for positive change and advancement.

One way to resolve the two sides of the narcissism argument is to note two things. *First*, if narcissism is trait-like then one can obtain identical scores, but some mainly from either the bright or the dark side. This implies variability within the narcissism dimension itself. *Second*, one has to consider other factors like cognitive ability, social conscience and conscientiousness. Thus a highly able, hardworking bright-side Narcissist could do very well in organizational settings whilst a less-able, less-hardworking dark-side Narcissist would inevitably fail.

THE NARCISSISTIC MANAGER

It should not be assumed that narcissism is necessarily a handicap in business. Indeed, the opposite may be true. If a manager is articulate, educated and intelligent as well as good-looking, his or her narcissism may be seem to be acceptable.

Rosenthal and Pittinsky (2006) list various American narcissistic business leaders who rise and seem driven by personal egoistic needs for personal power and admiration, not by any real concern for the welfare of those they lead. They note, however, the "upside" of narcissistic leaders, where the supreme self-confidence and dominance of these leaders really inspire their people. It can be that "mirror-hungry" narcissists help unstable societies of "ideal hungry" followers. Just as there are successful psychopaths, there may be *productive narcissists* who steady the nerves of organizations in flux and provide a powerful vision and agenda. Narcissists with vision and imagination can, for a short time at any rate, be very successful.

Rosenthal and Pittinsky (2006) argue that there may be an optimal conclusion for the rise of narcissistic leaders:

> We might expect narcissists to succeed in positions where charisma and extraversion are important (e.g. sales), or where self-absorption and grandiosity are important (e.g. science), rather than in positions that require building sustained relationships and trust. Narcissists are also likely to do better in situations in which their personal goals converge with those of their followers and institutions rather than situations in which their success is likely to come at the expense of those around them. Narcissists are apt to emerge, and often flourish, in times that call for a new order to be established, but they are unable to maintain the necessary stability once that new order has come to the fore.
>
> (p. 625)

Bright-side Narcissists can be good delegators, good team-builders and good deliverers. They can be good mentors and genuinely help others. However, subordinates soon learn things go wrong if they do not follow certain rules.

- Everyone must acknowledge who is boss and accept rank and hierarchical structure.
- They must be absolutely loyal and never complain, criticize or compete. They should never take credit for something but acknowledge

133

success is primarily due to the narcissist's talent, direction or insights.

- They should not expect the narcissist to very interested in their personality, issues or ambitions but they must be very interested in the narcissist's issues.
- They have to be attentive, giving and always flattering. They need to be sensitive to the whims, needs and desires of the narcissistic manager without expecting reciprocity.
- Narcissistic managers can be mean, angry or petulant when crossed or slighted, and quickly express anger, so subordinates have to be careful when working with them.
- They must ask for help, directions and clarity about objectives when they need it.
- They need to watch out that a narcissistic manager's self-preoccupation, need for approbation and grandiosity does not impede their business judgment and decision-making.
- They need to find ways of giving critical feedback in such a way that the manager both understands it and does not get offended.

The dark-side narcissistic manager tends to have shallow, functional uncommitted relationships. Because they are both needy and ego-centric, they tend not to make close supportive friendship networks in the workplace. They can often feel empty and neglected as a result.

Narcissistic leaders may have short-term advantages but long-term disadvantages, because the narcissist's consistent and persistent efforts are aimed at enhancing their self-image, which leads to group clashes. Campbell and colleagues (2005) note that narcissistic leaders often maintain positive feelings around the self with high positive and low negative affect, as well as high self-esteem. However, they bring "costs" because of their need to distort reality into a form con-ducive to self-enhancement. They also have the need to seek out positive social feedback whilst attacking or disparaging negative feed-back. Further, they experience long-term performance deficits because their illusion of success interferes without obtaining real success. Narcissists also trade interdependence and closeness for individual status and esteem. Finally, they adopt strategies that, whilst show-ing gains at the individual level, show losses at the group level. That is, they may gain themselves short-term advantage by looking skilful or tough or insightful, whilst these decisions actually have long-term disastrous consequences. Thus radical re-engineering may improve short-term profitability but lead to long-term chaos and collapse.

Kets de Vries (2006a) argues that a certain degree of narcissism is an essential prerequisite for leadership. He offers a psychoanalytic interpretation for the aetiology of narcissism which is, inevitably, bad parenting. It is seen as problems associated with two related issues – how narcissists perceive themselves as well as salient others; more specifically, how they come to cope with the reality that they are neither omnipotent nor omniscient and that their parents are not powerful and perfect. The child's life-long quest for admiration and approbation is often a mask for self-doubt or hatred, or feeling one is never properly loved for one's own sake alone.

Inevitably with psychoanalysis, both the neglected and the pampered child (too little and too much of a good thing) can lead to the development of narcissism. The indulgent, all-praising, pampering parents lead to exactly the opposite of what they want or expect. Excessive praise leads to feelings of superiority and destined greatness which, whilst being beneficial for really talented individuals, only serves to undermine those who cannot understand why the world does not react like their doting parents. The narcissist does a lot of transference – the unconscious redirection of early feelings (to the parent) to other people. The psychological imprints of early care-givers are thus manifest throughout adult life.

Whilst a "touch" of narcissism can be good for leaders, it can be problematic in the long run, particularly if the problem is severe. Because of their selfishness and egocentrism, narcissistic managers are more committed to their own welfare than that of their team or, indeed, the whole organization. Kets de Vries (2006a) also distinguishes between *constructive* and *reactive* narcissism.

The healthy constructive narcissist (that is, the person with high self-esteem) does take advice, accept feedback and responsibility for both success and failure. Their energy, zeal and larger-than-life enthusiasm and theatrics can be precisely what it takes to transform organizations. On the other hand, the reactive narcissist has a defective sense of identity and self-esteem. They can be troubled by feelings of anger and inadequacy as well as lingering, but intrusive, thoughts of both deprivation and emptiness. Their whole aim is to compensate for this sense, of inadequacy and insecurity. Hence the constant, pervasive and insistent need for praise. The childhood memories of being ignored, belittled or maltreated can, it seems, only be overcome by success in adulthood.

To some extent, one can see the narcissistic urges as highly motiva-tional. If narcissistic managers have a very high need for praise and recognition, this may well drive them to work hard to achieve worthy goals. In this sense, they can learn to earn recognition. But that need can turn to envy, spite, greed and vindictiveness.

When things are going well, the narcissistic manager can be good news. They can be upbeat and their sense of well-being spreads to others. However, even slight and temporary setbacks can cause dis-proportionate negative reactions. This might lead to outbursts of rage followed by feelings of dejection, depression and lethargy. However, the narcissist is a master at finding others to blame. They rationalize, they project and they explain away. Some get vindictive, attempting to "get even" with those whom they perceive to have slighted them. The major problem is that they do not learn from their mistakes.

Kets de Vries (2006a) uses political and business examples because both business and power provide a wonderful stage to see the vicis-situdes of narcissism acted out. The short-term expediency, the opportunism, the self-righteousness and self-centeredness of the nar-cissist lead to bad business decisions, poor problem-solving and low morale.

However, one really important feature in the narcissism-at-work scenario is the complicity of followers. It is said that we get the lead-ers we deserve. That is, if our expectations are unrealistic we tend to get very disappointed. Often, particularly in situations of difficulty or crisis, people at work have unrealistic expectations of their lead-ers. They want them to be superhuman and to ensure success and continuity.

Followers, according to Kets de Vries (2006a), encourage two types of behaviors in narcissistic leaders which are very bad for both leader and follower. First, there is the process of *mirroring*, where followers use leaders to reflect what they want to see. Narcissists get the admiration they crave and mutual admiration occurs. The problem is that man-agers can take their eye off the ball, being more concerned with policies and procedures which make them look good rather than serve the best interests of all stakeholders. Second, there is *idealization*, in which followers project all their hopes and fantasies onto the leader. Thus, leaders find themselves in a hall of mirrors which further decreases their grip on reality.

Where narcissistic leaders become aggressive and vindictive, Kets de Vries (2006a) claims that some followers, in order to stave off their anxiety, do identify with the aggressor. Followers impersonate the aggressor, becoming a tough henchman of the narcissistic manager. Inevitably, this only exacerbates the problem and begins to explain the vicious cycle of narcissistic management failure.

The central question for the work psychologist is how they can set up processes, apart from careful selection, that help prevent narcissist-induced management failure occurring.

Can one reduce the possibility of appointing, promoting or encouraging narcissistic managers? Clearly, this has a great deal to do with selection policies. However, Kets de Vries (2006a) offers three other strategies which may help to "downsize the narcissist".

1. Ensure distributive decision-making to ensure checks and balances. Thus, do not combine roles like CEO and chairman.
2. Educate the CEO and board to look out for signs of narcissism and to have strategies to put in place when they do spot the signs. This involves clear systems of accountability and involving shareholders in crucial decisions.
3. Offer coaching and counselling to those clearly identified as reactive narcissists, although few seem willing to accept help because they, by definition, rarely take personal responsibility for their failure.

Perhaps certain organizations attract narcissists more than others. It therefore is highly recommended that these organizations become aware of the psychological processes associated with narcissism, and are willing and able to do something about them.

UNANSWERED QUESTIONS

Rosenthal (2007) has suggested that the topic of the narcissistic leader is well worth exploring, and identified seven areas to examine:

1. The line between narcissism and healthy, optimal self-confidence and self-esteem. This differentiates between the so-called "bright-side", "charismatic", "constructive" or "productive" narcissists and those "dark-side", "destructive" narcissists. This is about drawing the line between confidence and arrogance, healthy and unhealthy, normal or abnormal. The question is whether those demarcations can be made accurately and whether they are situationally appropriate.
2. Whether there are optimal conditions for narcissistic leadership. That is, are there times in organizational life when narcissistic leadership is both desirable and effective? Thus, in times of crisis

or rapid growth, this style of leadership may be highly efficient, whilst in steady-state times when building sustained relationships and trust is important, it is much less so. Indeed, it is very debatable as to whether the narcissist is really capable of building sustained, trusting relationships.

3. Whether narcissistic leadership is effective only in the gaining, but not the maintaining, of power. That is, are they prone to a rapid rise-and-fall scenario because their self-defeating behavior soon overwhelms their supposed charisma? In this sense are they, from a stakeholder perspective, only very superficially attractive and desirable?

4. What is it about followers that causes them to choose narcissistic leaders? Is the aggressive, confident charismatic type exactly what people want and expect from their leaders? Is it because of their superhuman confidence that they appear so appealing? It has been suggested that a mirroring takes place, in that narcissistic followers choose narcissistic leaders. Thus, organizations – indeed, nations – may choose leaders to "sooth their own narcissistic insecurities" and even create other narcissistic enemies. However, it is likely that followers soon rebel against those they have elected, and blame them for living up to their quite obviously unrealistic expectations. Indeed, both parties' – narcissistic leaders and followers – self-loathing is projected onto the other with highly negative consequences.

5. Whether a criterion of productive or destructive narcissistic leaders is the extent to which they sacrifice all personal relationships (home and work) for "success". Many successful leaders have impaired personal relationships (multiple divorces; fractured broken families), but a central question is whether this is necessarily a sign of narcissism.

6. What can, or should, be done to prevent productive narcissists' destructiveness leading to serious "organizational damage". Thus, one may have a stable, non-narcissistic deputy or "side-kick", or one might encourage coaching for the narcissistic leader. Other possibilities include having various procedures which act as checks and balances to the narcissist's power-hungry and sometimes rash decision-making.

7. Most importantly, a good deal of this research is justified by finding historical examples to justify ideas. The better test is that of predictive validity; namely, being able to make accurate predictions about individuals that can be verified by research data.

CONCLUSION

It has only been comparatively recently that psychologists have begun to take an interest in clinical narcissism in the workplace. Many researchers have pointed out the paradox of narcissism at work as being that many traits and processes associated with narcissism can seem positive and beneficial, whilst others are the precise opposite. This paradox has been "solved" by trying to distinguish between the adaptive and maladaptive narcissist, though it is not clear whether this is merely a linguistic tautology. Could one call a constructive narcissist a narcissist? In this sense, it is also an oxymoron.

Conceiving narcissism as a self-esteem trait disorder does imply, as many personality psychologists have argued, that there is a clear continuum between healthy and unhealthy. The issue remains, however, where to draw the line.

It is also important to bear in mind the perspective of social and work psychologists who stress how situational and cultural variables moderate narcissism. That is, organizations may unwittingly reinforce narcissism, thus leading to their own destruction. They may, indeed, encourage or discourage certain processes (like performance appraisals) which make the problems of narcissists much worse.

They may agree to disband committees and allow narcissistic managers to make decisions on their own. They may allow and encourage expensive privileges for people once they achieve certain levels. They may inhibit upward or negative feedback reaching senior managers.

Certainly, narcissists create friends and enemies in organizations and can be a major contributing factor to the dysfunctional workplace (Langan-Fox et al., 2007). They certainly provide a serious management challenge to ensure their pathology works for, instead of against, the fortunes of the organization.

6

THE MACHIAVELLIAN LEADER

INTRODUCTION

The Prince was written by Machiavelli, arguably the first political scientist, in 1532. The author's name has been lent to a style of leadership and management associated with cynicism, deceit and guile. To be described as Machiavellian is to be insulted – it means being duplicitous, egocentric and manipulative. The Machiavellian is exploitative, competitive, and selfish.

Machiavellians make, but break, alliances, promises and rules. They make misleading statements, are high on blame and low on forgiveness. They seem deeply cynical. They may do particularly well in many organizations. In a dog-eat-dog corporate culture, Machiavellianism may be the only way to survive, let alone thrive.

Machiavelli advocated and recommended ways of acquiring and maintaining power in socially competitive situations. It was guilt-free expediency. It is about control and impression management. He suggested all leaders try hard to look bold, great and strong with a grand sense of their gravitas. Moreover, he was a powerful utilitarian who argued that the ends justified the means. Just as modern bankers argue that they are essentially motivated by either fear or greed, Machiavelli suggested it was love and fear.

Machiavellians attempt a detached, controlling coolness whilst simultaneously stressing the clearly non-meant sense of warmth or justice. They are then encouraged by Machiavelli to be crafty liars with superficial charm and great duplicitousness.

Machiavellians are not necessarily hostile, vicious or vindictive. They can and do function well in stressful, competitive, unstructured situations such as bargaining. Their coolness and emotional detachment may serve well to achieve a positive result. Their acuity and sensitivity may make them particularly skilful in negotiations. Coolness, perceptiveness and charm can be particularly useful in tough bargaining situations.

It is clearly the case that national and corporate cultures espouse Machiavellian values, or at least behaviors. There is often, in corporate life, a clear disparity between the PR and the actuality. The corporate mission statement and avowed values of openness, fairness and integrity bear no relationship to what goes on in the boardroom or any other part of the organization. Indeed, this may lead the naïve individual to give up their own ethical approach to business and cynically adopt the Machiavellian strategies of all those around them. They see how power and privilege operate in the organization. Hence complaints about "office politics". The following have been identified as Machiavellian traits:

- resistant to social influence
- hides personal convictions well
- changes positions in argument readily
- resistant to confessing
- highly convincing when telling truth
- suspicious of others' motives
- situationally analytical
- does not assume reciprocity
- withholds judgment of others' likely moves
- able to change strategy with situation
- says things others want to hear
- sensitive to information about others
- exploitative, but not viciously so
- exploits more if others can't retaliate
- not susceptible to appeals for compliance, cooperation or attitude change
- never obviously manipulative
- prefers fluid environment
- preferred by peers as leader
- preferred by peers as work partner.

Authoritarian, despotic and tyrannical leaders thrive in situations of flux, collapse and chaos. Where there is a deep chasm between hope and reality, wealth and poverty, virtue and corruption, and where social institutions fail or collapse, the Machiavellian steps in. When individuals are anxious or alienated, when isolated or dislocated, they are more prone to follow mass movements, to back strong leaders and to subject themselves to despotism.

Machiavelli saw despotic rule as a natural requisite at certain times. Despots might repress their citizens, but the arguable upside of despots is uniting people torn apart by strife, introducing law and order, erasing some types of corruption and protecting people against outside forces. Bad times call for strong leadership. But where he was wrong, according to Kets de Vries (2006a), is that Machiavellianism soon turns to full despotism and tyranny. He argues that:

> Gradually, the perks and privileges, appropriated by the ruling elite, become increasingly glaring. The leader and his henchmen engage in regressive activities, the arbitrary use of power, the grabbing of scarce resources, the repression of free will, and the violation of human rights, all of which mean misery for the populace and decline for the economy.
>
> (p. 203)

Despots are, however, different from Machiavellians or authoritarians and that difference is in their use of ideology. Despots offer utopian visions and supposedly virtue-based worldviews. These false dreams can foster a sense of togetherness and solidarity, but they always distinguish clearly between right and wrong. Despots, not authoritarians, rejoice in and force mind-control, media manipulation, the search for scapegoats, and so on.

PSYCHOLOGICAL RESEARCH

Psychological work in the area goes back to the early work of Christie and Geis (1970) who, in their first chapter of their celebrated book, noted four characteristics of people who had this style (trait, syndrome, disorder). They were:

1. a relative lack of affect in interpersonal relationships, low in empathy, little concern for morals, task oriented
2. a lack of concern with conventional morality; they are often amoral as well as immoral, with a utilitarian perspective
3. a lack of gross psychopathology; they have good reality checks and do not fit into any other established category

4. low ideological commitment: short-term, tactical goal achievement is their major task.

What is most important is to note the third point. Machiavellianism is a clinical condition. It is a belief and value system that underlies and "inspires" a behavioral pattern. Once this style had been identified, the authors set about trying to devise a robust measure. Psychologists, at least those from a psychometric tradition, seek first to define then 'operationalize' a concept. By the latter, they mean to measure it and then find what beliefs and behaviors it is associated with. This, of course, takes time, deciding on items, subscales (i.e. morality, tactics, views) as well as the ideal format – like a forced choice.

Studying the 20-item questionnaire helps us to understand the MACH philosophy. Note, the same statements are reversed (i.e. 2, 5, 8).

Survey Questionnaire

1. The best way to handle people is to tell them what they want to hear.
2. When you ask someone to do something for you, it is best to give the real reasons for wanting it rather than giving reasons which might carry more weight. (r)
3. Anyone who completely trusts anyone else is asking for trouble. (r)
4. It is hard to get ahead without cutting corners here and there.
5. Honesty is the best policy in all cases. (r)
6. It is safest to assume that all people have a vicious streak and it will come out when they are given a chance.
7. Never tell anyone the real reason you did something unless it is useful to do so.
8. One should take action only when sure it is morally right.
9. It is wise to flatter important people.
10. All in all, it is better to be humble and honest than be important and dishonest. (r)
11. Barnum was wrong when he said there's a sucker born every minute. (r)
12. People suffering from incurable diseases should have the choice of being put painlessly to death.
13. It is possible to be good in all respects. (r)
14. Most people are basically good and kind. (r)

15. There is no excuse for lying to someone else. (r)
16. Most people forget more easily the death of their father than the loss of their inheritance.
17. Most people who get ahead in the world lead clean, moral lives. (r)
18. Generally speaking, people won't work hard unless they are forced to.
19. The biggest difference between most criminals and other people is that criminals are stupid enough to get caught.
20. Most people are brave. (r)

They developed their scale over time. Here is a later version. Note 'r' means 'reverse', or is the opposite of Machiavellian beliefs. Again, it is a matter of agreeing or disagreeing with each item.

Mach-IV scale

1. Never tell anyone the real reason you did something unless it is useful to do so.
2. The best way to handle people is to tell them what they want to hear.
3. One should take action only when sure it is morally right (r)
4. Most people are basically good and kind (r)
5. It is safest to assume that all people have a vicious streak and it will come out when they are given a chance.
6. Honesty is the best policy in all cases (r)
7. There is no excuse for lying to someone else. (r)
8. It is hard to get ahead without cutting corners here and there.
9. All in all, it is better to be humble and honest than important and dishonest. (r)
10. When you ask someone to do something for you, it is best to give the real reasons for wanting it rather than giving reasons that carry more weight. (r)
11. Most people who get ahead in the world lead clean, moral lives. (r)
12. Anyone who completely trusts anyone else is asking for trouble.
13. The biggest difference between most criminals and other people is that criminals are stupid enough to get caught.
14. Most men are brave. (r)
15. It is wise to flatter important people.
16. It is possible to be good in all respects (r)

17. Barnum was very wrong when he said that there's a sucker born every minute (r)
18. Generally speaking, men won't work hard unless they're forced to do so.
19. People suffering from incurable diseases should have the choice of being put painlessly to death.
20. Most men forget more easily the death of their father than the loss of their property.

Christie and Geis (1970) end their groundbreaking book with a chapter called "Implications and Speculation". They start off by admitting concern about the exclusively negative connotations surrounding the concept. But are all 'Machs', as they call them, shadowy and unsavory manipulators? They seem self-insightful, more willing to admit unsavory traits and are impressive negotiators. Certainly, high and low Machs see each other differently. The former see the latter as naïve, out-of-touch and unrealistic, whilst the low Machs see their high Mach brethren as immoral, inhuman and lacking in both compassion and faith in others.

They end their book with a model explaining the different tactics of high and low Mach people in what they call "loosely" vs "highly" structured situations:

> The Mach's salient characteristic is viewed as coolness and detachment. In pursuit of largely self-defined goals, he disregards both his own and others' affective states and therefore attacks the problem with all the logical ability that he possesses. He reads the situation in terms of perceived possibilities and then proceeds to act on the basis of what action will lead to what results.
>
> (pp. 89–90)

Situations can be ordered along a dimension of loosely to highly structured. In highly structured situations the roles of the participants are clear, the way in which goals are achieved is clear, the reward associated with each goal is defined and there is little wiggle room or latitude for improvisation. Rules for behaviour are reasonably explicit and variation from them is penalised. Loosely structured situations on the other hand are characterised by ambiguity as to the role of the participants, the means to achieve goals, and their associated rewards. In the absence of formal rules, the situation permits a variety of ways of introducing structure and taking advantage of its absence.

(pp. 352–4)

The interaction model indicated that the greatest difference in the tactics used by high and low Machs occurs in loosely structured situations. We believe that this is supported by the experimental data and is consistent with results from field studies. A loosely structured situation puts the high Mach on his mettle. What are the limits? To what extent can the situation be exploited for one's own gain by imposing structure? The low Mach, rather than focusing on the structural aspects of the situation, is more likely to assume that a structure exists and is more amenable to others' (especially high Machs) interpretation of the structure. His susceptibility to affective involvement interferes with his ability to assay the situation in purely cognitive terms.

(p. 359)

This model leads the authors to ask under what conditions would a Mach show better or worse leadership behavior. They believe it has to do primarily with the structure of the organization.

Christie and Geis (1970) argued, 35 years ago, that the way society is moving, the Mach approach to leadership ensures they, or rather low Machs, will lose. It is their emotional detachment and their goal orientation that leads high Machs to be better leaders, even more so if they can 'fake' low-Mach empathy. They found Machiavellianism unrelated to intelligence but clearly related to job preference.

Over the years, there has been a lot of work on Machiavellianism and where it is "located" in personality space. McHoskey (2001) found Mach related to four of the personality disorders: borderline, paranoid, negativistic and anti-social. Wilson and colleagues (1998) found high Machs exploitative, low Machs cooperative. High Machs are chosen as aggressive leaders against enemies.

Nelson and Gilbertson (1991) revised the concept and made the distinction between *benign* and *predatory* Machs. They see the former as often good administrators, able negotiators and specialists. The latter, however, are characterized as careerists and opportunists.

In one imaginative study, Deluga (2001) prepared detailed profiles of 39 American presidents from standard biographical references and got people to rate them on Machiavellianism. Franklin Roosevelt was rated the highest on this trait. The most Machiavellian were always able to display considerable self-confidence, to have impressive management skills and to be very persuasive.

Interestingly, the most Machiavellian presidents were most success-ful legislatively. Their ability to build persuasive political coalitions, to make confident decisions in ambiguous but critical times and their emotional detachment from others clearly gave them particu-lar advantages. Machiavellian leaders often appear very charismatic. Their image-building, emotional intelligence and persuasive influence clearly make them appear charismatic.

Sutton and Keogh (2001) identified Mach in children. They used the Kiddie Mach developed by Christie and Geis (1970) shown below:

- Successful people are mostly honest and good.
- Most people are brave.
- It is possible to be good in every way.
- Most people are good and kind.
- The best way to get along with people is to tell them things that make them happy.
- It hurts more to lose money than to lose a friend.
- It is smart to be nice to important people even if you don't really like them.
- A criminal is just like other people except he is stupid enough to get caught.
- It is better to be ordinary and honest than famous and dishonest.
- It is never right to tell a lie.
- Sometimes you have to cheat a little to get what you want.
- You should always be honest, no matter what.
- It's better to tell someone why you want him to help you than to make up a good story to get him to do it.
- You should do something only when you are sure it is right.
- Most people cannot be easily fooled.
- Never tell anyone why you did something unless it will help you.
- Most people won't work hard unless you make them do it.
- Anyone who completely trusts anyone else is asking for trouble.
- It is smartest to believe that all people will be mean if they have a chance.
- Sometimes you have to hurt other people to get what you want.

As with the adult version, these beliefs fell into three categories or dimensions: lack of faith in human nature, dishonesty and dis-trust. They showed that these scores were significantly related to tough-mindedness (psychoticism) and lying (dissimulation). They found evidence of sex differences and speculated that boys experience injustice and feel disillusioned sooner and more dramatically than girls; also, that high-Mach boys avoid and suppress feelings and problems, whilst girls seek support. Non-anxious Machs have a callous-unemotional trait and tend to very disinhibited delinquency.

Similarly, Kline and Cooper (1983) found that, among students, Machs were anti-religious, hedonistic, radical and tough-minded. An interesting and more recent study by Austin and colleagues (2007) looked at the possible relationship between Mach and emotional intelligence. Machiavellians are manipulative, yet not empathic. They suggested that these had a low emotional quotient (EQ), being disagreeable and low on conscientiousness. They also developed an emotional manipulation scale and showed how this was related to Mach beliefs and behaviors. Their results show Machs are better at managing others' emotions than their own. In this sense, they speculate that there may be a dark side to emotional intelligence.

MACHIAVELLIANS AT WORK

Nicolo Machiavelli argued in *The Prince* that it is better for leaders to have a win-at-all-costs philosophy. His interest was in political power, but does his advice apply to leaders in business? Big companies are, indeed, like mini-states in both size and governance. A question of central interest is: Despite all claims to the contrary, do leaders essentially behave in ways to achieve, exercise and maintain power as Machiavelli suggested? Machs do well at work where work environments are loose, flowing and unstructured. The fewer the rules, constraints, checks and balances the better. They also do well in situations where the norm is face-to-face communication, where they can turn on their superficial charm.

Various researchers have looked at Machs at work. Graham (1996) noted that political skill was essential for many jobs, like project management. They need to be highly task-oriented; they need tight and efficient controls and they need to resist social influence. They need to be energetic and self-assured, focused on results and have good communications, negotiation and problem-solving ability. In fact, he found Mach scores did not relate to project management success, though he did speculate that this may be due to all project managers needing deceit, guile and manipulation to do their job well.

At the heart of Machiavellianism are the concepts of trust and reciprocity. People exchange goods and favors voluntarily and trust they will be reciprocated. "Cooperators" both trust and reciprocate; "cheaters" take advantage of extended trust. Cheaters are self-interested opportunists. At work, they are more upset by inefficiency than injustice. They are cynical, manipulative and unethical.

Becker and O'Hair (2007) looked at Machs' organizational good citizen behavior or the frequency of going above or beyond the call of duty to help their employer or co-workers. It concerned the extent to which Machiavellianism was related to acts of altruism, cooperation and helpfulness as well as gestures of goodwill. Inevitably, they expected Machiavellianism to be associated with little of the above but, paradoxically, to try hard to give the impression that they did. They were likely to try to cultivate a good impression, especially with the boss. Their "latitude for improvisation" makes them good impression managers.

Co-workers and subordinates, but not always bosses, know the selfish, misanthropic self-serving nature of Machs. This becomes very apparent when the multi-source (360 degree) rater feedback is done. The odd thing, of course, is that Machs often believe that they (really) are good citizens of the organization.

One recent study looked at the negotiation tactics of Machs (Al-Khatib *et al.*, 2008). The authors focused on things like competitive bargaining, inappropriate information-gathering, attacking opponents' networks, making false promises and misrepresenting information during a negotiation process. They believe that Machiavellianism may be situational and highly contingent on the magnitude of the issues at stake: that is, particular business situations seem to trigger Machiavellian behaviors.

THEORY X, CYNICISM AND OFFICE POLITICS

McGregor (1960) is remembered for his very simple but alluring distinction between theory X and Y. These were assumptions, beliefs, theories or schemas held by managers at work. People who hold theory X are, quite simply, cynical about workers. They believe employees, by-and-large, hate work, and therefore have to be coerced to do it. Further, they think all workers avoid taking on responsibility and have a tendency to follow the crowd.

Studies have shown theory X managers, who hold these cynical beliefs, are aversive, threatening and deceitful, partly because they believe anti-social and unethical behavior is effective at work. It is clear that Machiavellians are theory X managers. If clever and skilful, they can be very effective even if they are not liked. Further, they are nearly always known as being "political". They can be masters of office politics.

What are the key features of the concept of office politics? *First*, it is the secrecy, the covert agendas, the underhandedness of it all. Politics conducted in smoky rooms, behind closed doors, in private clubs, on the golf course. There are the insiders and the outsiders: the players and the pawns; those in the know and those in the dark. Office politics are about processes, procedures and decisions that are not meant to be scrutinized. Politics are about opaqueness, not transparency.

Second, there is impression management. Office politicians (all unelected) speak with forked tongue. The clever ones understand the difference between sins of omission and commission. What you see, hear and read is not what you get. Internal communications (except those carefully encrypted) are half truths, little more than management propaganda. Office politics are about censorship; about disguise.

Third, office politics are about self-interest. They are concerned with power and all the trappings, such as money and prestige; about selected groups hijacking activities, processes and procedures to secure their (and only their) interests. Covert groupings of individuals – based on clan, ideology or simply greed – cooperate with each other to obtain an unfair share of the resources of an organization. In this sense, office politics act against long-term organizational interests, at least from a shareholder perspective.

Politics cause distrust, conflict and lowered productivity. People do not openly share; they are guarded. They spend too much time and energy ingratiating themselves with the in-group and trying to work the system. The in-group are as much concerned with increasing or holding onto power as steering the company. The opposition is internal, not external. Office politics are dysfunctional.

But there is another perspective, and it is much more positive. Office politics are about building and strengthening networks and coalitions; about getting together movers and shakers prepared to do the hardest thing of all – make change happen. It can help driving through necessary but unpopular strategies. It is about identifying those with energy and vision – those who command various constituencies.

Politics is about power – the power to influence, persuade and cajole. Most organizations seek out and admire the CEO who is well-respected and connected. One who knows how to "play the game"; how to get people (investors, journalists and "real" politicians) on side. In this sense, being political is about being shrewd, proactive and strategic.

Hence, the success of Machiavellians. The more skilled they are at playing the game, the more they are likely to seize and retain that thing they most understand: power. They often use this power to further their own careers rather than being concerned for those that work for them or the organization as a whole.

CONCLUSION

Machiavellianism is a philosophy. It is a value or belief system that has a Hobbesian rather than Rousseauian view of Human Nature. To some, it seems like a form of naïve Darwinianism which has no place for altruism, selflessness or virtue.

Certainly, many well-known political leaders are clearly Machiavellians. They understand how power works and they make it work for them. Few of the leaders most people nominate as great are thought of as Machs; indeed, the opposite.

But could it be true that, whilst Machiavellians are unlikely to be particularly successful and certainly not admired in the business world, a "touch of" Machiavellianism may certainly help in the long and dangerous climb up the organization. Young managers jostle for power, for the limelight, for promotion. Machiavellians are feared more than respected. On its own it is unlikely to be a cause of derailment, but in conjunction with other disorders could prove to be a component of the whole derailment process.

PART III

7

SECTOR-SPECIFIC DISORDERS

INTRODUCTION

This chapter deals with five disorders and their relevant leadership styles. Each type of style is recognizable, particularly in certain sectors. Thus paranoids do well in the security business and hysterics in show business. Next, it is important to remember two things: first, that these disorders can (and often do) co-occur, giving each person a unique profile. Second, there is often a fine line between when these disorders may be considered healthily adaptive and when they can have a massive negative effect on leadership.

Certain jobs call for not only a very specific skill set, but also a particular set of attitudes and beliefs. Some worlds attract and reward the agreeable, empathic, caring individual, whilst others the opposite: skeptical, tough-minded, egocentric types. Some organizations have a corporate culture which perfectly fits individual preferences and values. In this sense, we select then get selected and socialized by organizations. Hence we have surprisingly homogenous groups, sectors and organizations. It is the thesis of this chapter that people with particular dark-side profiles are attracted to, and join, particular organizations where they may initially thrive. Certainly not all derail, depending on particular circumstances, though this also depends on the degree of their disorder.

PARANOID (ARGUMENTATIVE, VIGILANT)

Some jobs are all about secrets. People in R&D, those interested in national security, some finance organizations, and perhaps pharmaceutical companies are rightly concerned with security. Many organizations employ security people at the highest level to oversee complex organizations like airports or manufacturing complexes.

People in the security business have to be very vigilant. They often believe that potential spies are all around them. They are employed to make things safe and "brook no argument". They pride themselves on their toughness and realism. Indeed, many ex-military people as well as "spies" find good employment in that sector. They believe it is very important and difficult to keep things totally safe. This is, for them, their number one priority.

Many rely on elaborate electrical devices to ensure safety. Cameras, electronic gates and the like are used. Paranoia becomes normalized. The more paranoid one is the better. Paranoid people rise to the top. Indeed, Kets de Vries and Miller (1985) noted that whole organizations can become paranoid. They argue that when power is highly centralized in a leader with paranoid tendencies, there will tend to be a great deal of vigilance caused by distrust of subordinates and competitors alike. This may lead to the development of many control and information systems and a conspirational fascination with gathering intelligence from inside and outside the firm. Paranoid thinking will also lead to a centralization of power as the top executive tries to control everything himself (no one can be completely trusted). The strategy is likely to emphasize "protection" and reducing dependency on particular consultants, sources of data, markets or customers. There is likely to be a good deal of diversification, with tight control over divisions and much analytical activity. A leader who is obsessed with fantasies concerning distrust can set a very distinctive tone for the strategy, structure and culture of an organization.

The characteristics of these organizations are suspiciousness and mistrust of others; hypersensitivity and hyper-alertness; readiness to combat perceived threats; excessive concern with hidden motives and special meanings; intense attention span; cold, rational, unemotional, interpersonal relations. The paranoid organization is defensive and hypervigilant. It is pervaded by an atmosphere of distrust.

It is thought that between 0.5% and 2.5% of the population have this disorder, which must not be confused with the paranoid delusions of schizophrenics or the behavior of refugees and migrants, whose personal history leads to widespread mistrust. Paranoids are *super-vigilant*: nothing escapes their notice. They seem tuned into mixed messages, hidden motives, and secret groups. They are particularly sensitive to authority and power, and obsessed with maintaining their own independence and freedom.

Distrust and suspiciousness of others at work is their abiding characteristic. The motives of all sorts of colleagues and bosses are interpreted as malevolent, all the time. The "enemy" is both without and within.

They suspect, without much evidence, that others are exploiting, harming, or deceiving them about almost everything, both at work and at home. They are preoccupied with unjustified doubts about the loyalty or trustworthiness of subordinates, customers, bosses, shareholders, etc., on both big and small matters. They are reluctant to confide in others (peers at work) because of the fear that the information will be used against them: kept on file; used to sack them. They may even be wary of using email. They read hidden or threatening meanings into the most benign remarks or events from emails to coffee-room gossip, and they remember them. They are certainly *hypersensitive* to criticism. They persistently bear grudges against all sorts of people going back many years and can remember even the smallest slight. They perceive attacks on their character or reputation that others do not see and are quick to react angrily or to counter-attack. They seem *hyper-alert and sensitive*. They have recurrent suspicions, without justification, regarding the fidelity of their sexual or business partner and can be pretty obsessed with sex.

Paranoid individuals are slow to commit and trust, but once they do so are loyal friends. They are very interested in others' motives and prefer "watch-dog" jobs. They like being champions of the underdog, whistle-blowers on corruption. They are courageous because they are certain about their position. They are on the side of right: idealists striving for a better world. But they can be overly suspicious or fearful of certain people, which can manifest itself in an irrational hatred towards certain races, religions or political groups.

They are not compromisers and attack attackers. Many of their characteristics make them excellent managers: *alert, careful, observant* and *tactical*. But they can have problems with authority, and in dealing with those who hold different opinions from their own. However, they are more sensitive to the faults in others than the faults in themselves. The business world, they believe (sometimes correctly), is full of danger, dishonest people and those who are untrustworthy and will let them down. Because they believe others are out to harm them, they can be over-argumentative, bellicose, belligerent, hostile, secretive, stubborn and consumed with mistrust. They are not disclosive, they are suspicious of others and experts on projecting blame onto others.

Psychoanalysts believe the paranoid feel weak and dependent but sensitive to weakness in others and disclaim them for it. They yearn for dependency but fear it. Instead of showing personal doubt, they doubt others. Their self-righteousness, morality and punitiveness can be very attractive to some people.

Dotlich and Cairo (2003) sees the paranoid leader as manifesting habitual distrust. They are "inappropriately and egregiously suspicious" (p.53), which has an insidious effect on all those around them. They tend to see downsides to every action; to see others' exclusivity acting politically or in their own self-interest or with ulterior motives.

They are always critical in feedback and obsessed with what can (and will) go wrong. They identify three signs:

1. relentless skepticism about other people's motives
2. their direct reports become more and more highly defensive
3. they have increasing difficulty forging alliances with outside groups, companies and institutions.

They believe that, in certain occupations, people are trained to be distrustful and skeptical but that this can easily go too far. They believe the paranoid leader always needs to analyze the cause of their distrust and to recognize how much it is hurting their career. They need to be more positive and to imagine what effect their behavior has on others.

Miller (2008) calls the paranoid leaders "vigilantes" because of their "watch your back", "people can't be trusted" philosophies. They see deception, malevolence, and persecution everywhere, as their supersensitive and often malfunctioning radar is primed to pick up betrayal, duplicity and hostility. Of course, they project onto others those characteristics they don't like in themselves. They are often on a vendetta and should not be crossed lightly.

The war-room mentality of paranoid leaders means they fit well in competitive and combative sectors. Paranoid bosses demand total loyalty and, surprisingly, self-disclosure about your private life. However, the smallest and most trivial thing can turn the supportive boss into a suspicious enemy. They brood, bide their time and remember. They keep records to take revenge. Interestingly, they have got a good nose for insincerity and sycophants. They can be highly perceptive as to the motives of all those around them. Miller (2008) suggests they need to know who their enemies really are and beware black/white thinking.

According to Oldham and Morris (2000), the DSM-III-R describes the Paranoid personality as one who always expects to be cheated and exploited and, hence questions the loyalty of others all the time. These people bear grudges and remain unable or unwilling to confide in others. They may even counter-attack without any real justification.

Hogan and Hogan (2001) call this disorder 'Argumentative'. These types, they argue, expect to be wronged, to be betrayed, to be set up, to be cheated or to be deceived in some way. They see the world as a dangerous place, full of potential enemies, and they enjoy conspiracy theories; they are keenly alert for signs of having been mistreated. When they think they have been unfairly treated, they retaliate openly and directly. This may involve physical violence, accusations, retaliation or litigation. Retaliation is designed to send the signal that they are prepared to defend themselves. They are known for their suspiciousness, their argumentativeness, and their lack of trust in others. They are hard to deal with on a continuing basis because you never know when they are going to be offended by something (unpredictability), and because they are so focused on their own private agenda they don't have much time for others (unrewarding):

At their best they are very insightful about organisational politics and the motives of their counter players, and they can be the source of the good intelligence regarding the real agendas of others, and the real meaning of events. Although they are very insightful about politics, they are often not very good at playing politics. This is because they are true believers, they are deeply committed to their worldview, and they tend to be unwilling to compromise, even on small issues. Nonetheless, with their passionate commitment to a theory about how the world works, they can be visionary and charismatic, and people may be drawn to them ... Because they are unpredictable and not regarding to deal with, they have trouble maintaining a team over a long period.

(p. 48)

Paranoids mishandle stress by retreating, by withdrawing into their ideology and then attacking that which is threatening them. They are very persistent and tend to accumulate enemies. They are self-centered and ideology centered – all information and experience is filtered through their odd worldview and evaluated in terms of the degree to which it fits with, or threatens, that view, which somehow reflects on them.

To work with them, reporting staff have no alternative but to agree with them, because they will defeat your objections in a way that makes sense to them. Reports won't be able to persuade them that they are wrong, and risk alienating them by challenging them; and once they decide people can't be trusted, the relationship will be over. Reporting staff are either for them or against them.

According to Oldham and Morris (2000), the six traits and behaviors are clues to the presence of what they call the Vigilant style. The first of these is *Autonomy* as they keep their own counsel, require no outside reassurance or advice, make decisions easily, and take care of themselves. Next, they exercise *Caution* in all their dealings with others. They are also very *Perceptive* (good listeners), and also good at all forms of self-defense. Of course, they are also very *Alert to criticism*, becoming intimidated relatively easily. Finally, they place a high premium on *Fidelity and loyalty*. Vigilance can turn into paranoia and the latter to mistrust. Over time, the vigilant leader can become subclinically paranoid with disastrous effects for the organization.

SCHIZOTYPAL (IMAGINATIVE, IDIOSYNCRATIC)

In a knowledge-based economy, creativity and the ability to innovate are very desirable. Further, some organizations are very tolerant of rather odd behavior; they see it as a sign of genius. Schizotypal individuals may attract cult-like status, particularly in organizations that deal with "new-age" post-Christianity ideas.

There are cases of well-known people who suddenly seem to "lose the plot". However, whilst they might be tolerated and even respected for their oddities, it is rare that they become leaders of big organizations. They certainly have, however, with their unpredictable eccentricity, the capacity to derail small organizations.

This disorder, more common in males than females, has been estimated to affect about 3% of the population. In a sense, they are mild schizophrenics but do not show the gross disorganization in thinking and feeling or the severe symptoms of the latter. However, they all appear to be pretty idiosyncratic and, often, creatively talented and curious. They often hold very strange beliefs, enjoying the occult. They have odd habits, eccentric lifestyles and a rich inner life.

Schizotypal people have a rich inner life and often seek emotional experience. Hence they are drawn to religion and pharmacological techniques that promise "testing the limits". They seek rapture and nirvana.

Here the manager is marked by acute discomfort with, and reduced capacity for, close relationships. They show many eccentricities of behavior. They may look odd and have a reputation for being "peculiar".

They often have very odd ideas about business: how to succeed, who to hire, what controls what. They can have very odd beliefs or magical thinking that influences behavior and is inconsistent with business norms (e.g. superstitiousness, belief in clairvoyance, telepathy). They get into crystals, feng shui, etc., in a very big and serious way. They can have odd thinking and speech styles, being very vague or very elaborate. They can seem "other-worldly" and may be very difficult to follow. They can have unusual perceptual experiences – seeing things that are not there, smelling and tasting things differently. Some are very suspicious or paranoid around the home and office. They show inappropriate or constricted affect: that reacts oddly emotionally in various contexts. That is, they may become very emotional around some trivial issues but strangely and unpredictably cold about others.

Many organizations do not tolerate the odd behaviors of these idiosyncratic types. They dress oddly and work odd hours. They are not very loyal to their companies and do not enjoy the corporate world. They don't "connect" with staff, customers and their bosses. Their quirky quasi-religious beliefs estrange them yet more from the normal world of the other people. They are often loners.

Dotlich and Cairo (2003) label the Schizotypal leader as *eccentric*, enjoying being different for its own sake. There is all the difference between being creative, off-beat and quirky as opposed to weird, impractical and unrealistic. The trouble with eccentric leaders is that they are full of ideas and initiatives that go nowhere. Further, stakeholders are confounded by their non-conformist style. They seem unable or unwilling to prioritize, to collaborate and cooperate, being stubborn individualists, and therefore suffer from the problem that others don't take them seriously. Like all others, they need insight and self-awareness about the consequences of their actions. They need to see and close the gap between their intentions and their impact. They need dedicated staff who can and will execute their ideas. They also need to know the price they pay for being different. Oldham and Morris (2000) report the DSM criteria thus:

> A pervasive pattern of deficits in interpersonal relatedness, peculiarities of ideation, appearance, and behaviour, beginning by early

adulthood and present in a variety of contexts, as indicated by at least five of the following:

1. ideas of reference (excluding delusions of reference) (e.g., 'I'm sure those two people over there are talking about me')
2. excessive social anxiety, e.g., extreme discomfort in social situations involving unfamiliar people
3. odd beliefs or magical thinking, influencing behavior and inconsistent with sub-cultural norms, e.g., superstitiousness, belief in clairvoyance, telepathy, or 'sixth sense,' 'others can feel my feelings' (in children and adolescents, bizarre fantasies or preoccupations)
4. unusual perceptual experiences, e.g. illusions, sensing the presence of a force or person not actually present (e.g., 'I felt as if my dead mother were in the room with me')
5. odd or eccentric behavior or appearance, e.g., unkempt, unusual mannerisms, talks to self
6. no close friends or confidants (or only one) other than first-degree relatives
7. odd speech (without loosening of associations or incoherence), e.g., speech that is impoverished, digressive, vague, or inappropriately abstract
8. inappropriate or constricted affect, e.g. silly, aloof, rarely reciprocates gestures or facial expressions, such as smiles or nods
9. suspiciousness or paranoid ideation.

(p. 259)

Hogan and Hogan (2001) call these types *Imaginative* and describe them thus: they think about the world in unusual and often quite interesting ways. They may enjoy entertaining others with their unusual perceptions and insights. They are constantly alert to new ways of seeing, thinking, and expressing themselves, unusual forms of self-expression. They often seem bright, colourful, insightful, imaginative, very playful, and innovative, but also as eccentric, odd, and flighty.

These people are curiously interesting and may be fun to be around. But they are distractible and unpredictable and, as managers, they often leave people confused regarding their directions or intentions. They tend to mis-communicate in idiosyncratic and unusual ways. At their best, these people are imaginative, creative, interesting, and amazingly insightful about the motives of others but, at their worst, they can be self-absorbed, single-minded, insensitive to the reactions of others, and indifferent to the social and political consequences of their single-minded focus on their own agendas.

Under stress and heavy workloads, they can become upset, lose focus, lapse into eccentric behavior, and not communicate clearly. They can be moody and tend to get too excited by success and too despondent over failure. They do want attention, approval and applause, which explains the lengths to which they are willing to go in order to attract it.

To work with the imaginative, reports needs primarily to be a good audience, to appreciate their humor, creativity and spontaneity, and to understand that they do not handle reversals very well. They will not mind suggestions and recommendations regarding important decisions and, in fact, may even appreciate them. Reports should study their problem-solving style, listen to their insights about other people, and model their ability to "think outside the box". Oldham and Morris (2000), who call these types "idiosyncratic", note their social anxiety and frankly odd beliefs, perceptions, speech and mannerisms. They often have no close friends, odd speech, strange emotions and are often general suspiciousness.

The imaginative, idiosyncratic person is unlikely to reach very high positions in organizations, though they may be promoted in advertizing or academia. The absent-minded, nutty professor, the creative advertizing genius may share many schizotypical behaviors. If talented they may do well, but rarely as managers of others.

HISTRIONIC (COLORFUL, DRAMATIC)

In certain worlds – advertizing, media, fashion and the theatre – particular characteristics get people noticed. They are sometimes called outrageously disinhibited, emotional drama-queens. Often, they are skilled at attracting attention or inspiring people like themselves. Kets de Vries and Miller (1985) noted how a whole organization could become drama obsessed.

The dramatic organization is hyperactive, impulsive and uninhibited. In such an organization, decision-makers prefer to act on hunches and impressions, and take on widely diverse projects. Top managers reserve the right to start bold ventures independently; subordinates have limited power.

Such organizations are characterized by: self-dramatization and excessive emotional displays; incessant self-displays organized around crises; a need for activity and excitement; an alternation between idealization and devaluation of others; exploitativeness; inability to concentrate or sharply focus attention. This is not only the world of "AD-land" but, increasingly, that of e-commerce.

Dramatic managers are not risk averse. They often make rash, intuitive decisions, swinging company policy in radically different directions. They are impulsive and unpredictable. At their best, they can revitalize tired companies and provide the necessary momentum at crucial periods in a company's history (merger and acquisition or start-up). But, most of the time, they simply create instability, chaos and distress.

Histrionic leaders can be very inspirational. Combined with other talents, they can make brilliant speeches and stir great crowds. They love to be around their admirers and are unafraid to be emotional. But some of the most serious parts of management are often done very badly and they have a great capacity for derailment.

The term is derived from the Latin to mean "actor", but the original term was "hysterical", from the Latin root to mean "uterus". This disorder is found more frequently in women. They are attracted to "limelight" jobs and strive for attention and praise, but setbacks can lead easily to serious inner doubts and depression. Histrionics are certainly emotionally literate: they are open with all their emotions. But these emotions can change very quickly. These managers have excessive emotionality and attention-seeking. They are the "drama-queens" of the business world.

Most are uncomfortable in situations in which they are not the center of attention and try always to be so. They delight in making a drama out of a crisis. Their interaction with others is often characterized by inappropriate sexually seductive or provocative behavior. Needless to say, this causes more of a reaction in women than men. They display rapidly shifting and shallow expression of emotions. They are difficult to read. Most use physical appearance (clothes) to draw attention to self, but this may include body piercing or tattooing. They certainly get a reputation in the office for their "unique apparel". Many have a style of speech that is excessively impressionistic and lacking in detail. They always display self-dramatization, theatricality and exaggerated expression of emotion, usually negative. Even the dullest topic is imbued with drama. They are easily influenced by others or circumstances – and therefore both unpredictable and persuadable. Many consider relationships to be more intimate than they actually are. Being rather dramatic, they feel humdrum working relationships more intensely than others.

Histrionics do not make good managers. They get impatient with, and anxious about, details and routine administrative functions. They prefer gossip to analysis, and tend not to be good at detail. They are highly sociable and have intense relationships. They live to win friends and influence people by being very generous with compliments, flattery and appreciation. They hate being bored: life with them is never staid and dull. They don't like being alone.

Interestingly, the definition of themselves comes from the outside: they see themselves as others say they see them. They, therefore, lack a consistent sense of who they are. They need constant reassurance and positive feedback from others. And, because their heart rules their head, they can be impulsive, impetuous and impatient. They live not in the real world but in a storybook world.

At work they can be persuasive and insightful. They enjoy the world of advertizing, PR, sales and marketing but need strong back-up for things like plans, budgets and details. At work they are volatile, being known for being moody. They can be effusive with both praise and blame. But everything is an emotional drama and, emotionally, they can be both childlike and childish. They don't do stable relationships. At work they need to be the star, the center of attention, or else they can feel powerless or desperately unworthy. They are not introspective. And it is important not to overreact to their overreactions.

Dotlich and Cairo (2003) call the histrionic leader *melodramatic* because they are always trying to grab the center of attention. Those "over-the-top", showman types distract too much attention from what should be the focus of the business. They dominate meetings; use attention-seeking to try to create unquestioning compliance; they use their theatrical style to make them, rather than the business, the center of attention; they are more flamboyant than strategic and always "on", never reflective.

They have, according to Dotlich and Cairo (2003), four classic signs and symptoms:

1. lack of focus; confused priorities; wasted energy
2. a failure to develop people because they are too self-focused
3. they attract other show-offs, so executive teams mimic this unhealthy style

4. the elevate the expectations of others, develop a following but cannot, and do not, follow through on commitments.

They recommend some "corrective" actions: like seeing some feedback of themselves in action, identifying and, therefore, avoiding the situations that increase the melodrama; and making time to reflect and listen to others.

Miller (2008) calls histrionic types *emoters*. Their attention-seeking, intuitive, highly impressionistic style can lead to impulsivity and fickle decision-making. They are enthusiastic and fun-oriented; optimistic and energetic, but often very impractical. They tend to be personally poorly organized, which is not a recommendation for those who run organizations.

Because histrionic bosses don't deliver, with little follow-through, they cause many problems. Further, they can have difficulty separating work and pleasure; task and social. They need to be better prepared and find those with complementary skills. They have to learn to have fun but to know when it is, and is not, appropriate. Also, they need not take things personally.

Hogan and Hogan (2001) call these types *colorful* and seem persuaded that others will find them interesting, engaging and worth paying attention to. They are good at calling attention to themselves – they know how to make dramatic entrances and exits, they carry themselves with flair, self-consciously pay attention to their clothes and the way others react to them.

Histrionics are marked by their stage presence or persona, their self-conscious and distinctive aura – they perform extremely well in interviews, in assessment centers, and other public settings.

> They are great fun to watch, but they are also quite impulsive and unpredictable; everything that makes them good at sales (and selling themselves) makes them poor managers – they are noisy, distractible, over-committed, and love to be the centre of attention. They are not necessarily extraverted, they are just good at calling attention to themselves. At their best, they are bright, colourful, entertaining, fun, flirtatious, and the life of the party. At their worst, they don't listen, they don't plan, they self-nominate and self-promote, and they ignore negative feedback.
>
> (Hogan and Hogan, 2001, p. 49)

Histrionics deal with stress and heavy workloads by becoming very busy; enjoying high-pressure situations when they can then be the star. Breathless with excitement, they confuse activity with productivity and evaluate themselves in terms of how many meetings they attend rather than how much they actually get done. A key feature of these people that others may not appreciate is how much they need and feed off approval, and how hard they are willing to work for it. And this explains why they persist in trying to be a star after their lustre has faded. To work with them, reporting staff have to be prepared to put up with missed appointments, bad organization, rapid change of direction, and indecisiveness. This will never change, although it can be planned for. Yet by watching reporting staff you can learn how to read social clues, learn how to present your views effectively, forcefully, dramatically, and learn how to flatter and quite simply dazzle other people.

Oldham and Morris (2000) noted seven characteristics of this type, which they call *Dramatic*. First and foremost, they *live in a very emotional world.* They are noticeably emotionally demonstrative and physically affectionate. Second, they have *Rich imaginations*, are drawn to romance and melodrama, and seem to live all aspects of their lives vividly. Third, they are *Spontaneous*, being lively and fun-loving. Next, they certainly *Like to be seen and noticed* and can rise to the occasion. As a result, they always seek out *Applause*. Sixth, they pay a lot of attention to *grooming and physical presentation*. Last, they tend to be *Seductive, engaging, and charming tempters and temptresses.* There are drama-queens in all sectors, though they are likely to be found in the more human resource-oriented world. They can do very well in PR, marketing and training, particularly if they are talented. But they certainly remain hard work for their ever-suffering reporting staff.

PASSIVE-AGGRESSIVE (LEISURELY)

It is unusual for a passive-aggressive personality to reach really high levels in organizations. They can, however, rise to departmental head, where they can have a powerful effect on the organization overall. The more departments are interdependent, however, the more likely the passive-aggressive individual can derail the whole organization.

This personality type is very concerned about "doing their own thing". They demand the "right to be me". They have a right to do their thing in their way and no one has the right to deprive them of it. They believe, at work and in private relationships, nobody has the right to own them. They like the companionship of others but need strong defences against being ill-used. They are particularly sensitive to fairness.

They do not find the workplace of great importance. They can be good managers and workers. But they do not work overtime, take it home or worry much about it. They certainly will not do any more than their contract specifies. They do not work to please the boss or feel better about themselves. They are often heard saying, "It's not my job" and they tend to be suspicious of workplace authority. If their boss asks them to work harder, faster, more accurately, they feel unfairly treated, even abused. They are supersensitive to their rights, fairness and exploitation avoidance. They seem leisurely; they believe success is not everything. They tend not to be above middle-management levels because they are not ambitious or thrusting enough. For them, the game is not worth the candle.

Passive-aggressive types are not usually stressed. They sulk, procrastinate and forget when asked to do things they think are not fair. They are called "passive-aggressive" because they are rarely openly defiant, yet they are often angry. They snipe rather than confront. And they are often furious. They can be needy but resentful about those moods. They are, in essence, oppositional: not assertive. They often have downward job mobility.

The DSM-III-R describes Passive-Aggressive personality disorder a pervasive pattern of passive resistance to demands for adequate social and occupational performance, beginning by early adulthood and present in a variety of contexts. They are expected to have five of nine manifestations to "qualify" for this condition: procrastination (deadlines are not met); sulky, irritable, or argumentative; working deliberately slowly or shoddily on tasks they dislike; protesting that others make unreasonable demands on him or her; avoiding obligations; believing they are doing a much better job than anyone else believes; resenting suggestions on how to be more productive; obstructing the efforts of others; and unreasonably criticizing all those in authority.

Passive-aggressive leaders are labelled by Dotlich and Cairo (2003) as *passive resistant*. They are political and duplicitous, carefully fulfilling their own agendas. They come from and, indeed, perpetuate cultures where no one really says what they think. The essence of this (relatively common style) is saying one thing but doing another; having strictly private, non-shared agendas; always avoiding conflict and rarely openly expressing disagreement; and really caring little what others hope or expect.

This leadership style leads to people becoming angry, confused and very cynical. It leads to teams and partnerships falling apart and everything being seen as spin. They recommend that passive-aggressive leaders analyze the gap between how they are feeling inwardly and what they are saying or doing outwardly. They believe they should be encouraged to confront their egotism by putting themselves in place of the people they work with. They are also encouraged to confront their conflict avoidance and consider how successful leaders behave.

Miller (2008) calls the passive-aggressive leader a *spoiler*. They feel disadvantaged, vulnerable and as if life has been rigged against them, so they carefully and surreptitiously attack others. In essence, they carefully mask the opposition and rebellion against authority. So, they both shirk responsibilities whilst claiming others do so. They are, of course, brilliant at all types of sabotage.

Miller (2008) notes that their "martyred mewling" is mixed with a great skill at deflecting blame.

> They easily destroy team morale and generate a lot of animosity among co-workers. They are masters of procrastination. They'd rather be perceived as struggling but helpless to overcome the forces (oh, so unfairly) arranged against them, rather than make the transition into true health and independence because then they'd have the same responsibilities as everyone else and not be able to claim special privileges as a victim. In the workplace, these personalities often represent the classic wrecked-by-success syndrome: individuals who seem to be on the threshold of achieving their self-stated career goal, when – alas – forces beyond their control to conspire once again to bring them crashing down.
>
> (p. 96)

Clearly, it is not much fun working for the passive-aggressive boss who blames you for all his or her failures. Miller (2008) notes: "Remember, too, that for this personality, success implies expectation, expectation breeds fear, fear elicits self-loathing, and this self-loathing is then projected onto others including his employees. So, ultimately, he'll hate you for helping him because ultimately it demeans him. You may need to keep an accurate log of your actions and communications to protect yourself" (p. 97). His advice is, first, to get help and remember that "payback is a bitch", meaning you might get back what you hand out, so beware.

Hogan and Hogan (2001) call these people *Leisurely*. They argue that these types march to the sound of their own drum, they are confident about their skills and abilities, cynical about the talents and intentions of others – especially superiors, and they insist on working at their own pace. They tend to get angry and slow down even more when asked to speed up. They tend to feel mistreated, unappreciated and put upon; and when they sense that they have been cheated, they retaliate, but always under conditions of high deniability. They are, curiously, quite skilled at hiding their annoyance and pretending to be cooperative, and their peevishness and foot-dragging are often very hard to detect.

They are often late for meetings, they procrastinate, they work at around 80% of their capacity, and they are very stubborn and hard to coach. They will rarely directly confront others. Their prickly sensitivity, subtle cooperativeness, stubbornness, and deep absorption make them both unpredictable and unrewarding to deal with. As a result, they have trouble building and maintaining a team.

Passive-Aggressives handle stress and heavy workloads by slowing down, by simply ignoring requests for greater output, and by finding ways to get out of work. Because they seem overtly cooperative and agreeable, it takes a long time to realize how unproductive and refractory they actually can be. They are self-centered, they focus on their own agendas, and they deeply believe in their own superior natural talent and their right to leisure. They believe they have nothing to prove to themselves, are quite indifferent to feedback from others, and, therefore, become annoyed and resentful when criticized or asked for extra effort.

People need to be aware that passive-aggressives are not nearly as cooperative as they seem, and that they are only pretending to agree with you about work and performance issues. Also, people need to get passive-aggressive types to commit to performance goals in public, in front of witnesses, so that a community of people can hold them accountable. Social pressure won't change their views of the world, but it will serve to make their performance deficits less easily deniable.

Oldham and Morris (2000) claim the following five traits and behaviors are clues to the presence of what they, too, call the Leisurely style. A person who reveals a strong Leisurely tendency will demonstrate more of these behaviors more intensely than someone with less of this style in his or her personality profile. First, they have a belief in their right to enjoy themselves on their own terms in their own time. Next, they do what is expected of them and no more. Third, they can resist acceding to demands that they feel unfair. Fourth, they are not obsessed by time urgency or the demands of the clock. Last, they seem never to be over-awed by authority. There are many senior managers with this rather unattractive profile. Their "pathology" may have served them well, even if the burden of it has been "picked-up" by their long-suffering staff.

OBSESSIVE-COMPULSIVE (DILIGENT, CONSCIENTIOUS)

Of all the personality disorders, this is among the most widely-known and understood. This is, no doubt, the case because in so many business worlds careful thinking, bureaucratic form-filling and following set behavioral rules are required. The quality controller, the internal auditor, the health and safety inspectors are all required to follow rules vigorously and enthusiastically.

An obsessive-compulsive manager leads to the development of a compulsive organization. A compulsive organization emphasizes ritual; it plans every detail in advance and carries out its activities in a routine, pre-programmed style. Thoroughness and conformity are valued. Such organizations are hierarchical and generally have elaborate policies, rules and procedures. The strategies of compulsive firms reflect their preoccupation with detail and established rituals. Each compulsive organization has a distinctive area of competence and specializes in this area, whether or not the area is related to the marketplace.

For Kets de Vries and Miller (1985) these organizations are characterized by: perfectionism; preoccupation with trivial details; insistence that others submit to an established way of doing things; relationships defined in terms of dominance and submission; lack of spontaneity; inability to relax; meticulousness, dogmatism and obstinacy.

Compulsive managers are inward-looking, indecisive, cautious and fearful about making mistakes. They are deeply involved in the minutiae of facts and figures, and love promulgating rules and regulations to make their lives easier. They are often inflexible, oriented to the past and unwilling to change. They typically have excellent internal control and audit mechanisms and well-integrated procedures. But, all too often, they are anachronistic bureaucracies that seem out of touch with the flexible and adaptive companies of today. The faster the world changes, the more incompetent they are – change is an enemy not an opportunity.

The problem for certain organizations is that perfectionism is admired and rewarded. Those who most noticeably follow the rules and conform to even the smallest implicit and explicit behavioral norm become organizational heroes. They therefore climb the greasy pole, making the whole organization more compulsive.

This disorder is more common in men and around 1% of the population exhibit the symptoms. They are often known for their zealous perfectionism, for their attention to detail, for their rigidity and for their formality. They are also often the workaholics; those who really "live" the work ethic. They are competent, organized, thorough, loyal. They enjoy, even in their holidays and leisure time, intense, detailed, goal-oriented activity.

These managers show a preoccupation with orderliness, perfectionism, and mental and interpersonal control, at the expense of flexibility, openness and efficiency. They make for the most anal of bureaucrats. Always they are preoccupied with details, rules, lists, order, organization or schedules to the extent that the major point of the business activity is lost and forgotten. All show perfectionism that interferes with task completion (e.g. is unable to complete a project because his or her own overly strict standards are not met). And, of course, they demand it in others, however unproductive it makes them. These managers are frequently workaholics often excluding leisure activities and friendships. They are seriously driven workaholics. They have a well-deserved reputation for being over-conscientious, scrupulous, and inflexible about matters of morality, ethics or values.

Amazingly, they are unable to discard worn-out or worthless objects, even when they have no sentimental value. They hoard rubbish at home and in the workplace. They are reluctant to delegate tasks or to work with others unless those submit to exactly his or her way of doing things. They do not let go, and thus pay the price. They are misers towards both self and others; money is viewed as something to be hoarded for future catastrophes. Because they never fully spend their budget, they never get it increased. In short, they show rigidity and stubbornness ... very unpleasant to work for.

Conscientious, obsessive compulsives rise through the ranks through hard work. But, at certain levels, they start to derail because they have problems making quick decisions, setting priorities and delegating. They tend to want to check the details again and again. They function best as right-hand-man to leaders with strong conceptual skills and visions. They are very self-disciplined and put work first. They are often not very emotionally literate and can be fanatical and fundamentalist about moral, political and religious issues. They can find it difficult to relax and difficult to throw things away. Their relationships are marked by conventionality and coolness. They are faithful, responsible but unromantic and unemotional. They can be seen as mean, overcautious.

The obsessive-compulsive manager *must* have everything done *perfectly*. They get wrapped up in details and lose sense of direction and priorities. They can be tyrannical bosses, super-attentive to time, orderliness and cleanliness. They are driven by "oughts" and "shoulds" and expect others to be likewise. They make rules for themselves and others as they are rigid, perfectionistic and controlling. They are the overbearing, fault-finders of the business world. They are driven to achieve respect and approval, and to control their, and others', dangerous impulses, desires and feelings.

The scrupulously correct leader paradoxically gets the little things right whilst letting the big things go wrong. Dotlich and Cairo (2003) point out their irrational nitpicking; their detail obsessionality and their meddlesome hands-on approach. They tend to be detail focused, overmanaging of processes and too concerned with form over substance. Their discomfort with uncertainty and ambiguity leads to them over-structuring and regulating everything. They can't or won't delegate and don't seem to give people a sense of what is really important. Hence, quite often and very tellingly, they overlook the obvious. They are also prone to getting caught in a stress cycle.

Thus, Dotlich and Cairo (2003) encourage obsessionality to examine the costs (missed opportunities, diminished productivity, getting stressed out) of their style. They suggest that they try prioritizing key jobs, living with imperfectionism and giving up on their obsessional perfectionism: clearly, easier said than done.

Miller (2008) calls the obsessive-compulsive business leaders *derailers*. Cautious, devil-in-the-details, orderly perfectionists. They are attracted to, and rewarded for, high-level cognitive jobs such as those in engineering and finance. Their major dynamic is control. They need to control people and processes, to ensure that things are done properly, in the right order by the prescribed process. Failure to do that leads to anxiety.

Often, derailers are hard-working micro-managers. They can be exceptionally demanding, with all these familiar mottos about if a job is worth doing it's worth doing it very well. They can get a great deal out of their staff but at great cost. They are blunt and straight-forword, so followers know where they stand. Miller (2008) offers three pieces of advice for obsessives. First, quietly set the example you want your people to emulate. Second, set realistic objectives and standards. Third, critique with care.

Oldham and Morris (2000) describe the psychiatric criteria: perfectionism; preoccupation with details, rules, lists, order, organization or schedules; unreasonable insistence that others submit to very particular ways of doing things; excessive devotion to work; indecisiveness; scrupulousness, and inflexibility about morality, ethics and values; restricted, restrained or even virtually non-existent expression of affection; distinct lack of generosity with regard to time, money or gifts; and the inability to discard all sorts of rubbish.

Hogan and Hogan (2001) called these types *Diligent* because they are concerned with doing a good job, being a good citizen, and pleasing authority. They note that the Diligent type is hardworking, careful, planful, meticulous, and has very high standards of performance for self and other people. They live by these rules and expect others to do so too, and they become irritable and erratic when others do not follow their rules. What is most distinctive is their conservatism, their detail orientation, their risk aversion; but they are also thought of as reliable, dependable and predictable. They are often desirable organizational citizens who can always be relied upon to maintain standards, do their work competently and professionally, and treat their colleagues with respect.

Hogan and Hogan note that they are good role models who uphold the highest standards of professionalism in performance and comportment. They are popular with their bosses because they are so completely reliable, but not necessarily those who report to them. However, they are fussy, particular, nitpicking micro-managers who deprive their subordinates of any choice or control over their work. Their sin is micro-management. This alienates their staff, who soon refuse to take any initiative and simply wait to be told what to do and how to do it. Diligent, conscientious, obsessive-compulsives also cause stress for themselves; their obsessive concern for quality and high performance makes it difficult for them to delegate. It also makes it difficult for them to prioritize their tasks. They also have problems with vision and the big picture. Consequently, they have a kind of ambivalent status as managers and can function in some environments at certain levels.

Diligent obsessionals tend to become stressed by heavy workloads. They respond to increased workloads by working longer and harder (not smarter) and they fall further and further behind, and they find this intolerable. They often become a bottleneck to productivity – because everything must pass through them, be checked and revised by them, be approved by them, and they won't let anything go that isn't completed according to their standards. They closely supervise their staff. It can help to make suggestions regarding prioritizing work, and by putting tasks into context by reflecting on the big picture.

In everyday language, Oldham and Morris (2000) describe nine characteristics of these types: *Hard work*: dedication to work; Adhering to *Strong moral principles and values*; Ensuring that everything must be done the *"Right", correct, appropriate or sanctioned* way; *Perfectionism*; they show a *Love of detail*; they also strive for *Orderliness and tidiness*; next they celebrate *Pragmatism*; and *Prudence*; finally, they are characterized by *Accumulation* of lots of worthless junk of all kinds. The diligent, conscientious type can do very well in business. Certain jobs demand obsessive compulsive-checking such as health and safety, quality control. But, like all the other disorders, it is too much of this trait that leads to serious problems both for the individual and their staff.

CONCLUSION

Reading some of these profiles may lead one to believe no one with their traits, dispositions and tendencies could possibly end up in a senior management position. Others point out that the recognized incidence of these disorders in the population is very low: 1%–3%.

However, two points need to be restated. *First*, a person's preferences and predilections in part determine what sort of job they seek out. Argumentative, vigilant, paranoid individuals may thrive in the espionage, military or security sector. It certainly may help those who work in, for or with the Mafia or some sort of "associated organizations".

Similarly, creative, imaginative idiosyncratic people may make brilliant artists, inventors, and research and development specialists given, naturally, that they have other specific competencies and skills. They may be good science fiction writers or inspire political and religious movements. They may do well in the fashion or theatre industries, or even alternative medicine. However, if very extreme, it is unlikely they will ever really be able to accept the demands and responsibilities of senior management positions.

Histrionic, show-off, limelight-seeking types may do well in sales, or the arts. Combined with talent, their apparent self-confidence and social skills may mean they end up successful motivational speakers or religious evangelists. They may make reasonably successful lecturers or trainers, if they are prepared to put in sufficient hard work to provide the details their self-presentation preference glosses over.

Passive-aggressive leaders are so common that this disorder has disappeared from modern psychiatric manuals. It seems, indeed, as if some cultures almost encourage it. Few entrepreneurs are passive-aggressive, but these types can climb the management hierarchy in bureaucracies.

One of the best-known of all disorders is OCD. Many people have encouraged obsessionality in various forms. There are, no doubt, careers ideally suited to those "brushed with" this preference. They may thrive in quality control, internal audits, health and safety. They may make excellent proof-readers, complex timetable designers or stock-checkers. Some occupations need the detail-oriented, orderly checker.

Second, the issue is the same with all these types and a theme of the book. Although many researchers write typological language, they think along dimensions. The idea of *optimal* not maximal is important. Having some or enough of these "markers", one may be served well. Indeed, being high on some dimensions may be particularly useful in certain sectors. However, having too much could lead to either failure to achieve high positions in management – or, more likely, management derailment.

8

SIX MORE ODDBALLS

INTRODUCTION

As we have seen, the clinically-oriented observers of leadership derailment have used the Personality Disorders as a useful and comprehensive framework to describe failure (Dotlich and Cairo, 2003; Miller, 2008). It seems clear that around five of the disorders are most likely going to "help" a person *in the short run* to become a leader. These are most likely to be in rank order: psychopathic, narcissistic, paranoid, histrionic and schizotypal personality disorder. However, in certain situations and jobs other types might rise to the top.

Recall again the central tenet of all working in the area. All these behavioral dispositions lie *on a dimension*. A modest amount of the behavior pattern does no harm and, indeed, may be helpful. Too much – often caused by stress – is derailing.

One issue that is important is that the agreed "list" of personality disorders varies as psychiatric manuals change. Thus, some disorders (i.e. passive-aggressive) disappear, others get relabelled, whilst some new ones appear. Hence, not all books see the disorders framework as useful for describing leader derailing characteristics.

SCHIZOID (SOLITARY)

These are the cold fish of the personality disordered world: distant, aloof, emotionally flat, often preferring the affection of animals to that of people. These are the solitary loners of the personality disorders world. They are very self-contained: they do not need others to admire, entertain, guide or amuse them. And yet they report being free of loneliness. They seem completely dispassionate. They are doers and observers not feelers. They seem stoical in the face of pain and passion. Relationships? They can take them or leave them. They don't really understand emotions.

Dotlich and Cairo (2003) call this style *aloofness* because CEOs with this disorder disengage and disconnect. In times of difficulty they retreat, distancing themselves from others. Dotlich and Cairo argue there are five signs and symptoms of this disorder: they become invisible when needed most; they ignore conflict; they cause others to work less hard; false assumptions and miscommunications become rampant and a culture of lacking in passion arises. They recommend three ways to prevent failure: map out your network of support, rehearse your messages and pay attention to your impact on others.

Miller (2008) calls schizoid leaders *oddballs* who like to do things in their way at their pace. They are very unlikely to become leaders except when conscripted because of their imagination, reliability or skill. They tend to treat their following with benign neglect. Miller (2008) believes they should have a schedule for "people time", use alternative forms of communication which suit them well and practise their social skills. The personality website uses the mnemonic DISTANT

D: detached (or flattened) affect
I: indifferent to criticism and praise
S: sexual experiences of little interest
T: tasks (activities done solitarily)
A: absence of close friends
N: neither desires nor enjoys close relations
T: takes pleasure in few activities.

Here, the manager or leader seems detached from social relationships. They often have a restricted range of expression of emotions in interpersonal settings. They seem more emotionally flat than is necessary. They are thought of as unresponsive, and disparately low in EQ.

They neither desire nor enjoy close relationships at work, including being part of a family. They are never team players and hate the idea of being so. They almost choose the solitary activities, feeling uncomfortable even in informal gatherings. They have little, if any, interest in having sexual contact with others ... perhaps not a bad thing at work. They take pleasure in few, if any, activities. They seem joyless, passionless and emotionless. They lack close friends or confidants other than first-degree relatives. They are isolates at work but apparently not unhappy with their friendlessness. They appear indifferent to the praise or criticism of others. Absolutely nothing seems to get them going. They show emotional coldness, detachment or flattened emotionality.

Schizoid people are not team players; neither are they sensitive or diplomatic. They are not aware of office politics. Hence, they may be more successful in solitary careers. They are not anti-social but asocial. They are the "hollow man": empty, flat, emotionally unmovable. They may have a rich fantasy life but a very poor emotional life.

According to Oldham and Morris (2000), who call schizoids the *solitary* style, the DSM manual specifies the diagnostic criteria as a pervasive pattern of indifference to social relationships and a restricted range of emotional experience and expression. They seem neither to desire nor enjoy close relationships, choosing solitary activities. They seem not to experience strong emotions, and appear indifferent to both praise and criticism. They often have no close friends or confidants, possibly because they are so aloof and cold.

Hogan and Hogan (2001) call these types *self-absorbed*, self-focused, indifferent to the feelings or opinions of others – especially their staff. They are introverted, misanthropic, imperceptive and lacking in social insight. They appear thick-skinned and indifferent to rejection or criticism. They prefer to work alone, and are more interested in data and things than in people. They tend to work in finance, accounting, programming and information technology, where their progress will depend on their technical skills and not their social insight. They are often uncommunicative and insensitive, which makes them unpredictable and unrewarding, and they have trouble building or maintaining a team.

They can be very tough in the face of political adversity; they have a hard surface, and they can take criticism and rejection where others would tremble. They can also stay focused and on task, and not be distracted by tumult, emotional upheavals and stressful meetings; through it all, they will continue to do their jobs. But because they are indifferent to others' needs, moods or feelings, they can be rude, tactless, insensitive and gauche. They are therefore very poor managers. They are unperturbed by daily stress and heavy workloads; at the same time, they are insensitive or indifferent to the stress levels of their staff. When the pressure is really on, they retreat into their office, begin handling matters themselves, and stop communicating – which leaves others at a loss to know what they want or need. Always extremely self-centered and self-reliant; they do not need emotional support from others, and they don't provide any to others. They primarily don't want to be bothered by other peoples' problems, they just want to do their work.

To work with the detached, reports should stay task-oriented and questions and comments be job related. They will ignore requests for more and better communications, and will tend to work by themselves. Reports should observe what they do, so that they do not act that way themselves, and, develop lines of communication to other people in the organization so that you will have a source of advice during times of trouble. Oldham and Morris (2000) note:

> The following five traits and behaviours are clues to the presence of the Solitary style.
>
> 1. *Solitude.* Individuals with the Solitary personality style have small need of companionship and are most comfortable alone.
> 2. *Independence.* They are self-contained and do not require interaction with others in order to enjoy their experiences or to get on in life.
> 3. *Sangfroid.* Solitary men and women are even-tempered, calm, dispassionate, unsentimental, and unflappable.
> 4. *Sexual composure.* They are not driven by sexual needs. They enjoy sex but will not suffer in its absence.
> 5. *Feet on the ground.* They are unswayed by either praise or criticism and can confidently come to terms with their own behaviour.
>
> (pp. 264–5)

They have seven tips for dealing with these types:

> Let this person be ... They may not mix much in the Real World or react deeply to you, but they are very competent and responsible, and their inner worlds can be very interesting.
>
> 1. Do not assume that the Solitary person is uncomfortable or unhappy because he or she is alone ...
> 2. Do not assume that the Solitary person in your life is uncomfortable with you because he or she prefers to spend much time outside your presence or just sitting quietly instead of interacting with you ...

3. Look for signs of caring that are different from the standard I-want-you, I-need-you, I-love-you …
4. Ensure this person plenty of time to be alone. Anyone with even a small amount of Solitary style requires time to him- or herself to feel sane, well adjusted, and productive …
5. Take up hobbies or find activities to occupy yourself while the Solitary person is off on his or her own.
6. When you need to work out a problem with a non-emotional Solitary person, appeal to logic instead of emotion.

(pp. 275–6)

Again, there may be jobs where detached, solitary ways of behaving may be adaptive. The R&D scientists, the meteorologists on an uninhabited island or the artistic crafts person may work very well alone. It is when they are promoted to the position of managing teams that problems arise.

BORDERLINE (EXCITABLE, MERCURIAL)

These are people "living on the edge". Around 2% of the population have this order, more common in women than men. The term "borderline" originally referred to the border between neuroses and psychoses. There are often signs of other disorders: mood, depression, histrionics. People like Marilyn Monroe, Adolf Hitler and Lawrence of Arabia have been diagnosed with this disorder, being impulsive, unpredictable, reckless. Most of all, they tend to have problems with their self-image, often "splitting" their positive and negative views of themselves. They can vacillate between self-idealization and self-abhorrence.

They show chronic instability of interpersonal relationships, self-image and emotion. They are also marked by impulsivity in their daily behavior. Sometimes they show frantic efforts to avoid real or imagined abandonment by managers, their staff, and so on. They can become dependent and clinging. They often show a pattern of unstable and intense interpersonal relationships characterized by alternating between extremes of love and hate; worship and detestation. Most have identity disturbance: markedly and persistently unstable self-image or sense of self. They are not really sure who they are and assumed identity can easily change. They are impulsive with money, sex, booze, driving and are, in every sense of the word, accident-prone.

They might spend lavishly the one day and be miserly the next. At extremes, they can show recurrent suicidal behavior, or threats. Most noticeable is their marked change of mood (e.g. intense episodic dysphoria, irritability or anxiety, usually lasting a few hours and only rarely more than a few days). They seem to be on an emotional rollercoaster, with ups and downs even in the same day. They often talk about chronic feelings of inner emptiness. Unfortunately for their reports and managers, they have inappropriate, intense anger or difficulty controlling anger (e.g. frequent displays of temper, constant anger, recurrent physical fights).

These mercurial types are on the rollercoaster of life. They are intense and demanding. Their emotional world is geological: full of volcanic explosions and movement of tectonic plates. They can blow hot and cold; fire and ice very quickly. They are driven by emotions and find emotional significance in everything. Hence, they are very moody. People can drop from idols to "bad objects" in the space of days. But because they cannot control their emotional states, they are frequently in torment.

They act on impulse and they can have a real self-indulgent side. They can change their life-style quite easily and do not have a strong sense of self. In this sense, they can be a little unsure of their identity. At work they can be passionately involved with others. They can really admire their bosses when praised, but this can just be a phase. They insist on being treated well and have a keen sense of entitlement. They can easily see themselves as more important than others do. As managers, they get very involved with their staff and expect total dedication. When their unrealistic expectations are not met, they can get very moody and churlish.

Their sense of who they are, what they believe, what is the meaning of their life is ever-changing. They do not like mixed feelings, ambiguity or solitariness. They prefer to see the world in terms of good and bad. They can have great difficulty concentrating.

Dotlich and Cairo (2003) call these leaders *volatile*, with sudden and unpredictable mood shifts. They can easily explode, making others bewildered by unpredictability. They are, in some sense, bi-polar, vacillating between optimism then pessimism; energy and enthusiasm, then intimidation and lethargy. They document three tell-tale signs and symptoms. *First*, others "hold back" in their interaction (for fear of outbursts); *second*, everyone seems to be involved in distracting mood management and, *third*, others become more distant. Staff don't want to invest constant effort into the baggage that comes with volatility.

They recommend self-awareness and self-regulation for volatile leaders, like empowering a trusted adviser to provide votability alerts like stepping in or out of particular situations. The heroic, idea-generating, charismatic but volatile leader often makes a seriously bad manager.

Miller (2008) calls Borderline bosses *reactors*. He notes their tendency to "splitting", which is the sudden and dramatic changes between idealization and devaluation of individuals. Because they can be very passionate, both positively and negatively, they are, for others, extremely unpredictable. They have an unstable self-identity combined with a frequent dread of being alone. They can go into rages, go back on their word and look to others for self-affirmation all the time. Miller (2008) believes the only hope for the Borderline, reactor boss is to get professional help and give people the benefit of the doubt.

Some experts believe that the term "personality disorganization" is best suited to this disorder because they seem midway between the functional and dysfunctional. Oldham and Morris (2000) summarize the diagnostic criteria as a pervasive pattern of instability of mood, interpersonal relationships and self-image. Those with the disorder show a pattern of unstable and intense interpersonal relationships; impulsiveness with respect to spending, sex, substance use, shoplifting, reckless driving, binge eating; marked shifts in mood lasting a few hours and only rarely more than a few days; inappropriate intense anger or lack of control of anger; recurrent suicidal threats or behavior, or self-mutilating behavior; a marked and persistent identity disturbance with respect to self-image, sexual orientation, long-term goals or career choice, friends or values; chronic feelings of emptiness or boredom; and, finally, frantic efforts to avoid real or imagined abandonment.

The website on personality disorders suggests the following way to remember this disorder:

A: abandonment
M: mood instability (marked reactivity of mood)
S: suicidal (or self-mutilating) behavior
U: unstable and intense relationships
I: impulsivity (in two potentially self-damaging areas)
C: control of anger
I: identity disturbance
D: dissociative (or paranoid) symptoms that are transient and stress related
E: emptiness (chronic feelings of).

Hogan and Hogan (2001) call these types *Excitable*, as they expect to be disappointed in relationships; they anticipate being rejected, ignored, criticized or treated unfairly. They are on guard for signs that others will treat them badly. They erupt in emotional displays that may involve yelling, throwing things and slamming doors. Because they are so alert for signs of mistreatment, they find them everywhere, even when others can't see them. They are neither predictable nor rewarding to deal with. As a result, they have a lot of trouble building and maintaining a team – the fundamental task of leadership.

They can be sensitive to the plight of others; they have some capacity for empathy; because they know that life is not always fair, then can genuinely feels others' pain. They sometimes tend to be enthusiastic about, and to work very hard on, new projects. But, they are seriously high maintenance – they require a lot of handholding and reassurance, and they are seriously hard to please.

They do not handle stress or heavy workloads very well, and they tend to explode rather easily. Also, they are hard people to talk to and to maintain a relationship with. Consequently, they change jobs frequently and they have a large number of failed relationships. They are so easily disappointed in working relationships, their first instinct is to withdraw and leave. They are all self-centered – all information and experience is evaluated in terms of what it means for them personally – and they take the reaction of others personally. They personalize everything, but they do so privately, what others see are the emotional outbursts and the tendency to withdraw. To work with excitable managers, reports must be prepared to provide them with a lot of reassurance, keep them well-informed so at to minimize surprises, and give them a lot of preview so they know what is coming. Think of trying to soothe a fretful child.

In lay language, Oldham and Morris (2000) suggest these types, which they call Mercurial, have the following characteristics: *Romantic attachments*; *Intensity* as nothing is taken lightly; *Emotionally active and reactive*; *Lack of constraint* because they are uninhibited, spontaneous, fun-loving and undaunted by risk; *Activity* being always lively, creative, busy and engaging; *Imaginative and curious,* always experimenting with other cultures, roles and value systems.

Oldham and Morris (2000) also provide six tips on dealing with the Borderline personality. Be prepared for acceptance and rejection. Don't react to changeable moods. Ask them to explain their behavior and feelings. Beware of their letting things at work slide. Finally, always show love, devotion and dedication.

The borderline manager is unlikely to be very senior but, if they are bright and have frequently left jobs, they may be appointed to leadership roles they are very unsuited to fulfil. They certainly are relatively easy to spot, but really unpleasant to work for.

AVOIDANT (CAUTIOUS, SENSITIVE)

This disorder is equally common in men and women and is believed to affect between 0.5% and 1% of the population. People with this disorder appear to be social phobics, in that they are socially isolated and withdrawn. Feelings of possible rejection drive them to situations where they are likely to be shunned. They seek acceptance, approval, affection.

Miller (2008) calls those with Avoidant tendencies *shrinkers*. He notes that, because of their social inhibition, they tend to lower-level jobs with minimal interpersonal contact. However, it can be their intelligence and technical skills that thrust them into the limelight and a position of power. They experience many deficits like not giving clear goals or constructive feedback. Further, unscrupulous workers can find the avoidant boss an easy target because, being unconfrontational, people are allowed to get away with too much.

Miller (2008) believes that avoidant bosses can do better if they "regularize" with better schedules and standardized procedures. This tends to reduce their anxiety and, therefore, improve their performance. Often, they lack social skills because having avoided people they have had limited practice. Hence, they are encouraged to listen and observe people more closely.

The website suggest CRINGES is a good way to remember the key characteristics of this disorder:

C: certainty (of being liked required before willing to get involved with others)
R: rejection (or criticism) preoccupies one's thoughts in social situations
I: intimate relationships (restraint in intimate relationships due to fear of being shamed)
N: new interpersonal relationships (is inhibited in)
G: gets around occupational activity (involving significant interpersonal contact)

E: embarrassment (potential) prevents new activity or taking personal risks

S: self viewed as unappealing, inept, or inferior.

These individuals show social inhibition, feelings of inadequacy and hypersensitivity to negative evaluation. They are supersensitive, delicate flowers.

They avoid occupational activities that involve significant interpersonal contact, because of fears of criticism, disapproval or rejection. Any chance of negative feedback is to be avoided. They are unwilling to get involved with people unless certain of being liked, which is pretty difficult at work ... indeed, anywhere. They show restraint within intimate relationships because of the fear of being shamed or ridiculed. They are cold fish. They seem always preoccupied with being criticized or rejected in work situations. They are inhibited in new interpersonal situations because of feelings of inadequacy. They see themselves as socially inept, personally unappealing or inferior to others. It can be puzzling to wonder how they ever became managers in the first place. Certainly, low self-esteem people rarely make it to the top in business.

These rather sensitive types seek safety: in people and environments they know and trust. But they can easily become anxious, guarded and worried. Beneath a polite and cool facade they can feel very uneasy. They cope with their anxiety by being prepared for everything. They like life, their friends and work to be safe, secure and predictable. They do not like the new: strangers, unfamiliar people or ways of working. They prefer what they know and they try to make work a home away from home. They can be effective, reliable and steady, and show little need for variety and challenge. They like routine and are pleased to help their seniors. But they are not political in organizations and can take refuge in their professionalism. They do well in technical fields that require routine, repetition and habit.

But the avoidants are so afraid of rejection they live impoverished social lives. The paradox is that they avoid close relationships that could bring them exactly what they want: acceptance and approval. Because they feel isolated, unwanted, incompetent, they are sure others, will reject them and often they are rejected because of their cold, detached behavior. They are supersensitive to negative feedback and want unconditional love. Yet they believe one cannot really be loveable unless one is without imperfections. They are often very self-conscious and can feel strong self-contempt and anger towards others. Allergic to social anxiety, they routinize themselves in a safe world.

Dotlich and Cairo (2003) call these types *excessively cautious*, and believe many CEOs are like that because of the constant scrutiny that they are under. They over-analyze and procrastinate. Requiring second, third, then fourth opinions before making a decision can have (very) serious (negative) consequences. They stall, procrastinate and never give the go-ahead until it is too late. They believe there are three important subtle signs of this disorder. *First*, an unwillingness to fire anyone. *Second*, lots of effort through committees, timetable etc that achieves very little. *Third*, a serious, conspicuous and important absence of strong opinions in debate. Dotlich and Cairo recommend that often these "Mr Nice Guy" leaders need to prioritize, focus on past success, confront their worst fears and try something new. Ponderous cautiousness is a serious management derailer. Oldham and Morris (2000) summarize the diagnostic criteria as a pervasive pattern of social discomfort, fear of negative evaluation and timidity. They are easily hurt by criticism or disapproval; have no close friends or confidants; seem unwilling to get involved with people unless certain of being liked; avoid social or occupational activities that involve much interpersonal contact; seem always reticent in social situations because of a fear of saying something inappropriate or foolish; fearful of being embarrassed by blushing or crying; and, finally, exaggerating the potential difficulties, physical dangers, or risks involved in doing something ordinary but outside his or her usual routine.

Hogan and Hogan (2001) call this type *Cautious*, and stress their fear of being criticized, shamed, blamed, humiliated or somehow disgraced. "They do not handle failure, rejection, or criticism well; as a result, they are constantly on guard against the possibilities of making errors, mistakes, or blunders, that might cause them to be publicly embarrassed. Because they are so alert to possible criticism, they see hazards and threats everywhere, even when others cannot see them. They respond to the possibility of being criticized by hand wringing, perseverance, freezing, becoming very cautious, and by taking no action at all. When they are threatened, they will also forbid their staff from taking any initiative. These people are unpopular managers because they are so cautious, indecisive, and controlling."

Avoidant types can be prudent, careful and meticulous about evaluating risk. They rarely make rash or ill-advised moves, and they can provide sound, prudential advice about intended future courses of action. However, they avoid innovation, resist change, even when it is apparent that something needs to be done. They seem particularly threatened by the new, the different and the strange, and they

187

vastly prefer to react rather than take initiative. If their working world is stable, they can thrive: if not, their behavior may be maladaptive.

Under stress, avoidants begin to adhere to established procedures, and will rely on the tried and true rather than on any new technology or other procedures. They may try to control their staff, in fear that someone on the staff will make a mistake and embarrass them, especially with their seniors. They do exactly what their seniors tell them and they enforce standard rules and procedures on their staff and others over whom they have any power. They hate to be criticized; what others will see is cautiousness, rigidity, adherence to standardized procedures, and resistance to innovation and change.

To work with the cautious type, reports need to keep them well-informed about activities that concern them – where negative outcomes could reflect on them, and to consult them about intended future actions. When rapid action is needed, or when some form of innovation needs to be implemented, it is best to avoid them or put in writing the fact that you recommended action or innovation, then be prepared for nothing to happen.

The following five traits and behaviors are clues to the presence of what Oldham and Morris (2000) call the *Sensitive* style. First, they like *Familiarity* because they are comfortable with, even inspired by, habit, repetition and routine. Next, they prefer to interact with those close to the *family* and/or a few close friends. Third, they *care deeply about what other people think of them*. Fourth, they show *Circumspection*, behaving with deliberate discretion in all their dealings with others. Finally, they always take care to maintain a courteous, self-restrained demeanour.

Oldham and Morris provide seven tips for dealing with these types. First, count your blessings for knowing these types; second, accept their shortcomings; third, avoid emotional stress by not trying to get them to do things that they do not want to do; fourth, compromise; fifth, act as a guide to the unfamiliar for them; sixth, strive to reassure them that everyone is going to like them; and, finally, express the problems openly and directly. Frankly, few cautious, sensitive, avoidant personality-disordered types make it to the top. Those that do soon find they can't "hack-it", so leave.

DEPENDENT (DEVOTED)

People with this disorder are more heavily reliant on other people for support or guidance than most. Like young children, they can be clinging, submissive and subservient in all relationships, fearing separation. Dependents are carers – most happy helping others be happy. Others give meaning to their lives. They worry about others and need others. They find contentment in attachment and define themselves by others. They are not good at giving (or receiving) criticism and negative feedback. At work they are cooperative, supportive, caring and encouraging. They do brilliantly in jobs like nursing, social work and voluntary organizations.

Dotlich and Cairo (2003) note many CEOs are eager to please, trying to anticipate and meet the expectations of others. This does not have to mean their bending over backwards to please is always unadaptive. But it can be, because they tend to quash debates, dissenting or anxiety-provoking ideas. They can be so flexible and adaptable that nobody knows where they will, or do, stand. They seem too concerned with unhappiness, believing that work happiness leads to satisfaction, rather than the other way around. So, like all others, their behaviors are self-defeating and self-destructive.

Ironically, they lose the support and loyalty because one can't keep all people happy. By trying to avoid unpleasantness and disappointment they only increase it. Further, and more importantly, they seem unwilling to stand up for their people. They refuse to make all important, often company-saving, tough people-decisions. Their fear of tension means the business culture loses energy, edge and fire. They have to be taught the skills of assertiveness and the importance of a robust defense in things they really believe in.

Miller (2008) calls dependent bosses *clingers*. They fear being disliked or disrespected, and are almost only in leadership roles because of their skills or knowledge, or occasionally by default. If supported, they can be loyal and fair, but they seem too dependent on guidance and reassurance from those above them to make bold courageous moves. They need to learn that "every interaction does not have to be a popularity contest" (p. 27).

The website http://www.personalityresearch.org/pd.html believes the mnemonic RELIANCE a good way to diagnose the dependent personality disorder.

R: reassurance required for decisions

E: expressing disagreement difficult (due to fear of loss of support or approval)

L: life responsibilities (needs to have these assumed by others)

I: initiating projects difficult (due to lack of self-confidence)

A: alone (feels helpless and discomfort when alone)
N: nurturance (goes to excessive lengths to obtain nurturance and support)
C: companionship (another relationship) sought urgently when close relationship ends
E: exaggerated fears of being left to care for self.

These managers have a pervasive and excessive need to be taken care of by others. This leads to submissive and clinging behavior, and fears of separation.

These managers suffer analysis paralysis. They cannot make decisions on their own without continual advice and reassurance from others. They need to assume responsibility for most major areas of their lives. Inevitably they are good at delegating. But they seem always to need help and reassurance. Most have difficulty expressing disagreement with others because of fear of loss of support or approval. They publicly agree whilst privately disagreeing. This, of course, makes them difficult to read. They all have difficulty initiating projects or doing things on their own (because of a lack of self-confidence in judgment or abilities rather than a lack of motivation or energy). So they resist change, particularly where it leads to them being isolated or threatened. Some go to excessive lengths to obtain nurturance and support from others, often humiliating themselves in the process. All feel uncomfortable or helpless when alone, because of exaggerated fears of being unable to care for themselves at work (and home).

Dependent people do not make good managers because they are too quick to be apologetic, submissive and self-deprecating. They attach themselves to others who may all too easily take advantage of them. Kind, gentle, generous and full of humility they do not believe in themselves. They have very low self-confidence in all aspects of life and acquire self-esteem through their attachments to others. Despite their smiling exterior they often feel depression and dejection. Further, they can doom the relationships they value so much because they are too clinging and eager to please.

Oldham and Morris (2000) noted the non-psychiatric diagnostic criteria as a pervasive pattern of dependent and submissive behavior. Dependent people seem unable to make everyday decisions without an excessive amount of advice or reassurance; they allow and even encourage others to make the most of his or her important decisions; they "agree with" people even when they believe they are wrong: they have difficulty initiating projects or doing things on his or her own;

they volunteer to do things that are unpleasant or demeaning; they can feel uncomfortable or helpless when alone; they often feel devastated or helpless when any close relationship ends; they seem frequently preoccupied with fear of being abandoned; and, finally, they are always easily hurt by criticism or disapproval.

Hogan and Hogan (2001) note that dependent people are deeply concerned about being accepted, being liked and getting along, especially with authority figures. They are hyper-alert for signs of disapproval, and for opportunities to ingratiate themselves, to be of service, to demonstrate their fealty and loyalty to the organization. When they think they have given offence, they redouble their efforts to be model citizens. People notice their good nature, their politeness, their cordiality and their indecisiveness. As managers, they will do anything their boss requires, which means that they are reluctant to stick up for their staff or challenge authority, and this inevitably erodes their legitimacy as leaders.

They are polite, conforming and eager to please. They rarely make enemies and they tend to rise in organizations. But they have problems making decisions, taking initiative, or taking stands on tough issues. Thus their sections tend to drift, and they can have trouble maintaining a team.

They respond to stress by freezing and becoming passive, and by hoping that someone else will take initiative, step up, make a decision, assign responsibility and get things moving. They are too reliant on the initiative of others and can become a bottleneck for productivity and a source of delay and lost time.

They are deeply concerned with pleasing authority, which, in turn, is pleasing to authority, but they provide little leadership for those who must work for them. To work with them, reports must be prepared for indecisiveness, inaction and lack of leadership. They must also be prepared to take initiative when processes get stalled, but accept the fact that they won't be supported, should their initiative fail or backfire. Hogan and Hogan (2001) believe that to work with these people you must be prepared to flatter them, to agree with them, to be exploited, to allow them to take credit for your accomplishments and allow them to blame you for their failures. Along the way, however, you will profit from observing their pluck, stamina and ability to manipulate others to their ends.

Oldham and Morris (1997) noted seven typical characteristics of what they call the Devoted style: *Commitment to others* and dedication to the relationships in their lives; a preference for *Togetherness*;

Teamwork because they are cooperative and respectful of authority and institutions; *Deference*, being happy to seek out others' opinions and to follow their advice; *Seeking Harmony* by promoting good feelings between themselves and the important people in their lives; *Showing Consideration*, being thoughtful of others and good at pleasing them; and, finally, *Self-correction* in response to criticism.

Oldham and Morris also offer four tips on dealing with these types. First, let them help and do not feel guilty for accepting it but, second, do not take the attentions of this person for granted. Third, when you need to resolve a conflict or deal with unpleasant personal business, contribute as much reassurance as you can. Finally, take the stated opinions of this person with a grain of salt, because they will express an opinion that he or she thinks you want to hear. This personality disorder is nearly always associated with being a number two rather than a number one in any relationship. Even so, they may have a staff that they inevitably do not manage well.

SELF-DEFEATING (SELF-SACRIFICING)

These are the self-sacrificing altruists of the personality disordered world. They achieve meaning in life and satisfaction through serving others and sacrificing for them. They may feel undeserving of attention and pleasure, and unworthy of love; therefore, they have to earn it. They work long and hard for others and give their all in relationships. But they do not want thanks or attention and feel discomfort with positive compliments or praise. They seem guilty but they can be seriously neglected and under-recognized, which does cause pain and confusion. They tend not to have their own needs met. They see life as tough, unfair and uncompromising, and their job is to help those less fortunate than themselves. They are good under stress but can get resentful if consistently ignored.

To a large extent, the self-defeating personality is ideal at work. Hardworking, respectful, adaptable; they are, however, very concerned about the value and meaning of the work. They make reliable, loyal, undemanding, non-assertive workers. However, they rarely realize their potential: they turn down promotion for others.

Self-defeatists rarely end up as a manager or leader. But their dedication and loyalty may mean they end up in middle-management positions. But, inevitably, they have problems with delegation and discipline and take on too much themselves. They may feel, quite rightly, that their staff are ungrateful and underperform. Some, but a minority, may demand that staff expect their subordinates to adopt similar self-sacrificial behavior to theirs.

Because they have problems with success, they may suffer the imposters syndrome and consciously or unconsciously self-destruct. And, of course, they are immensely vulnerable to exploitation by others. Their generosity makes them masochists, which was the term previously used for this disorder. Oldham and Morris (2000) note the eight diagnostic criteria as a pervasive pattern of self-defeating behavior of contexts. The person may often avoid or undermine pleasurable experiences, be drawn to situations or relationships in which he or she will suffer, and prevent others from helping them. First, they, paradoxically, choose people and situations that lead to disappointment, failure or mistreatment. Second, they always reject or render ineffective the attempts of others to help him or her; Third, following positive personal events, they respond with depression, guilt or a behavior that produces pain. Fourth, they incite angry or rejecting responses from others and then feel hurt, defeated or humiliated. Fifth, they reject opportunities for pleasure. Sixth, they fail to accomplish tasks crucial to his or her personal objectives, despite ability. Seventh, they seem uninterested in – or worse, reject – people who consistently treat him or her well; and, finally, they engage in excessive self-sacrifice that is unsolicited by the intended recipients of the sacrifice.

Oldham and Morris (2000) specify seven characteristics in everyday language of the Self-Sacrificing type: first, unstinting *Generosity*, they do not wait to be asked; second, *Service* because their "prime directive" is to be helpful to others; third *Consideration*, being always ethical, honest and trustworthy; fourth, *Acceptance of Others*, being non-judgmental, tolerant of others' foibles and never harshly reproving; fifth, *Humility*, being neither boastful nor proud; sixth, showing *Endurance* by being long-suffering; finally, they can seem *Artless*, being naïve and innocent.

Oldham and Morris also offer seven tips in dealing with them. First, remember to recognize and acknowledge this person's efforts. Second, try to find a comfortable give-and-take formula. Third, learn how to translate "Self-Sacrificing language" into what it really means. Fourth, try not to reject what this person wants to give, and do not be embarrassed by their constant attention. Fifth, be careful, however, not to take advantage. Sixth, insist on being more helpful yourself. Last, talk about it because, unless you provide this feedback, the person may be unaware that you want something other than what he or she is giving to you. The self-defeating person is frankly unlikely to make it to senior management positions ... ever.

SADISTIC (AGGRESSIVE)

The sadistic personality-disordered individual is aggressive. They are strong, forceful, courageous, pugilistic and confident. They want to be leader, "top dog". They have a need to dominate and organize others. Hence they are autocratic, dictatorial and can be immoral. They give orders, make rules, run the show.

At work they are ambitious and purposeful. They have the drive for power. They thrive in the win-lose, dog-eat-dog, rough-and-tumble of the business world. They are neither squeamish nor sentimental and can be very tough. They thrive when they have clear goals and directions. And the end justifies the means, which is where the problems can begin.

They can make brilliant managers: goal-oriented, organized, disciplined. But they focus on results not feelings. They demand total loyalty and hard work and have little patience with errors, inefficiency, waste or failure of any type. They also do not like being bored. The most serious source of stress for them is losing power. They need to know how to manipulate power.

They have strong emotions but strong control over them. They tend to be more crafty and shrewd than physically aggressive, but they do bully, hurt and humiliate others who are subordinate to, and dependent on, them. They are disciplinarians who can easily inflict pain. Hence they can be very malevolent.

According to Oldham and Morris (2000), the diagnostic criteria are a pervasive pattern of cruel, demeaning and aggressive behavior. The sadistic use physical cruelty or violence for the purpose of establishing dominance in a relationship; humiliate and demean people in the presence of others; treat or discipline someone under their control unusually harshly; are unashamedly amused by, or take pleasure in, the psychological or physical suffering of others (including animals); lie for the purpose of harming or inflicting pain on others; get other people to do what they want by fear, intimidation or terror; restrict the autonomy of people in any close relationship; and tend to be fascinated by violence, weapons, martial arts, injury or torture.

Oldham and Morris (2000) specify six criteria of the Aggressive style as they call them: first, *Command*, they take charge; second, a preference for *Hierarchy*, a traditional power structure; third, they are *Highly disciplined* and impose rules of order; fourth, they like *Expedience* and are highly goal-directed; fifth, they show *Guts* because they are neither squeamish nor fainthearted; sixth, they like *The rough-and-tumble*, action and adventure.

Oldham and Morris also record seven ways of dealing with those types. Know yourself. Beware of competing with them. Know the precise parameters of your job and/or your role so that you do not overstep the boundaries. Be strong and maintain your self-esteem. Do not aim to win. Appeal to reason, not to feelings. Look for ways to cope creatively with his or her possibly harsh rules and regulations. Accept that they have a temper and avoid pushing the predictable buttons that will ignite it. The bullying, aggressive sadist has often punched, clawed and scratched their way to the top. They are very difficult to work with and soon derail established working groups.

CONCLUSION

Two things must be kept in mind when considering all the above. The first is that if people are intelligent and educated, then moderate amounts of these disorders should not necessarily handicap them as leaders. The "usefulness" of these traits does not, however, depend on their "age and stage", workplace and ambition. However, if they experience acute or chronic stress, it is quite possible that their dark side appears.

Second, of the six types mentioned in this chapter, it is really only the aggressive and borderline types that will likely reach positions of leadership. However, given that leadership has also to do with followership, the mental health of a leader's followers will naturally influence their successes as a leader.

Every manager has a dark-side profile. They may be high, medium or low on each of the disorders. It is certainly possible to be high – and therefore potentially prone to derailment – on more than one at a time. They make an individual doubly vulnerable. It is also worth bearing in mind that these "dark-side" traits may be non-threatening – indeed, normal – whilst the individual is not under stress or pressure. It is when they are threatened that these dark-side tendencies manifest themselves. Of course, what makes them threatened may itself be a function of these disorders. Further, it should be accepted that senior management is a very threatening occupation.

It is possible to profile an individual in terms of abilities, traits and disorders. It is their unique, and not very changeable, fingerprint. It makes them predictable and it can be both their source of strength and/or weakness. As noted in the previous chapter, it is the dark trio that is most obviously associated with management failure. However, many people reading the descriptions of the types of disorders in this chapter will, no doubt, recognize them in some of the managers they have had. Further, they are probably able to describe how (and now why) various situations and circumstances that led to their derailment, even demise.

PART IV

9

THE COGNITIVELY CHALLENGED LEADER

INTRODUCTION

Some leaders fail because they are not up to the job. There are various polite euphemisms and English expressions that state this: "He is a sausage short of a fry-up"; "The lift does not go to the top floor"; "The lights are on but no one is home"; "She's a few pixels short of a wide-screen". They are low wattage, dim, short-changed, thick, unintelligent. All these expressions mean leaders are "underpowered" for the job. They do not have the analytic and reasoning ability, the processing capacity or the knowledge base to make timely, wise decisions. The cognitively challenged leader crops up in organizations that promote on loyalty rather than ability, or where socio-political or technological changes make the world completely unpredictable.

This chapter will consider some of the findings of research in the area of intelligence, as well as examine some of the major issues in the area. One inescapable conclusion is that by *ignoring, downplaying or not assessing leaders' cognitive ability or intelligence, they get elected, chosen or promoted only to fail at a later point.*

Leaders have to "size up the situation". This may involve analyzing data or trends. They also have to make plans, often of considerable complexity. In business they must be good at "tumbling numbers", understanding spreadsheets, understanding and mastering new technology. More importantly, they have to make wise, timely, informed and often risky decisions. They need accurately to examine and appraise complex, ill-defined and new problems. They need to be able to interrogate data and people. They need to understand what is known and unknown about issues, that there are different philosophic issues and perspectives, but come to a conclusion. They need to be good at problem-solving; efficient and accurate. But they also need to be able to articulate their position and to draw upon past experience. They need to know how to learn; what to remember and how to store experience. In short, they need to be bright, *bright enough to* cope with all aspects of the job.

The more complex the task, the more things change; the more novel the problems presented, the brighter leaders have to be. Neither charisma nor conscientiousness can make up for cognitive, analytic ability.

Managers continually have to learn new facts and new skills. There are general interpersonal skills but also very specific business skills. But there are individual differences in educability. People differ in their self-discipline (conscientiousness), their self-confidence (neuroticism), their insightfulness and their rationality (intelligence). Some are better and more comfortable around skill learning, or what Hogan and Warrenfeltz (2003) call "knowing how" as opposed to conceptual learning or "knowing that". Managers need the will but also the ability to learn how to lead. The former relates to personality and motivation, the latter to intelligence. Certainly, intelligence testing has had a chequered and controversial history in psychology. Yet research from *many scholars* over *many areas* in *many countries* and *over a century* has demonstrated the pervasive influence of intelligence in *all walks* of life, from health and happiness to wealth and welfare. It is a basic building block for the differential psychologist. It is, quite simply, the most easily and reliably measured individual-difference variable with the most reliability and validity.

Those investigating the relationship between cognitive ability and job performance have agreed on the basis of the data numerous times. First, validities, the correlation between test and scores and business performance, is around the 0.3 to 0.5 mark and higher for training than job performance. Second, predictive validity increases with job complexity. Intelligence predicts better when leadership situations are seriously complex. Third, the validity generalizes well across countries, criteria, jobs, settings and industries. It doesn't matter what sector, task or country: intelligence still predicts well. Fourth, intelligence is, quite simply, the *best predictor of overall job and training* (and specific task) performance. Fifth, measuring very specific abilities (like verbal or numerical ability) does not give much incremental advantage over general IQ or mental ability scores. Special abilities are related to general ability and measuring 10 overall is good enough.

There are many fundamental psychometric questions about intelligence which get asked again and again: Consider the following ten:

1. *Do intelligence tests have good reliability?* Yes. Only high anxiety or situationally induced low motivation cause test-retest correlations to drop below $r = 0.90$
2. *Are IQ scores stable over (life)-time?* Yes. By late childhood, tests reasonably accurately predict adult scores as many as 50 years later.
3. *Do intelligence tests have adequate validity?* Yes. They predict school success (around $r = 0.50$) and how long people remain in school ($r = 0.70$), and many other educational, or organizational and social variables. They even predict longevity.
4. *Do intelligence tests predict job performance and academic success?* Yes. And how good a leader is.
5. *But are there not multiple intelligences?* No. Not in the sense that most people are very good at some cognitive tasks and very bad at others. Generally, we find that scores on all sorts of (good) IQ tests correlate positively and significantly with one another. That is, people perform at a broadly similar level across all tasks (vocabulary, maths, etc.).
6. *Are all IQ tests equally good?* No. It takes quite some effort to develop, refine and produce a test that gives an all-round picture of a person's cognitive functioning.
7. *So why aren't leaders given IQ tests?* Good question. The answer is threefold: ignorance and prejudice on the part of selectors and electors; the belief that educational achievement, self-confidence or social class are a proxy for intelligence; fear of embarrassment or litigation if one had to tell an executive they are not bright enough for the job.
8. *Are tests not biased against certain groups like ethnic minorities, dyslexics, etc.* No. There is ample evidence from disinterested experiences to dismiss this claim.
9. *So how bright do leaders have to be? That is, what is bright enough?* This does depend on the job. But it is likely that for senior positions they need to be in the top 10%–20% of the population.
10. *Can you teach people to be bright? That is, is intelligence pretty well fixed (from late adolescence) or can you improve it?* In part yes, in part no. Intelligence is traditionally made up of two parts – fluid or efficient problem-solving ability and knowledge/vocabulary. Data suggest the latter can be taught more than the former. Practice can increase IQ tests scores, but only to a limited extent.

Most people are familiar with the many and frequent objections to tests. Consider the following, *all of which are erroneous*:

- All IQ tests are timed, but the ability to think fast is not necessarily the ability to think well.
- All tests are culture-bound – devised for, and by, white middle-class (males) to their advantage.
- All they measure is how rich a person's parents are/were and how much education they had.
- There are many very different types of intelligence and no one test (or even battery) can properly measure them.
- The more you practise, the higher your score. They therefore measure only effort not ability.
- We all know seriously bright people who never excel at school or in jobs. Test scores predict nothing.
- Test scores change. You can increase your intelligence. Scores should measure potential, not how well you do today.

Eysenck (1998) in his last book lists five widely-held and false beliefs about intelligence with his comments:

1. *Psychologists disagree about the nature and definition of intelligence.* Eysenck points out that debates about certain aspects of intelligence have little to do with fundamental agreement on the basics. Also, with few exceptions, all experts in the area largely agree with one another.
2. *IQ tests measure nothing important; merely the ability to do IQ tests.* "Nobody who has even the most passing acquaintance with IQ testing would ever make such an outrageous statement" (p. 8).
3. *The notion that differences in IQ are largely determined by heredity has been disproven.* "Quite the contrary is true." Indeed, the pendulum has swung dramatically against the environmentalist position, in the world of intelligence, but also everywhere else in psychological research.
4. *IQ testing was invented to maintain the "status quo" and strengthened the ruling class.* Eysenck argues that IQ testing leads to meritocracy and social mobility. In other words, it has the precise opposite effect, by identifying a person's potential, whatever their background, and giving them a chance to realize that potential.
5. *IQ testing was introduced to bolster the claims of the white race to superiority.* Eysenck points out that the data, in fact, suggest that

the Japanese and Chinese score higher than White Americans or Europeans for the job.

It is these myths that frustrate researchers as well as selectors who try to select the best candidate.

INTELLIGENCE AND IQ: WHAT MANAGERS SHOULD KNOW?

Nettlebeck and Wilson (2005) have recently written a clear, helpful paper on what teachers should know about intelligence. The issues are identical for managers and represent a sensible overview in everyday language.

They acknowledge that IQ tests have been, are and no doubt will be misused and misinterpreted. But, they argue that, for little more than an investment of an hour or two's testing, one can gain insights that are unlikely to be achieved even with long periods of detailed observations. Further, they remain happy with the definition of the intelligence as "ability to understand complex ideas, to adapt effectively to the environment, to learn from experience and to engage in various forms of reasoning to overcome obstacles by taking thought" (Neisser, 1967, p. 7).

Their bottom line is the same as that of all researchers: IQ test scores tap a general ability that predicts life success in all cultures at all times. IQ tests are as valid as medical tests like mammograms or home pregnancy tests. Further, it is also widely accepted that there is some, as yet not fully identified, universal biological substrata that underpins intelligence, meaning that "being clever" is cross-situational, cross-temporal and cross-cultural. IQ scores account for about 25% in the variance in school and work performance. There is no single better predictor of this stable individual characteristic, which is measurable very accurately at age 10 years.

Nettlebeck and Wilson (2005) argue that IQ scores are not the same as intelligence: "Intelligence is best defined in terms of multiple domains configured within a hierarchical structure that accounts for different degrees of commonality among, and specificity between, those domains. IQ, on the other hand, has, until fairly recently, amounted to little more than an average outcome from an abridged range of those domains" (p. 613).

Individual IQ remains stable over the lifetime but there is evidence that IQ in the world population is rising (the Flynn effect). This is probably due to a combination of factors like improved educational opportunities, increased competition and work demands, techno- logical advances, better health care, better nutrition and improve- ments in child-rearing practices. Flynn believes people now invest more of their mental capacities into better abstract problem-solving and take up and enjoy more intellectual challenges. Thus, tests will need to be, and have been, recalibrated as long as IQ appears to rise.

Nettlebeck and Wilson (2005) also address the general vs multiple intelligence theory, which goes back to the 1920s with all the greats in the area like Spearman, Thorndike and Thurstone. They are scathingly dismissive of Gardner's (1999) theory ("A person doing well in one domain tends to do well in others" (p. 615)), but accept Carroll's (1993) model, which has a strong general intelligence factor with eight or nine additional broad forms of intelligence. Thus, they believe any really adequate psychometric description of intelligence is dependent on a large array of tests for all differentiated cognitive abilities. One criterion for inclusion should be tests that definitely strengthen the general fac- tor (are highly correlated), but also add specificity. At the heart of this research endeavor is the attempt to expand the definition, measure- ment and theory of intelligence beyond that which simply predicts academic achievement and which admits numerous environmental influences. Few of those in applied fields would have problems with this concept.

Their take on emotional intelligence is that it is important and useful only to the extent that it adds something to explaining and predicting real-life outcomes over and above that of IQ and personality traits. That has yet to be proven.

One interest of all applied researchers is the question of whether the new electronic and neurological technologies can provide new and improved ways of assessing intelligence; namely, the biological indices of brain function and structure. This remains both a hope and goal, but progress is slow. At this stage, most progress appears to be more in the improvement of current tests, even of an "elementary" nature, than the invention of robust tests with predictive validity.

Can IQ be enhanced or improved by formal education and training as well as work experience? There is now ample strong evidence that IQ is stable over the life span. Yet this does not mean that IQ is fixed and unchangeable from a very early age and resistant to improvement via education. Certainly, duration of education correlates with adult IQ, income and organizational level, but this could simply mean brighter children stay in school longer. Yet there is evidence that education has noticeable and measurable beneficial effects on IQ. What education and training does is provide IQ-relevant knowledge, and inculcate specific modes of thought and self-discipline.

Nettlebeck and Wilson (2005) end their review by addressing the uses for IQ tests. First, they argue tests can be used to clarify the existence of some "exceptionality", which presumably could be positive or negative. Second, they can diagnose the source of certain difficulties. They do, however, warn that assessment should always involve other activities as may be found in assessment centers. They conclude: "Our support for these tests is contingent on two provisos. First, they must be consistent with current hierarchical, multifaceted theory that includes a general ability. Second, the child's cultural background must be the same as that within which the tests were developed" (p. 626). This is good advice for testing adults in workplace settings as well.

RECOGNIZING THE DIM LEADER

What are the signs of not being bright enough? How does one diagnose the problem correctly? Many leaders are bright enough to know that they aren't. They become skilful at covering up their faults and being highly reliant on others to help them. Indeed, they often get usurped and de-throned by brighter colleagues called in to support them.

What are the signs and symptoms of lack of ability?

- *Speed*: Dim managers are slow at picking things up, seeing the big picture. Some are impulsive, very far from slow. But they are slow to see patterns, solve problems, see threats and opportunities. They are quite simply inefficient processors of data.
- *Accuracy*: Dim managers are often wrong. They make mistakes. Their analysis is simple-minded, superficial and full of illogical inferences. They are often intolerant of ambiguity, unable to see subtle or nuanced issues. They overlook, downplay or ignore important issues because they are too difficult to process.
- *Learning*: Dim managers are less trainable and benefit less from experience. They are slow learners. Indeed, many eschew any form of learning or training because it shows them up as "below par", slow learners.

- *Change/Risk*: Because they have difficulty in learning, they don't like new things – ideas, technology, processes – because they find it difficult trying to master them.
- *Expression*: Dim leaders are often poor at articulation. Whilst they may master motivational scripts and can inspire support with passion, once the issues become more complex that power of persuasion declines. This may be all the more apparent in written text.
- *Wit*: Kipling talked of having one's wits about one. Whilst humor may not be an important criterion for leadership, it surely is advantageous. Funny ("ha ha" or peculiar) is different from witty: it can be learned, wit can't. Few, if any, dim people are known as witty.

EXECUTIVE INTELLIGENCE

Business psychologists have begun to sit up and pay attention to the psychometric data. Menkes (2005) writing in the *Harvard Business Review* described what he called "executive intelligence". He points out the familiar experience of the executive who is academically brilliant, but ineffective, because of poor decision-making. The gist of the argument is in the subedited "highlight" that accompanies the main heading of his article: "It's all very well to be kind, compassionate and charismatic. But the most crucial predictor of executive success has nothing to do with personality or style." Menkes argues that all managerial work falls under three headings: tasks, people and self, which is very like Adair's (2002) famous, three-circle model: task, team and individual. Menkes (2005) lists various things that intelligent leaders do, under headings making up seven facets to this three-dimensional model. He argues, for instance, that executives:

1. accomplish tasks: this involves various core cognitive skills which include:
   - critically examining underlying assumptions
   - identifying probable unintended consequences
   - distinguishing primary goals from less relevant concerns
   - anticipating probable outcomes
   - recognizing people's underlying agendas
2. work with, and through, others: these are people skills and they include:
   - recognizing the underlying agendas of others
   - considering the probable effects of one's actions

   – recognizing personal biases or limitations in one's perspectives
   – pursuing feedback that may reveal an error in judgment and making appropriate judgments
3. judge oneself and adapt one's behavior accordingly including:
   – seeking out and using feedback
   – recognizing when it is appropriate to stand one's ground and resist the arguments of others
   – acknowledging personal errors and mistakes.

Menkes (2005) acknowledges what psychometricians have argued for years: "Yes despite these very real shortcomings, IQ tests are still a better predictor of managerial success than any other assessment. The business world's reluctance to use intelligence testing of any kind ... has robbed companies of a powerful tool for evaluating candidates for employment or promotion" (p. 106).

He also wisely notes that interviews – even structured interviews – do not work as well as testing because interviewers rely on the confidence and articulateness of candidates rather than looking for their abilities. He *favors situational* analyses where executives are presented with typical business problems and asked to analyze them. However, he does recognize the difficulty (in achieving reliability) and expense of this method of measuring cognitive skill, and argues this analysis can be done in verbal, face-to-face tests, rather than with paper- or computer-oriented ones.

Hogan (2007a) takes a similar approach. He developed a test of business problem-solving called the Hogan Business Reasoning Test (HBRI). The test measures three types of reasoning:

1. **Strategic reasoning**: concerns being able to evaluate current business practices from a strategic perspective, and understand how recent trends and technological innovations may impact future business development. High scorers focus on long-term issues, and find solutions that integrate the need of different business units. They quickly recognize novel problems and seem innovative, curious, tolerant of ambiguity and interested in feedback.
2. **Tactical reasoning**: concerns being able to reach sound, defensible conclusions using the data and information that are available. High scorers focus on short-term issues, solving them one at a time. They excel at anticipating the consequences of decisions and the obstacles to their implementation. They bring discipline to the

decision-making process and seem steady, precise, detail-oriented and professional.

3. **Critical thinking**: concerns being able to define and solve complex problems. High scorers can balance short- and long-term goals, can link innovation with implementation, are able to recognize assumptions, understand agendas and evaluate arguments. The Critical thinking score is composed of the Tactical and Strategic reasoning scales. Critical thinking predicts overall performance across many jobs.

The test measures three types of data: (1) verbal information based on conversations, emails and written reports; (2) quantitative information that comes from tables, data in financial reports and statistical analyses; and (3) graphic information that comes from charts, graphs and figures. The overall structure of the HBRI is illustrated below. Further, the test is used to suggest a cognitive style. Cognitive Style concerns a person's characteristic ways of thinking about and solving problems in the workplace. Cognitive Style is the interaction of Strategic and Tactical Reasoning. The table below illustrates the four Cognitive Styles that result from this interaction.

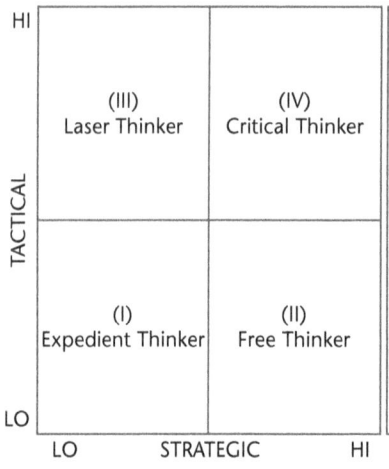

HI	(III) Laser Thinker	(IV) Critical Thinker	**I Expedient thinker:** Tendency to analyze problems in an opportunistic way, to choose answers that are quick and easy to make, intuitive rather than reflective choices, leading to poor-quality solutions.
TACTICAL			**II Free thinker:** Tendency to identify important problems but ignore the obstacles to their solution and minimize the importance of the detailed steps needed to solve them.
	(I) Expedient Thinker	(II) Free Thinker	**III Laser thinker:** Tendency to focus on a problem and the obstacles to its solution, without putting the problem in a larger context and evaluating the need for its immediate solution.
LO			**IV Critical thinker:** Ability to contextualize problems correctly in terms of the short- and long-term benefits of their solution, then solve them effectively.
	LO	STRATEGIC	HI

Source: Hogan Assessments, with kind permission.

This is typical of the imaginative work done by Hogan, who is an expert himself in leadership derailment. After years of "discomforture" with even mentioning ability in executive selection, the data are now overwhelming that intelligence is a very important predictor of success and equally, therefore, that lack of intelligence is an important predictor of failure. No wonder, then, that popular business magazines and test publishers have addressed the problem. Hogan, Barrett and Hogan (2009) believe good (business) judgment is a function of both personality and intelligence. The latter they divide into two components: *problem-finding* and *problem-solving*, both equally important in business. The former is about seeing errors, gaps and inconsistencies in the literature; the latter, solving serious problems once they have been identified. But personality affects thinking style, such that anxious people become analytically uneven and defensive, whilst conscientious perfectionist people become slow and even complicate issues. Those with inappropriate self-confidence and enthusiasm tend to be careless and over-reaching in their plans and ambitions.

WHAT THE EXPERTS SAY

The publication of a highly controversial book on intelligence (*The Bell Curve*, Herrnstein and Murray, 1994–) and a passionate, although not necessarily well-informed, debate – led over 50 of the world's experts on intelligence to write to the *Wall Street Journal* on 15 December 1994. Their 25-point summary is an excellent and clear statement on what psychologists think about intelligence. The most relevant are set out here.

The meaning and measurement of intelligence

1. Intelligence is a very general mental capability that, among other things, involves the ability to reason, plan, solve problems, think abstractly, comprehend complex ideas, learn quickly and learn from experience. It is not merely book learning, a narrow academic skill, or descriptive of test-taking smarts. Rather, it reflects a broader and deeper capability for comprehending our surroundings – 'catching on', 'making sense' of things, or 'figuring out' what to do.
2. Intelligence, so defined, can be measured, and intelligence tests measure it well. They are among the most accurate (in technical terms, reliable and valid) of all psychological tests and assessments. They do not measure creativity, character, personality or other important differences among individuals, neither are they intended to.

---

3. While there are different types of intelligence tests, they all measure the same intelligence. Some use words or numbers and require specific cultural knowledge (such as vocabulary). Others do not and, instead, use shapes or designs and require knowledge of only simple, universal concepts (many/few, open/closed, up/down).

4. The spread of people along the IQ continuum, from low to high, can be represented well by the bell curve (in statistical jargon, the "normal curve"). Most people cluster around the average (IQ 100). Few are either very bright or very dull: about 3% of Americans score above IQ 130 (often considered the threshold for "giftedness"), with about the same percentage below IQ 70 (IQ 70–75 often being considered the threshold for mental retardation).

5. Intelligence tests are not culturally biased against African-American or other native-born, English-speaking people in the USA. Rather, IQ scores predict equally accurately for all such Americans, regardless of race and social class. Individuals who do not understand English well can be given either a non-verbal test or one in their native language.

6. The brain processes underlying intelligence are still little understood. Current research looks, for example, at speed of neural transmission, glucose (energy) uptake and electrical activity of the brain.

Practical importance

7. IQ is strongly related, probably more so than any other single measurable human trait, to many important educational, occupational, economic and social outcomes. Its relation to the welfare and performance of individuals is very strong in some arenas in life (education, military training), moderate but robust in others (social competence), and modest but consistent in others (law-abidingness). Whatever IQ tests measure, it is of great practical and social importance.

8. A high IQ is an advantage in life because virtually all activities require some reasoning and decision-making. Conversely, a low IQ is often a disadvantage, especially in disorganized environments. Of course, a high IQ no more guarantees success than a low IQ guarantees failure in life. There are many exceptions, but the odds for success in our society greatly favor individuals with higher IQs.

9. The practical advantages of having a higher IQ increase as life settings become more complex (novel, ambiguous, changing, unpredictable or multifaceted). For example, a high IQ is generally necessary to perform well in highly complex or fluid jobs (the professions, management); it is a considerable advantage in moderately complex jobs (crafts, clerical and police work); but it provides less advantage in settings that require only routine decision-making or simple problem-solving (unskilled work).

10. Differences in intelligence certainly are not the only factor affecting performance in education, training and highly complex jobs (no one claims they are), but intelligence is often the most important. When individuals have already been selected for high (or low) intelligence and so do not differ as much in IQ, as in graduate school (or special education), other influences on performance loom larger in comparison.

11. Certain personality traits, special talents, aptitudes, physical capabilities, experience and the like are important (sometimes essential) for successful performance in many jobs, but they have narrower (or unknown) applicability or "transferability" across tasks and settings compared with general intelligence. Some scholars choose to refer to these other human traits as other "intelligences".

Implications for social policy

12. The research findings neither dictate nor preclude any particular social policy, because they can never determine our goals. They can, however, help us estimate the likely success and side-effects of pursuing those goals via different means.

CLASH OF VALUES

Those favorable to the idea of using cognitive ability/intelligence tests at work in assessment, promotion and selection note test scores are the *best single predictor* of job performance (efficiency, productivity, profit) (Hulsheger, Maier and Stumpp, 2007). Those who are unfavorable stress racial/ethnic minority discrimination, inequity and unfairness. This represents a severe, and perhaps irreconcilable, clash of values (Murphy, 2002).

Cognitive ability tests do show adverse impact. But racial differences in test scores are larger than in measures of job performance. Thus, a workforce based on actual performance would be less racially segregated than one based on ability tests. Yet there remains a powerful applied quandary:

> If you emphasize efficiency criteria, and are willing to live with adverse impact, your choice is easy – that is, rely heavily on cognitive ability tests. If you emphasize equity criteria and are willing to live with lower levels of performance, longer training time, more errors, and so forth, your choice is also easy – that is, remove cognitive tests and other selection devices that have strong cognitive components (e.g. scores on cognitive ability tests are correlated with scores on structured interviews and on assessment centres). Many decision makers care about both efficiency and equity, and the choice faced by these decision makers is necessarily more complex.
>
> (Murphy, 2002, p. 178)

One solution is to try to find non-cognitive, non-discriminatory tests that predict work performance. Indeed, the problem seems so intractable that, Murphy (2002) argues, one cannot avoid *value trade-offs* but has to learn how to make value-based, trade-off decisions. He cautions against values distorting the evidence and suggests that, when organizations choose either to use or not use tests, they should make the values underlying this decision explicit and public.

Hough *et al.*, (2001) reviewed all the issues, evidence and lessons learned around the topic of adverse impact. The more specifically the nature of work is specified, and the more salient and valid instruments are chosen, the better. The data looking at both crystallized intelligence (namely, verbal ability, quantitative ability, science achievement) and fluid ability (spatial ability, memory, mental processing speed) reveal systematic and replicable race, gender and age differences. There are also personality and physiological differences between these groups. They suggest various possible ways to reduce negative impact including test coaching for applicants; improving test-taking; motivation of applicants; using different criteria for different groups distinguishing between task and contextual performance. They also consider in detail statistical methods for detecting and reducing adverse impact, such as test score banding and predictor/criterion weighting.

We know the single best, most powerful predictor of success at work. It remains shocking that we do not use it more. Anyone who has worked with or for a dim leader or manager knows the cost of their poor, slow problem-solving and decision-making.

FLUID AND CRYSTALLIZED INTELLIGENCE

Since the turn of the century another, and important and widely accepted, distinction has been made between *fluid* and *crystallized* intelligence by Cattell (1987). The analogy is to water – fluid water can take any shape, whereas ice crystals are rigid. Fluid intelligence is effectively the power of reasoning, and processing information. It includes the ability to perceive relationships, deal with unfamiliar problems and gain new types of knowledge. Crystallized intelligence consists of acquired skills and specific knowledge in a person's experience. Crystallized intelligence thus includes the skills of an accountant and lawyer, as well as a mechanic and salesperson.

Fluid intelligence peaks before 20 years and remains constant, with some decline in later years. Crystallized intelligence, on the other hand, continues to increase as long as the person remains active. Thus, a schoolchild is quicker than a retired citizen at solving a problem that is unfamiliar to both of them, but even the most average intelligence older person will excel at solving problems in his or her previous area of occupational specialization.

In some cases, people try to solve problems by thinking about them in familiar terms – that is by using crystallized intelligence. Most intelligence tests use both types of intelligence, though there is a clear preference for fluid intelligence tests. Thus, consider the following:

a. Underline which of these numbers does not belong with the others:

625, 361, 256, 193, 144

b. Underline which of the following cities is the odd one out:

Oslo, London, New York, Cairo, Mumbai, Caracas, Madrid.

The former is a measure of fluid, the latter of crystallized intelligence.

These two types of intelligence are highly correlated, although they are conceptually different. Usually *what* you have learned (crystallized intelligence) is determined by *how well* you learn (fluid intelligence).

Other factors, like personality, do play a part – introverts like to read, study and learn, whilst equally bright extroverts like to socialize, have fun and experiment. Introverts who like learning thus often do better at tests of crystallized intelligence. Further, self-evidently, motivation is important – a highly motivated adult will learn more efficiently and effectively than an adult less interested in learning.

Thus, one good reason to have a measure of crystallized ability is that a tendency to work hard is a good measure of scholastic and business success – and hard work results in better scores in tests of crystallized ability. Another reason is that even short *vocabulary tests* give very reliable scores.

With changing technology, the value of crystallized intelligence may be dropping. Crystallized intelligence comes with age and experience. It is a repository of knowledge. Yet, if that knowledge can be cheaply, accurately and efficiently stored by computers, and accessed by high fluid intelligence 'Young Turks', whence the usefulness of the years of experience?

Skeptics may argue that computers could also assist in fluid intelligence problems, thus making that sort of intelligence equally less valuable. Yet, in the business world, it seems to be less and less the case.

Furnham (2001) has argued that it is the business CEO's fluid intelligence, personality and motivation that appear to be the key to success. In a different age, when education came through the apprenticeship system, the value of crystallized intelligence was particularly great. It still is in some sectors. Being a wine-buff, an antiques expert or a skilled musical performer all mean long hours of attempts to accumulate wisdom. Skills need to be practical and knowledge always increased. In the cut and thrust of a quick-changing business, crystallized intelligence is of less use – save, of course, a good memory for how things did not work out in the past. Tomorrow belongs to the quick-witted, agile, fluid thinkers and less to the salty old stalactites and stalagmites, who cling to the cave walls gradually getting bigger.

What is, however, very clearly apparent is that, despite problems that need to be overcome, like potential litigation over test bias, organization psychology can add a great deal by carefully assessing employer and employee intelligence.

Over the years, in a systematic and research programmatic way, Ackerman and colleagues have tried to map out and explain the relationship between concepts like intelligence, interests, knowledge and personality. In a very important historical and conceptual overview,

Ackerman and Heggestad (1997) found evidence of what they called *trait complexes*. These are clusters of personality and ability traits and interests that have striking overlap or commonalities. These were labeled social, clerical, conventional, science/maths and intellectual/cultural. They argue that it is possible that ability, interest and personality develop *in tandem* because ability and personality predict success (and failure) in a particular task domain, and interests determine the motivation to attempt the task. Success thus leads to increased motivation and interest, and vice versa.

Ackerman and colleagues looked at academic and occupational knowledge as a way of understanding conceptually how ability and non-ability traits interact. They proposed PPIK theory, which sees intelligence as Process, Personality, Interests and Knowledge. Knowledge is accumulated only through expanded effort over time. Personality traits influence the process of acquiring knowledge. Ackerman and Rolfhus (1999) found knowledge in 20 areas (from astronomy and biology through to physics and world literature) was predicted by a combination of general intelligence, crystallized abilities, personality, interests and self-concept. Rolfhus and Ackerman (1999) found further evidence for PPIK theory. Domain knowledge (i.e. of biology or business management; music or physics) is logically and statistically related to general intelligence, verbal abilities, trait openness, Typical Intellectual Engagement and specific vocational interests.

Beier and Ackerman (2001) add further evidence to the call for expanding the type of knowledge included in adult intelligence assessment, especially the type of knowledge important for success in work and adult life. It is essentially as *investment theory* that suggests knowledge represents an individual's choice to invest cognitive resources, effort and time in acquiring knowledge about the world.

In one sense, controversy has been good for intelligence researchers because it has given them an opportunity to articulate in straightforward language what the research data reveal.

INTELLIGENCE RESEARCH AND TESTING AT WORK

Most people understand intelligence to be about learning, adaptation and problem-solving. It is about being good at abstract reasoning, decision-making, and speed of uptake. Fundamental differences in definitions revolve around how wide or inclusive it should be. Thus some researchers want social competence, creativity, practical solving all to be included in the definition. Some even favor dropping the term altogether and prefer something which is less "hot" or more politically correct: that cognitive ability, capacity, and so on.

Lay people use the term to describe people, though they do not always understand the mechanism or process by which it is possible to deduce or measure that one person is significantly more intelligent than another. A lot of focus has been on the use of tests and the meaning of the scores. However, it is difficult to deny the accumulated evidence that intelligence scores do have predicted significance: that is, that administered and scored at time 1; the predictable behavior, educational and work achievement at time 2 (Mackintosh, 1998; Deary, 2000; 2001).

Reviewers have pointed out there are many correlates of IQ scores. Ree, Earles and Teachout (1994) listed 10 categories of psychological outcomes:

- Abilities (reaction time, analytic style, eminence)
- Creativity/artistic (craftwork, musical ability)
- Health and fitness (infant mortality, dietary preference, longevity)
- Interests/choice (marital partner, sports participation, breadth and depth of interest)
- Moral (delinquency (−), racial prejudice (−) values)
- Occupational (SES, occupational status, income)
- Perceptual (myopia, field-independence, ability to perceive brief stimuli)
- Personality (achievement motivation, altruism, dogmatism) (−)
- Practical (social skills, practical knowledge) and other (motor skills)
- Talking speed, accident proneness (−)

Various reviews published in the 1960s and 1970s suggested that intelligence (and personality) tests did not predict organizational outcomes very well. Further, the socio-political zeitgeist of these times discouraged many business people from trying to measure intelligence. Major controversies about intelligence and race suggested that tests were significantly biased, as well as lacking in predictive validity.

However, things were to change dramatically with the paper by Hunter and Hunter (1984), who presented a re-analysis of earlier databases plus some further data. In their analysis, they took into account various statistical factors that impact on the size of correlations: size of sample, restriction of range and reliability of data. Based on data from 30,000 people and 425 correlations, their "bottom-line" figure for the correlation between supervisor-rated job performance and IQ was $r = 0.53$. They broke this down for various job families. The highest correlation was for salespeople ($r = 0.62$) and nearly all were over $r = 0.40$. Thus for service workers it was $r = 0.49$, trades and crafts workers $r = 0.50$ and vehicle operators $r = 0.46$).

As Brody (1992) notes, despite some criticisms of their methods Hunter and Hunter (1984) demonstrated quite clearly that IQ scores related logically and consistently to many kinds of job performance. By the end of the century, reviewers like Ree and Carretta (1998) felt able to conclude: "Occupational performance begins with learning the knowledge and skills required for the job and continues into on-the-job performance and beyond. We and other investigators have demonstrated that g predicts training performance, job performance, lifetime productivity, and finally, early mortality" (p. 179). More recent reviews are even more positive about the role of intelligence in all aspects of life.

INTELLIGENCE AND OCCUPATIONAL PERFORMANCE

Do tests predict behavior at work? If they do, how do we explain this? And what else predicts work-related behavior and success? There is a very long and important literature on IQ and education which, of course, informs the concept of training at work. The efficiency, speed and generalizability of learning via training is, indeed, related to intelligence. Estimates differ between about $r = 0.30$ to $r = 0.60$ (Ree and Carretta, 1998).

Ree and Carretta (1998) noted that intelligence predicts performance *and* promotion. That is, longitudinal studies have shown that brighter individuals attain higher occupational status. Thus, intelligence predicts job knowledge, which predicts job performance.

Researchers have been interested in this question since at least the First World War. There have been various studies and meta-analyses of various sorts which can probably be divided logically into three time periods: the 1920s to the 1970s; the 1980s and 1990s; and post-millennium work. The amount of work, the quality of the data and the sophistication of the analysis has all systematically improved.

A central, often unanswered question is *how* intelligence predicts overall or specific job performance. This, in the first instance, can best be done via path analysis. Hunter (1986) showed that intelligence strongly predicted job knowledge, which predicted both "objective" job performance and supervisors' ratings.

Borman *et al.* (1993) tested a model which went thus: IQ (ability) results in a person having an opportunity to acquire job experience as a supervisor. It also predicts an increase in job knowledge. Experience, in turn, leads to a further increase in job knowledge. Experience, ability and knowledge predict proficiency. Thus intelligence predicts job performance. Ree, Carretta and Teachout (1995) also argued that intelligence predicts job knowledge prior to training as well as job knowledge acquired during training.

Thus it seems that intelligence predicts learning, knowledge and proficiency which, in turn, usually predicts learning from experience. That is, bright people learn faster, demonstrate salient skills and get promoted. This adds to their knowledge and experience, all of which influence supervisor ratings or any other measure of job performance.

After some important early work which, because of both poor measurement and poor meta-analytic techniques, seemed to suggest both personality and intelligence tests had poor predictive validity in predicting behavior at work, the situation has changed. Over the last 20 years, there have been around a dozen good large meta-analyses looking at the validity of cognitive ability tests.

Whilst these analyses used different tests, they were all reliable and highly intercorrelated (Hulsheger, Maier and Stumpp, 2007). However, it is possible to divide the tests essentially into those that measure general mental ability compared to specific cognitive abilities.

The best known meta-analyses from the 1980s were those by Hunter and Hunter (1984) and Hunter (1986), though there were others before these. Although there were some trends, what was noticeable was the variability in the correlations between IQ test scores and job performance: some very high, others very low. This led to the "doctrine of situational specificity" which argued that the relationship was dependent on the particular job, job performance criteria and IQ test itself. However, this, in turn, led to the development of meta-analysis which, through various statistical and "corrective" techniques, aims to show the true operational validity between general mental ability (GMA) and work outcomes (Hunter, 1986; Hunter and Hunter, 1984; Hunter and Schmidt, 1976, 1990; Schmidt and Hunter, 1977, 1984, 1998).

Ones, Viswesvaran and Dilchert (2006), in an excellent comprehensive and up-to-date review of the meta-analysis, were concerned with cognitive ability, selection decisions and success at work. In doing so, they examined many different areas and came to clear conclusions:

- Based on data of well over a million students, they note GMA is a strong, valid predictor of exam success, learning and outcome at school and university, regardless of the speciality or subject considered.
- Training success at work, as measured by such things as supervisor ratings or job knowledge acquired, is predicted by GMA and the more complex the job, the more powerfully it predicts.
- Regarding job performance, cognitive ability tests predict outcomes across jobs, situations and outcomes – that is, validity is transportable across occupational groups and is cross-culturally generalizable.
- Tests of specific ability do *not* have incremental validity over general measures and, although they may be more acceptable to job applicants, the relative importance of these abilities alters over time.
- Intelligence predicts job performance well because it is linked to the speed and quality of learning, adaptability and problem-solving ability.
- Cognitive ability tests are predictively fair to minority groups but can have an adverse impact, which is a sensitive political issue.
- In short, GMA is one of the best, if not the best, predictor of success in applied settings.

Various meta-analyses have been done over the last five years that have attempted a critical, comprehensive overview of the role of intelligence (often called "general mental ability" or "cognitive ability test results") in predicting work-related outcomes.

Some reviewers have tended to concentrate on data from one country, like America (Schmidt and Hunter, 2004), Britain (Bertua *et al.*, 2005), Germany (Hulsheger *et al.*, 2007) or from wider areas like the European Community (Salgado *et al.*, 2003). Despite these differences, the results were essentially the same and all reviewers argued for the

TABLE 9.1 **The meta-analytic results of operational validity of overall and specific measures**

	Performance	Training
GMA	0.62	0.54
Verbal	0.35	0.44
Numerical	0.52	0.48
Spatial/mech	0.51	0.40
Perceptual	0.52	0.25
Memory	0.56	0.43

practical use of cognitive ability tests, which are quite clearly good predictors of both overall job performance as well as training success.

Salgado and colleagues (2003) looked at the predictive validity of GMA, as well as specific cognitive abilities like verbal, numerical, spatial-mechanical, perceptual and memory, to predict measureable job performance and training success. Different selection and personnel practices could, they argue, lead to difference when comparing American and European data. Following the rigorous demands of meta-analysis from over 250 studies that tested over 25,000 Europeans, they found an operational validity of 0.62, which they note "means GMA is an excellent predictor of job performance" (p. 585), noting also that "GMA is the best predictor of job performance" (p. 585). The validity of the five specific measures varied from 0.35 for verbal to 0.56 for memory. The data on training ratings were broadly similar, if slightly lower (0.54 for GMA; 0.44 for verbal and 0.34 for memory).

Salgado and colleagues' conclusion is that, internationally, GMA measures are the *best predictors* of work performance. That is, despite differences in tests used; measures/conceptualizations of job performance and training; differences in unemployment rates, cultural values, and demographics, still GMA wins out as the best individual difference psychometric measure. Indeed, the results are strikingly similar to earlier data coming out of America (Hunter, 1986; Hunter and Hunter, 1984; Kuncel *et al.*, 2001; Viswesvaran *et al.*, 1996). They conclude that, because of the predictive validity of GMA at work across cultures, one can easily conceive of a scientifically feasible general theory of personnel selection. They also point out: "tests of specific abilities such as verbal, numerical, spatial-mechanical, perceptual and memory failed to demonstrate higher validity than GMA measures. It is thus prudent to reiterate the main practical implications of this finding that GMA tests predicted these two criteria most successfully" (p. 594).

Another meta-analysis focused exclusively on British data. This had 283 samples of, in total, over 13,000 people (Bertua *et al.*, 2005). This analysis looked at the predictive validity of specific abilities (i.e. verbal, numerical, etc.) as well as GMA over seven main groups (clerical, engineer, professional, driver, operator, manager, sales). As in all meta-analyses, they found GMA and abilities valid predictors of job performance and training success (performance $rho = 0.48$; training $rho = 0.50$).

They also found, as one may predict, the greater the job complexity, the higher the operational validities between the different cognitive tests and job performance and training success.

TABLE 9.2 Correlations between overall and specific IQ measures and job performance and training

	Performance	Training
GMA	0.48	0.50
Verbal	0.39	0.49
Numerical	0.42	0.54
Perceptual	0.50	0.50
Spatial	0.35	0.42
Average	0.42	0.49

Thus these results were broadly in line with those from both Europe and America. Once again, the conclusion is that GMA measures may be the best single predictor for personnel selection for all occupations. They recommended the use of psychometrically proven measures of GMA for use in selection "regardless of job type, hierarchical seniority, potential future changes in job role composition or whether the tests are principally for general or specific cognitive ability" (p. 403).

In their meta-analysis of German data examining both training success (of 11,969 people) and job performance (746 people), Hulgsheger, Maier and Stumpp (2007) found validities of 0.47 for training success and 0.53 for job performance. They found also, as they suspected, that job complexity did moderate that relationship. Their results were therefore strikingly similar to those shown in other countries.

Thus over the past quarter-century there is a "large and compelling literature" showing that intelligence is a good predictor of both job performance and training proficiency at work (Dragow, 2002). Extensive meta-analytic reviews have shown that intelligence was a good predictor of job performance, but particularly in complex jobs. Although debated, researchers suggest the correlation between intelligence and job performance is around $r = 0.50$ (Schmidt and Hunter, 1998). The central question is what other factors, like personality or social/emotional intelligence (sometimes called 'social skills'), accounts for the rest of the variance. But referring to g, or general intelligence, Dragow (2002) is forced to conclude "for understanding performance in the workplace, and especially task performance and training performance, g is the key .... g accounts for an overwhelming proportion of the explained variance when predicting training and job performance" (p. 126).

A recent survey of over 700 American applied psychologists showed considerable consensus that cognitive ability (intelligence) tests are "valid and fair; that they provide good but incomplete measures that

TABLE 9.3 **The meta-analytic results for GMA over the eight occupational groups**

	Performance	Training
Clerical	0.32	0.55
Engineer	0.70	0.64
Professional	0.74	0.59
Driver	0.37	0.47
Operator	0.53	0.34
Manager	0.69	
Sales	0.55	
Miscellaneous	0.40	0.55

different abilities are necessary for different jobs, and that diversity is valuable" (p. 660).

One hundred years after Spearman (1904) published his paper "General Intelligence: objectively determined and measured" in the *American Journal of Psychology* there were various celebrations, conferences and special issues to celebrate the fact. One paper entitled "Academic performance, career potential, creativity and job performance: can one construct predict them all?" concluded, *yes*! (Kuncel, Hezlett and Ones, 2004).

Leading researchers in the area, Schmidt and Hunter (2004), also came to a clear conclusion based on 100 years of work. It is that:

> The research evidence [shows] that GMA predicts both occupational level attained and performance within one's chosen occupation and does so better than any other ability, trait, or disposition and better than job experience. The sizes of these relationships with GMA are also larger than most found in psychological research. Evidence is presented that weighted combination of specific aptitudes tailored to individual jobs do not predict job performance better than GMA alone, discomfirming specific aptitude theory. A theory of job performance is described that explicates the central role of GMA in the world of work. These findings support Spearman's proposition that GMA is of critical importance in human affairs.
>
> (p. 162)

Thus, for complex, senior jobs the correlation between GMA and job performance is around 0.50. Further intelligence is a more powerful predictor than personality. It is because people with higher GMA acquire job knowledge more efficiently (faster and more) that it is such

a good marker of career success. Job experience does relate to job performance but it declines over time, unlike the intelligence–performance
relationship, which increases.

Since the turn of the millennium, there have been some excellent
reviews on the subject of intelligence at work. Below are quotes from
those reviews:

> There is abundant evidence that general cognitive ability is highly
> relevant in a wide range of jobs and settings and that measurements
> of general cognitive ability represent perhaps the best predictors
> of performance. Ability–performance relations are essentially linear
> and the correlation between general cognitive ability and per-
> formance appears similar across jobs that differ considerably in
> content. There is some evidence that ability–performance correla-
> tions tend to increase as jobs become more complex but few other
> consistent moderators of the ability–performance correlation have
> been reported. Finally, the incremental contribution of specific abil-
> ities (defined as ability factors unrelated to the general factor) to the
> prediction of performance or training outcomes may very well be
> minimal.
>
> (Murphy, 2002, p. 175)

> Given the overwhelming research evidence showing the strong link
> between general cognitive ability (GCA) and job performance, it is
> not logically possible for industrial–organizational (I/O) psycholo-
> gists to have a serious debate over whether GCA is important for
> job performance. However, even if none of this evidence existed in
> I/O psychology, research findings in differential psychology on the
> nature and correlates of GCA provide a sufficient basis for the con-
> clusion that GCA is strongly related to job performance. From the
> viewpoint of the kind of world we would like to live in – and would
> like to believe we live in – the research findings on GCA are not
> what most people would hope for and are not welcome. However, if
> we want to remain a science-based field, we cannot reject what we
> know to be true in favour of what we would like to be true.
>
> (Schmidt, 2002, p. 187)

> "the utility of g," is that g (i.e., possessing a higher level of g)
> has value across all kinds of work and levels of job-specific expe-
> rience, but that its value rises with *a*) the complexity of work,
> *b*) the more "core" the performance criterion being considered (good
> performance of technical duties rather than "citizenship"), *c*) the

more objectively performance is measured (e.g. job samples rather than supervisor ratings). Predictive validities, when corrected for various statistical artefacts, range from about .2 to .8 in civilian jobs, with an average near .5. In mid-level military jobs, uncorrected validities tend to range between .3 and .6. These are substantial. To illustrate, tests with these levels of predictive validity would provide 30% to 60% of the gain in aggregate levels of worker performance that would be realized from using tests with perfect validity (there is no such thing) rather than hiring randomly.

(Gottfredson, 2003a)

THE STRONG CASE FOR MEASURING INTELLIGENCE

Gottfredson (2003a) argues that *life is a mental test battery*. By this, she means that the business of living involves solving various problems and completing various tasks. Jobs, like good psychometric IQ tests, have a variety of performance tasks which are judged against an accepted standard. The more demanding the job, the brighter people have to be. Jobs operate like "differentially g loaded mental tests" because workers' differences in job performance simultaneously measure their differences in intelligence. Being more intelligent gives one a competitive edge for performing the job's core technical duties. Superior knowledge and extensive job experience, she argues, may sometimes hide a lower intelligence level, but never nullify or compensate for it. Brighter workers apply past knowledge more effectively, and deal with novel problems more effectively and efficiently.

In a series of extremely important, critical and comprehensive papers, Gottfredson (1997; 1998; 2002; 2003a; 2003b) has made an overwhelming case to measure general (g) intelligence and to take it into consideration in everyday management decisions.

Intelligence, she notes, has pervasive functional importance in people's lives. This is particularly true at work. "Intelligence turns out to be more important in predicting job performance than even personnel psychologists thought just two decades ago" (Gottfredson, 1997, p. 81). Interestingly, it was civil rights laws and regulations aimed at reducing discrimination that encouraged researchers to look very closely at this area. Looking at this research, she came to various very important conclusions:

1. The prediction validity of intelligence is ubiquitous. Across all jobs and all ratings of success, intelligence is very important.

2. The predictive power of intelligence rises with job complexity. The more intellectually and technically demanding the job, the more important is intelligence for success.
3. The validity of intelligence is high compared to other factors like personality, particular aptitudes or vocational interests.
4. Intelligence is important in a causal sense. More surprising, differences between individuals do not decrease with training (the less good become better and the good remain much the same) but can increase. Intelligence is a major source of enduring, consequential differences in job performance.
5. Higher levels of intelligence are required as people rise up the occupational ladder. Occupations both attract and accommodate individuals from a wide range of IQ levels but job incumbents are more homogenous than applicants. But there do appear to be minimum IQ thresholds that rise steadily with job level.
6. Higher intelligence reflects higher trainability. That is, intelligence predicts a person's capacity to learn: trainability.
7. The essence of intelligence at work is the ability to deal with complexity, which is an individual's ability to acquire, apply, organize, recognize, select and update on salient work-related information; in other words, to manipulate information mentally.
8. Complexity is the key feature in the workplace. It is the major distinguishing factor between jobs. It is all about information processing.
9. As social, cultural and work-life becomes more complex, the role of intelligence inevitably increases.
10. Where people have little time and ability to learn and be trained, it is best to focus on specific training for specific skills.

Gottfredson (2002) believes it is vitally important for personnel psychologists and managers to understand the role of intelligence at work. In a wonderfully clear and important synthesis, she outlines the real importance of g (or general intelligence) at work (Gottfredson, 2002; pp. 44–6). This is well worth repeating in full.

Major Findings on g's Impact on Job Performance a Utility of g

1. Higher levels of g lead to higher levels of performance in all jobs and along all dimensions of performance. The average correlation of mental tests with overall rated job performance is around .5 (corrected for statistical artefacts).

2. There is no ability threshold above which more g does not enhance performance. The effects of g are linear: successive increments in g lead to successive increments of job performance.
3. a) The value of higher levels of g does not fade with longer experience on the job. Criterion validities remain high even among highly experienced workers. b) That they sometimes even appear to rise with experience may be due to the confounding effect of the least experienced groups tending to be more variable in relative level of experience, which obscures the advantages of higher g.
4. g predicts job performance better in more complex jobs. Its (corrected) criterion validities range from about .2 in the simplest jobs to .8 in the most complex.
5. g predicts the core technical dimensions of performance better than it does the non-core "citizenship" dimension of performance.
6. Perhaps as a consequence, g predicts objectively measured performance (either job knowledge or job sample performance) better than it does subjectively measured performance (such as supervisor ratings).

Utility of g Relative to Other "Can Do" Components of Performance

7. Specific mental abilities (such as spatial, mechanical or verbal ability) add very little, beyond g, to the prediction of job performance. g generally accounts for at least 85–95% of a full mental test battery's (cross-validated) ability to predict performance in training or on the job.
8. Specific mental abilities (such as clerical ability) sometimes add usefully to prediction, net of g, but only in certain classes of jobs. They do not have general utility.
9. General psychomotor ability is often useful, but primarily in less complex work. Its predictive validities fall with complexity whilst those for g rise.

Utility of g Relative to the "Will Do" Component of Job Performance

10. *g* predicts core performance much better than do "non-cognitive" (less *g*-loaded) traits, such as vocational interests and different personality traits. The latter add virtually nothing to the prediction of core performance, net of *g*.

11. g predicts most dimensions of non-core performance (such as personal discipline and soldier bearing) much less well than do "non-cognitive" traits of personality and temperament. When a performance dimension reflects both core and non-core performance (effort and leadership), g predicts to about the same modest degree as do non-cognitive (less g-loaded) traits.

12. Different non-cognitive traits appear to usefully supplement g in different jobs, just as specific abilities sometimes add to the prediction of performance in certain classes of jobs. Only one such non-cognitive trait appears to be as generalizable as g: the personality trait of Conscientiousness/integrity. Its effect sizes for core performance are substantially smaller than g's, however.

Utility of g Relative to the Job Knowledge

13. g affects job performance primarily indirectly through its effect on job-specific knowledge.

14. g's direct effects on job performance increase when jobs are less routinized, training is less complete, and workers retain more discretion.

15. Job-specific knowledge generally predicts job performance as well as does g among experienced workers. However, job knowledge is not generalizable (net of its g component), even among experienced workers. The value of job knowledge is highly job specific: g's value is unrestricted.

Utility of g Relative to the "Have Done" (Experience) Component of Job Performance

16. Like job knowledge, the effect sizes of job-specific experience are sometimes high, but they are not generalizable.

17. In fact, experience predicts performance less well as all workers become more experienced. In contrast, higher levels of g remain an asset regardless of length of experience.

18. Experience predicts job performance less well as job complexity rises, which is opposite the trend for g. Like general psychomotor ability, experience matters least where g matters most to individuals and their organizations.

Quite simply, for Gottfredson (2005) all of life is a mental test battery. In this sense, a higher intelligence is related to most advantages in life. The better paid, more demanding, more socially desirable jobs recruit workers from the higher reaches of the IQ distribution. Intelligence provides the competitive edge for a job performance particularly in high-level, more technically demanding jobs. Being intelligent provides a big, but not decisive, advantage. Intelligence has a large causal effect on one's career.

Gottfredson (2005) believes that jobs act as a template for understanding the role of intelligence in all daily life. Intelligence relates to functional literacy, which has many educational, health and social relationship concomitants. Indeed, Gottfredson and Deary (2004) showed that intelligence is a good predictor of health and longevity. The central question, of course, is why this is true. It seems that less intelligent people adhere less often to treatment regimens; learn and understand less about how to protect their health; seek less preventive care, even when free; and less often practise healthy behaviors for slowing and preventing chronic disease.

APPLICATIONS AND IMPLICATIONS OF TESTING AT WORK

Is it advisable to use cognitive tests to make selection, training and promotion decisions? If so, what tests should be administered to whom for what purpose? Are the potential negative consequences greater than the benefits? Could one make a good economic, as opposed to legal, argument for testing in the workplace?

Viswesvaran and Ones (2002) examined in detail eight issues surrounding the use of ability testing in the workplace. It was a summary of 11 excellent articles including many important papers (i.e. Murphy, 2002; Reeve and Hakel, 2002; Schimdt, 2002; Tenopyr, 2002).

What is the predictive value of intelligence (general mental ability) tests for real life outcomes and work behavior?

Results show consistently that intelligence is positively related to educational level, income and health behaviors, and negatively related to delinquency, disciplinary problems and health issues. People need a level of ability to thrive in a particular work environment: more cognitive demands, more ability required. To many, this is self-evident.

But there are three criticisms. The *first* is the size of correlation between intelligence and job outcome – in other words, the strength of that relationship and the amount of variance being accounted for.

Some argue that the relationship is too weak or too small and may only account for 25% of the variance. Thus, hard work, honesty and training could all easily compensate for relatively low intelligence in a competitive working environment.

A *second* criticism concerns the sort of relationship to look at. If you examine the relationship between intelligence and work outcomes of job incumbents and find them small, that should be no surprise, because if they have been well-selected there should be little variance. That is, they should all be within the appropriate intelligence range. On the other hand, if all job applicants are tested, that would yield a far better index. Equally, we need to consider how reliable the measurement of the criterion work outcome/variable is. Critics argue, then, that if we correct for range restriction (of those in the job) and the unreliability of the outcome measure, we will see a much stronger relationship between IQ and work. The *third* critique, quickly dismissed by Viswesvaran and Ones (2002), is that intelligent behavior at work is the result of more than just what intelligence tests measure.

Do overall IQ test scores predict better than measures of specific abilities?

This question is whether very specific tests of verbal, or mathematical or spatial ability will relate to work outcomes more strongly and logically than general IQ test results. It is agreed that there are non-cognitive factors that do predict job performance in addition to GMA. But are there very specific abilities that predict success in all jobs (rather than very specific jobs)?

Whilst there may be good reasons to use very specific ability measures, like those of verbal reasoning or mathematical ability (for face validity, legal reasons), to give incremental validity over a GMA, the evidence suggests that its advantage is small. This could be for many reasons: restriction of range in certain occupational samples; a limited number of criteria. Nevertheless, based on the current data, it is fairly difficult to provide evidence to justify the tests of specific ability above that of GMA.

How good are the criteria (job/training performance)?

The central question here is how reliable, representative and parsimonious are the traditional outcome measures? There have always been doubts about the narrowness of these measures that neglect, for instance, both team and organizational effectiveness. Few researchers are completely happy with the criteria but find it difficult to discover better ones.

Is the utility evidence for GMA convincing?

Is it possible to place monetary values on the consequence for an organization choosing people of high, average or low intelligence based on the provided predictive validity of IQ test/job performance links. This is not a methodological issue but one of focusing only on organizational productivity, as opposed to health or harmony. Utility evidence is, therefore, a value statement. However, it is frequently done and yields some startling results, usually showing the great economic benefits of testing.

Are the negative reactions to GMA tests a result of group differences?

That is, is the debate about black/white differences and the association of such concepts as "adverse impact", bias, discrimination and fairness" the real cause of public cynicism and skepticism about tests? Put another way, would the controversies about intelligence be less intense and passionate if there were no evidence of group differences?

The problem is of logic: GMA predicts work performance better than specific ability measures, but there are recognized, replicable group differences in IQ not due (solely) to measurement bias. Yet, it seems that negative attitudes to testing go beyond the race (and sex) issue. They may be caused by historically recorded abuses of testing, as well as the philosophy of equality and equal opportunity that eschew selection on ability. Another reason is that most people believe that IQ is not the only important predictor of educational, job and life success. Indeed, it is not even the most important predictor.

Is the theoretical knowledge of GMA adequate?

At the heart of the problem is the very meaning of the concept of GMA. That is, researchers seem not to understand the process or mechanism that leads to GMA or, indeed, its association with job success. There may be interesting statistical evidence of behavioral and biological correlates of GMA scores, but how it operates remains unclear. Defenders say we know as much about the construct as many others in psychology, whilst critics detect a theoretical dark hole at the center of all this research.

Is there promise in various new methods of testing for GMA?

That is, using different technologies – biological, computational, video-based – will we be able to measure intelligence more reliably, and, presumably, understand GMA? The question is whether changing the measurement changes what is measured. Some have hoped that tests using different media would reduce group differences; however, some believe all they have done is increase measurement error. Nevertheless, as Viswesvaran and Ones (2002) have noted, "Whether these potentially more invasive assessments are developed and become available for use depends on how society decides to balance the privacy rights of individuals against the needs of organisations" (p. 224).

What is the current status of non-GMA predictors and substitutes or supplements to GMA?

The search for other good predictors has been long and hard. Thus can personality variables, work samples or some measured motivational variable act as a substitute or supplement to GMA as an accurate predictor? Can we find factors that increase predictive validity yet reduce group differences? Many have been suggested, from tacit knowledge, through working memory capacity to psychomotor ability. The problem is that few (good) studies attempt to compare the predictive validity of alternative tests with GMA. Two issues are important here according to Viswesvaran and Ones (2002); first, not to confuse constructs and methods and, second, to examine predictor intercorrelations. Further, there are important consequences of choosing people on the basis of the supplementary predictor. Thus, Conscientiousness is thought to be a better predictor of GMA; that one would have an organization full of ambitious, hardworking, persistent, dutiful and perhaps dependent people rather than fast, accurate, effective problem-solvers.

CONCLUSION

Few areas of psychology attract as much discussion and debate as the topic of intelligence. More academic researchers have been attacked (physically), hounded, sacked and vilified by what they have written about intelligence. The area that inevitably causes most passion is that of sex and race differences in intelligence. There is also, still, considerable debate about the role of intelligence testing in educational settings.

There are essentially two issues: an empirical issue and a social policy issue. Most of the debate is about the latter not the former, though there remains considerable controversy about the predictive power of intelligence tests.

The data on general intelligence as a predictor of work-related behaviors are, however, very clear. There are very few researchers who have inspected recent meta-analyses who could not be impressed by the fact that, without doubt the best single predictor of success at work (particularly in senior, complex jobs) is intelligence. This is neither to deny that there are not other important factors, nor that it is patently obvious that not all intelligent people do particularly well in the workplace. Intelligence is relatively easy to measure reliably and accurately. Intelligence test scores are influenced by other factors (like personality) but not to any great extent. Intelligence is cognitive capacity and refers both to efficient problem-solving and accumulated knowledge.

However, the science and the practice of intelligence testing remain far apart because of the history of misunderstanding, misapplications and political differences. The signs are hopeful for the future, where differential psychologists and people at work could benefit from some of the most valid and predictive of all measures in the workplace.

Most people have encountered the cognitively challenged leader. They appear most frequently in old-established, change-resistant organizations, in monopolistic organizations and in corrupt societies. Change, competition and good selection usually mean they don't get through the net.

However, the famous Peter principle illustrates the well-known issue. Peter, himself a psychologist, noted how many very senior people or leaders seemed incompetent at their job. He felt the problem lay in the fact that they had been over-promoted. All were incompetent because competent leaders kept being promoted until a point where they no longer were competent enough.

How common is the problem? Many of the most spectacularly derailing leaders are bright, often very bright. Further, they are good-looking, confident and charming. Here, it is their personality that lets them down, not their ability.

As we age, our capacity for cognitive processing decreases. We become slow, forgetful and dependent on others. It is sad to witness very clever people decline, and it often illustrates how important their intelligence was to how they became good leaders.

Certainly, any diagnosis of the cause of leader derailment needs to consider the role of cognitive ability. All leaders need to be bright enough to fulfil the complex role involved in senior leadership positions in all sectors.

10

PREVENTING AND MANAGING DERAILMENT

INTRODUCTION

Certainly, prevention is better than cure. For some organizations, diagnosis is harder than treatment. It can take organizations some time to realize that individual senior managers and leaders are driving them on the path to disaster. This is particularly the case when failing leaders have had such a "stellar career", where they have appeared to have the Midas touch. Alas, that Midas touch can so easily look like the false claims of alchemy.

It is important, once again, not to fall for the classic attribution error of seeing the cause of all problems to be exclusively *within* the personality, values or abilities of leaders. As noted in Chapter 1 ("The toxic triangle"), it is always *three* factors that are essentially responsible for the emergence, rise and ultimate failure of a particular leader. Some leaders are set up to fail. Others have impossible tasks trying to lead corrupt, incompetent organizations that resist appropriate processes and procedures. Economic, political and social forces can conspire to ensure that, in effect, no leader can succeed. Also, organizational culture, procedures and governance play an important role.

However, there is a difference between failed and derailed leaders. The former is usually associated with poor judgment or lack of ability. Failure is usually associated with the *absence* of a quality. Derailment, on the other hand, is associated more with the *presence* of a quality.

Oldham and Morris (2000), in their brilliant "self-help" book on personality disorders, noted temperamental characteristics on which people differ:

1. **Activity level.** Every infant has a characteristic activity level, from slow to speedy.

2. **Regularity.** Some are regular in their eating, sleeping and other biological functions, others unpredictable.
3. **Approach/withdrawal.** When presented with a new toy, food, person or other stimulus, does the baby respond positively and with interest (approach), or negatively and fearfully (withdrawal)?
4. **Adaptability.** Does the child learn and adjust to new situations and tasks easily, or does he or she have difficulty adjusting to change?
5. **Threshold of responsiveness.** What does it usually take to get a "rise" out of a baby or boss – a strong sensory stimulation such as a loud noise, or a mild one such as a soft voice? Does the person become over-stimulated easily by sensory experiences.
6. **Reaction intensity.** Some react loudly to everything, whereas others typically are less intense in their positive and negative reactions.
7. **Mood.** Even babies have characteristic mood patterns, varying from predominantly cheerful to frequently unhappy. Some adults are moody, unstable, unpredictable, volatile.
8. **Distractibility.** Does the child tend to focus on tasks at hand, or is he or she easily distracted?
9. **Attention span and persistence**. How long does the baby typically stick with an activity, and will he or she persist despite difficulties? (p. 386)

They note that these can be dimensionalized into simpler groups like inhibited vs uninhibited. Others include flexible vs inflexible, variety-seeking vs repetitive, adaptable and stress prone. They stress the importance of biology and genetics, but also the importance of protective environments early in life. Personality styles and disorders affect all aspects of life – self-perceptions, relationships, work, and so on. This is a useful attempt to give the less "psychologically minded" in selection an opportunity to think through some of the important characteristics that they should look for and avoid in senior leaders. Imagine using the nine dimensions to rate a future chief executive rather than a set of bland business competences. Would this provide a good warning of derailment?

Miller (2008) has pointed out that every workplace is a community, family, tribe or village populated by "colourful characters". He argues that *hindsight, insight* and *foresight* prevent the appointment of dysfunctional leaders. He notes that a person's temperament, ability and values determine their job choice. He looks at 10 personality disorders categorized into five groups:

1. Shrinkers and clingers: avoidants and dependent disorders
2. Emoters and reactors: histrionic and borderline disorders
3. Preeners and predators: narcissistic and anti-social disorders
4. Detailers and vigilantes: obsessive-compulsive and paranoid disorders
5. Oddballs and spoilers: schizoid and passive-aggressive.

Miller (2008), in a series of practical chapters, offers advice about managing difficult, disturbed and dysfunctional bosses and employees. Naturally, one has to look at the particular problem that is manifest: workplace aggression, misconduct or marginal performance. Various pretty standard recommendations are made including: selection and screening; education and training; coaching and counselling; discipline; as well as psychological evaluations through psychological services. As have others, Miller (2008) offers simple but sound advice for managers under stress:

• Show yourself by being visible and accessible
• Give and get (earn) respect by treating people fairly
• Demand excellence, expect it and reward it
• Ask for, and use, feedback
• Maintain a culture of knowledge acquisition
• Pick your battles (issues) and fight them wisely.

Preventing and curing derailment involves some psychological-mindedness into the ability and personality of individuals. This process may be facilitated by the use of carefully chosen psychometric tests or by employing experts with the necessary training and skill. Given the cost of derailment, it seems like a good investment.

DISCRETIONARY INCOMPETENCE

Most people know the quote that "power corrupts and absolute power corrupts absolutely". It is true that the more power, influence and control that a leader has, the more likely the potential derailer is to derail.

Some jobs, some positions, some institutions offer both senior and junior people considerable choice, discretion or latitude of action. However, most organizations have "good governance" processes and procedures that attempt to restrict possible leadership misbehaviors, like the pursuit of personal power or gain. There are mechanisms like governance rules, a board of directors (including non-executive directors), as well as shareholder votes that are designed specifically to reduce the excesses of executive direction.

Kaiser and Hogan (2007) note that leader discretion moderates any relationship between a leader's characteristics and organizational outcomes. High discretion reduces the role of the leader's dark side having a negative impact. They argue that organizational policies aimed at leader discretion affect their behavior in organizations as well as their decision-making and, hence, leadership of organizations.

More discretion leads to more individuality and the personal influence of the leader's values and styles. Their dark side then becomes most manifest. Kaiser and Hogan (2007) highlight three higher-order factors that can easily appear when leaders have too much discretion. The *first* is a tendency to intimidation. Being aloof, insensitive, inflexible or overbearing, they are very poor at building and managing teams and the socio-emotional skills associated with good leadership. They are bullies who seem impervious to feedback.

The *second* type are seductive and flirtatious. They often have charisma and personal magnetism. But they are prone to hubris, overconfidence and general recklessness. The *third* are the diligent, dutiful ingratiates with high standards and a taste for perfectionism. Their problem is not seeing the big picture.

Kaiser and Hogan (2007) note that all organizations need to be aware of, and attempt to curtail, leaders' selfishness. They do so best by astute selection, good governance techniques and strictly performance–contingent compensation. The latter point is to link pay to long-term profitability rather than short-term revenue generations. The idea is not to inhibit but restrain; not to tie the hands of leaders but make sure that they have sufficient discretion to make wise decisions. It has been called doing due diligence and ensuring good governance.

CORPORATE GOVERNANCE

One of the simplest but most profound prophylactics against the problem of leadership derailment is good corporate governance. This is, in essence, a set of rules and laws, procedures and processes that dictate how an organization is administered, controlled and directed. The aim is to ensure all stakeholder welfare by holding key individuals accountable.

Shapiro and Von Glinow (2007) asked a neglected question: "Why [do] bad leaders stay in good places?" – meaning, how do corrupt, incompetent or devious leaders hold onto power in otherwise "good" organizations. They argue that this depends on both the awareness and willingness of others (usually senior managers) to report misconduct. *One explanation*, they argue, lies in the processes of organizations where all appraisals are about telling subordinates how and what they should be doing, but never the other way around. That is, there is no mechanism for upward appraisal. *Second*, there is no internal "whistle-blower" mechanism that allows a concerned employee to report on leader derailment. *Next*, there needs to be some way of measuring how leaders are using their (often considerable) legitimate and coercive power to silence, bully or exclude employees willing to report on their misdeeds.

Most organizations have boards, though they can have different names like cabinets or "top teams". Their job, led by the CEO, is to ensure organizational survival and growth. The idea is that healthy board functioning and outcome is a part function of the policies, processes and procedures that it follows. However, retrospective studies have shown that, often, non-executive directors and directors themselves share the pathology of the derailed leader. Equally, there is evidence that clever leaders often skilfully court the board to their own advantage.

Traditionally, they are key principles of corporate governance, such as ensuring leaders and boards respect the right of all shareholders and stakeholders in the organization. Corporate governance sets out the roles, rules and responsibilities of the board. Most importantly, they aim to ensure integrity and ethical behavior. It is about accountability and transparency.

It is done by some way of monitoring the board of directors by using internal auditors, by making sure power for various issues is shared in the organization. It is claimed that corporate governance is clearly, systematically and logically related to the performance of the organization, though the data are mixed.

The issue is always the appropriate balance between over- versus under-regulation. There is always a cost to supplying the information required for good corporate governance. There are monitoring costs. It can be that paying too much attention to internal auditing and the supply of accounting information taxes the organization too heavily.

Some leaders feel quite rightly that they are handicapped, even trapped, by the requirements of corporate governance. They feel they cannot act quickly or boldly enough to do what has to be done. They see governance not as a wise system of checks and balances, but as a suffocating system of bureaucracy that leads to long-term failure. Certainly, the excesses of anti-social or narcissistic leaders can, in part, be controlled by light but effective governance procedures.

Often, business and political leaders have a lot of decisional and behavioral latitude. But can this discretion, this latitude, be a significant derailer? Discretion is freedom, freedom is power and power can corrupt. Some senior jobs involve a great deal of responsibility but not a lot of discretion. Rules and regulations, ever-watchful shareholders and the media, as well as financial and other constraints, simply reduce the opportunities of the grown-ups to misbehave, make mistakes or simply "lose the plot".

The more the constraints, the less the latitude, the less important the personality and values of those at the top. This applies to both good *and* bad leaders. That is, job autonomy mediates the relationship between personality and performance. But as functional autonomy and job discretion increase, job roles and all performance criteria become more vague. The model goes like this:

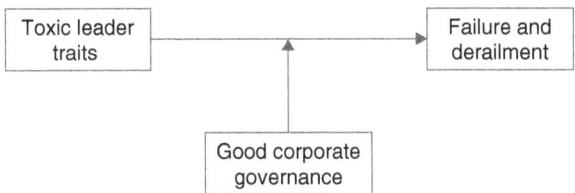

That is, that quirky, unconventional and toxic leaders whose motives, styles and traits could easily lead to organizational failure or instability may be very efficiently controlled or detected by the enforcement of simple, sensible corporate governance policies and procedures that are properly "policed" and enforced by outside and disinterested groups.

Some organizations attempt to "constrain" their leaders by checks and controls. Some really do link the pay and perks to actual performance. Others make sure various board appointees, such as non-executive directors, hold CEOs responsible for their actions.

Some organizations are quite rightly very concerned about the possible egotism, selfishness and self-serving attitudes of the potentially megalomaniac CEO. They want greater alignment, greater cooperation. They, therefore, take a real interest in corporate governance.

They encourage shareholder activism. They attempt various types of restriction, depending on the type of organization and sector. Some have the threat of serious retribution for pervasive greed or incompetence.

So, the paradox is this – it is often the discretion and latitude that organizations permit which really influence the impact that CEOs can have. Tie their hands and it matters little what ability, values and style they bring. Give them their head and they can really "do the business". Their individuality counts, but can cost.

Smaller, newer organizations in certain sectors, such as computers, telecommunications and biotechnology, tend to have weaker cultures and fewer control mechanisms. The job of a CEO is not that difficult to describe, although it is difficult to fulfil. The *first* task is to build, motivate and direct a functional team. The *second* is to set directions, objectives and strategy. The *third* is to get the structure and processes right: lean, mean, efficient so that there are logical, flexible policies for allocating resources, and so on.

It seems quite self-evident that the personality, ability and values of the CEO can make a huge difference to the fate of organizations. Indeed, personality, more than knowledge or ability or values or experience, because there is usually more variability in personality. Personality is the primary source of difference in our leaders, neither education, nor vision, nor even ability.

Personality influences leadership style and, the more latitude and discretion leaders have, the more their personality and style matter. Some like to make decisions by consensus, others by experts, others by their own judgment. Some are communicative, others secretive. Some love strategy, divergent thinking, the big picture. Others are detail oriented.

Leadership weaknesses (vanity, micro-management, paranoia, etc.) are most apparent in work situations where there are few constraints upon them. The aloof, intimidating, overbearing leader who is insensitive to people issues can be disastrous. These types often surround themselves with "yes men", demand personal loyalty and play power games. Why do shareholders, voters, corporate governance regulators ever allow that? Who, then, is to blame? Clearly, bad governance is a major factor in the derailment story.

Others – the magnetic, charismatic, grandiose visionaries – behave like rock stars. Their issue is themselves, not their organization. Self-promotion needs checks and balances. And then there is the diligent, dutiful, perfectionist control freak who looks in, not out. They eschew strategy and "what if" thinking, to their considerable cost.

One mechanism most stakeholders have is the under-used *probationary period*, as well as a fixed renewable contract.The next best thing is the serious business of establishing functional governance mechanisms. The board should be such a mechanism, but only when it is not personally chosen by the CEO, and where it has very clear accountability for overall performance and the openly stated power (and obligation) to sanction the CEO where necessary.

Of course, there is a balance between constraining and tying the hands of a CEO, who is little more than spokesperson for others, and giving a CEO total discretion to pursue personal passions. There are lots of temptations at the top of the totem. It's very important to be aware of the potential downside of discretion and the disasters which can arise from too much decisional latitude.

PATHOLOGICAL BOARDS, TOXIC TEAMS AND LEADERS

Executive teams frequently have real and continuous problems, and these can be both chronic and acute. Rather than being a forum where educated, experienced and rational adults meet to try to make wise and perspicacious business decisions, they appear to be places of dissimulation and dishonesty, intrigue and backbiting, fear and loathing. For some boards, the prognosis of developing into a healthy team is poor unless something drastic is done quickly and rationally.

Just as politicians have cabinets, so organizations have boards: groups of senior people representing major sections of the organization (marketing, finance, etc.). Their role is primarily decision-making, but also support of the leader who is, or at least should be, "first among equals". Often, one board member gets elected to the "prize of leadership" in the same way that it is from the College of Cardinals that the Pope gets elected. There is, therefore, considerable, unhealthy competitiveness among the board for the top position.

It is often crucially important that the executive board is fit, focused and functional. The dysfunctional team can, in a surprisingly short time, lead an organization into terminal decline. Shareholders know this to their cost.

What are the typical problems of executive teams and how to deal with them? A number are immediately identifiable.

Bloated membership

It has been said that the only thing worse than not being on the board is being on the board. Everybody wants to sit on the board and be "on the top team", but there is an optimal number for an efficient team – somewhere between 7 and 12. Too big and they split, a few become silent and others very vocal. Any CEO needs to be clear about who is on the board and why, and resist the cancerous growth of those who feel, want or believe they deserve to be at the heart of power. The solution: be clear about membership and limit it to an optimal number. The question is: who does this, when and how can changes be made? The trouble is, being on the board is too bound up with power, prestige and money.

It is very important that those on the board bring in their expertise and ability, but just as importantly they need to bring in their motivation to succeed through appropriate cooperation. It is all very well having the optimal number, but unless they pull together in the process, the board will not succeed. Often, they need help with their team processes.

Naked ambition

Many board members yearn for the top job. They see their career clocks ticking and feel the urge for the money, power and prestige of the top job. There is no easy solution to dealing with the pathologically ambitious, but at least bringing succession planning out into the open helps control some blind ambition. The teams need to specify a timetable, personal criteria for the top job and the process by which the boss is appointed. Again, the question is: *who* does this?

It is important the process is open and apparently fair. Nepotism, pusillanimous chairpeople, even laziness are reasons for massive boardroom squabbling. "Nights of the long knives" do no one any good.

Conspiracy of silence

Surprisingly, perhaps, senior managers often cope with issues by never mentioning them: this is the well-known "elephant in the room" syndrome. Just as talk about money and death may be taboo in certain circles, teams often deal with emotional issues by ignoring them. As parents attempt to control a five-year-old's first attempts at shock-swearing by selective deafness, so boards often refuse to discuss issues. These may be around success planning, personal pathology, relationships at work or the future of the company. It is surprising how often powerful adults resort to such primitive coping strategies to deal with issues.

The way to stop groups conspiring to be silent is to bite the bullet and, where appropriate, put the issues on the table. There needs to be a rule about what can and cannot be discussed, when and why. It is often the personal pathology of the CEO that dictates what is taboo or not. Consultants who deal with top-team pathology or boardroom malaise are often astounded by the history of "non-discussables". Interestingly, it is often tough professional women – so often missing from boards – who deal with the problem best. This is an issue of emotional quotient (EQ) rather than intelligence quotient (IQ) – and real balls.

Resisting centrifugal forces

Board members can, quite literally, head off in different directions. Their values and priorities can soon lead to the executive team losing its cohesiveness and focus. This is most frequently the problem where individuals have difficulty delegating. Thus, directors manage, managers supervise, supervisors deliver. Delegation should liberate board members to concentrate on what they do: strategy, the vision thing.

The CEO must become aware of the existence and power of these forces upon the members of the board and, therefore, of the necessity to ensure uniformity of approach. Members are pulled in different directions at the same time, and need help with the focus and alignment.

Ambiguity of roles

This problem is not unique to top teams but can be very destructive. Executive team members are answerable to many different constituencies. More importantly, it is not always clear how decisions are made. Executives need to specify very clearly how the group is to make decisions and, of necessity, stick to them.

Decision-making is the essence of the board's duty, and decision-making involves a pretty clearly followed process. This concerns things like goal analysis; a decision about how to decide (should decisions be made by individuals or by groups? should outside experts be consulted?); the generation of alternatives; the choosing of alternatives;

and so on. Some decisions are relatively minor and may be made by the chairperson or, indeed, specialist board experts. Others need to be considered by everybody, but it is important to know what type of decisions require what sort of response by whom, and when.

Personal agendas

The boardroom is an ideal place, some believe, to have fun promoting personal causes – they ride hobby horses. These can be inspired by ideology or aggrandizement. To have important and powerful people pay attention to one's personal issues is too attractive an opportunity to miss for some directors whose politico-religious or other crypto-philosophical agendas can hijack board meetings for hours. The solution is quite simple – have a clear agenda and stick to it. Boards need to be told on a regular basis what they are there for.

It is too easy to see the problems of the board in terms of the lack of ability, or simply the pathology, of the CEO or the individual members. Some directors do make it to board level with remarkably mediocre ability. Others have exploited their personal pathology, like narcissism or paranoia, to rise in the organization, but, hopefully, they remain in the minority – though in some companies this is far from clear.

It is the role of the chairperson to get the best out of the board through optimal membership, appropriate control and openness. Getting members focused and clear about their roles and joint agenda is easier said than done with self-important grown-ups, but it is essential if boards are to function effectively. Sometimes, the chairman is "first among equals". Often, they are too weak or too much of a bully to use the assets of the board well.

The board is a team like any other. They work in an organization that hopefully has good governance processes and procedures that are aimed to guarantee the long-term success of the organization. However, the journey to the board is often a long and arduous one marked as much by capriciousness, politics and opportunism as a healthy Darwinian selection process. To uninformed and naïve outsiders they are places of calm, rational, high-order decision-making. To some insiders they are a battleground of naked egotism and power-lust.

The question is how to ensure a potentially dark-side leader first creates and uses his or her team and, secondly, how to help them if things go wrong. Many derailing leaders are bullies or charmers who ignore, coerce or intimidate their board members into being little more than "yes men". They "side-step", overrule or simply ignore those who dare to oppose them. Challengers, in time, get replaced by those sycophants, if the leader is in charge of their appointment. Hence, it becomes important not only to have rules and regulations about appointment to the board, but also that this is done by independent, trained and informed outsiders.

Second, boards that "get into trouble" may be very beneficially helped by "process consultants", who help boards understand and change their dynamic. There are those skilled in this task, often with systems or psychodynamic training, who can help boards confront and then change their pathological behavior. Naturally, toxic leaders will resist their being called in, so the task is to find a mechanism whereby they cannot do this.

SIX PREVENTIVE OPPORTUNITIES

There are, classically, at least six organizational operational points/ processes where it may be possible to detect or avoid the problem of derailment. They are:

1. *Recruitment.* Whilst it must be recognized that there are "sick pathological" organizations that can derail anybody, it is equally true that there are people more or less prone to derailment. Given that there are known "markers" of derailment, it maybe useful for recruiters to have this in mind in their activities. Recruiting people from particular backgrounds increases the likelihood that they share certain values and assumptions that may or may not be related to later derailment. The deeply ambitious, partly-socialized cynic may come from particular cultural milieu. Being aware of this will help avoid some derailers. Also, being aware that some organizations are clearly attractive to derails is also important.

2. *Selection.* Selection is about selecting "in" and selecting "out". Many leaders who later derail were selected because nobody was responsible for selecting out those prone to, or susceptible to, serious derailment. We are now clear about what the markers are. Further, we now have robust and reliable instruments that can help detect those more prone to derailment. The paradox that too much of a good thing may lead to failure has alerted many selectors to being much more vigilant about the idea of maximal not optimal abilities, traits and aptitudes.

3. *"On boarding".* Often, the induction process in any organization is brief and superficial. In some organizations, it is almost the first

test: find out the who, what, where. Some old cynics enjoy watching newcomers make gaffs. Is this a useful Darwinian process or a waste of time? The issue is about setting expectations and clarifying issues. If people are not appropriately inducted, they have to rely on hearsay and gossip for an understanding on how to begin their job. It smacks of unprofessional behavior right from the beginning. It can hasten derailment.

Conger and Fishel (2007) stress the importance of the much neglected "on boarding" process, which includes setting clear goals and objectives, learning the written and unwritten rules, establishing expectations and learning how the organization gets things done through networks and stakeholder relationships.

4. *Planning development.* Most people are appointed to a job or role which itself may change quite quickly. However, the expectation for most people is that they have joined the organization and will progress on some path. Despite the fact that, often, much effort is put into recruitment and selection, the idea that development is planned at this stage is forgotten. Opportunities are lost. The question is: who does the planning? The individual, his or her boss or HR? The answer may be all three. Interestingly, most young(ish) managers have a plan themselves, but few check it for realism. Many derail because nobody has taken responsibility for planning their development within the organization.

5. *Performance managing.* This is about setting clear, attainable targets; discussing with people all issues around their performance (honestly and regularly) and rewarding them equitably. They need good feedback on their performance and, where necessary, help and training to acquire new skills. Most managers dislike and distrust a bureaucratic HR system, which means they don't really manage their people, establishing a culture of non-, as opposed to the mis-, management of people. Often, potential derailment can be at least indentified, if not "fixed", in this process.

6. *Career pathing.* Even in current times, people expect a career in organizations. They expect promotion within and between job functions, and that hard work and loyalty is rewarded by promotion. The central question is: which career path is best for each individual? Should they, or indeed can they, switch from being a specialist being a generalist? When are they at their peak/optimal level? What assignments would best develop and test them? Are their career-path hopes realistic?

The above six "opportunities" are, or should be, standard management practices. Looking back at subclinical psychopaths, narcissists and Machiavellians, it remains a mystery why their "antics" are not picked up earlier. People will always slip through the net. Bold, articulate, self-confident people can "bluff" their way through selection or appraisal interviews. They can charm, cajole and cover up a wide range of derailing, delinquent and dastardly activities.

MITIGATING DERAILMENT

There are various ways of trying to prevent or recover derailed managers. Typically, these involve selection, coaching and training, and transitioning.

Selection

One of the themes of this book, and the area as a whole, is that most derailed managers have been, earlier in their careers, classified as high-flyers or those with high potential. Most have been correctly judged to be technically very capable, as well as highly ambitious. Further, they often have a good track record in their early jobs, even if the records are not very thorough.

However, as later problems show, they appear to be not very self-aware and are very defensive about their errors. As noted in the introductory section of this chapter, because most selectors select in, not out, those problems are overlooked.

Derailed leaders can bankrupt organizations. Those in the selection business often use particular formulas to demonstrate the cost-effectiveness of employing their methodology.

It is paradoxical that, often, more money is spent selecting graduate trainees than CEOs. That is, unless "headhunters" are used. They can quickly "use up the budget" by providing a short-list of eligible candidates, though the precise "formula" that they are using to do this is unclear. How vulnerable to, and perceptive of, toxic, anti-social managers are headhunters?

The question of cost is a simple equation around the benefits of getting the right person vs the cost of getting the wrong person. There may well be a false economy in quick, cheap methods. The sheer amount of money spent, however, cannot, in itself, guarantee anything. The issue must be the judicious spending of sufficient resources of time and money.

Headhunters might charge as their fee 10% to 25% of the first year's salary of the person chosen. This is the same concept as that used by estate agents (realtors). The more expensive the leader, the more is spent on finding/selecting him or her. However, headhunters do recruitment, not selection. It is essential that money is wisely invested in selecting between short-listed candidates. Further, the effort needs to be put into both select-in and select-out.

How much time and money is spent by the task-force looking at potential derailers? This is the central question. And it is one asked by shareholders of organizations that have selected flawed leaders whose later derailment was extremely costly.

The following are simple, but important, recommendations for the selection of leaders.

With regards to references, these can be invaluable if used appropriately. They are very cheap, observer ratings of those who have considerable data on the individual under question. Hopefully, they have seen him or her behave under all sorts of situations: of threat and stress; where moral judgments have to be made; how they cope with "triumph and disaster"; what they confess as their aims and ambitions. In short, they possess the best possible historical behavioral data on the individual in question.

However, the way in which they are traditionally used renders them practically worthless for three reasons. *First*, the candidate nominates them and usually chooses his or her friends and confidants. *Second*, they are often reluctant to tell the whole truth ("warts and all") about their friend. *Third*, they are rarely asked perspicacious questions and encouraged to write a few paragraphs as they please.

To overcome these problems, the following four steps may help to provide invaluable data:

1. The *selector*, not the candidate, chooses the referees based on the person's job history. You do not rely on the candidate to give you a short-list. Choose those who know them in different contexts. Be careful not to choose those with a grudge, who are jealous or those who are close friends. The task is to get reliable, accurate and predictive evidence of past behavior, which is the best predictor of future behavior.

2. Have six to a dozen references. Reference data are cheap to gather, especially if done by phone. The concept of 360-degree feedback or

multi-source reporting suggests that different people know different things about the candidate as a function of their relationship to him or her. Bosses, colleagues/peers, and subordinates/reports know different things. Subordinates know about their management style, peers about their values and abilities, bosses about how efficiently their team works. Select people from different groups and preferably from different organizations.

3. Establish what, and how much, they know about the person. The quality and quantity of data may vary considerably between individuals. It may be that the individual's first two bosses hardly know them at all and the only data they have are "hearsay" and "gossip". Thus, a first question is about their knowledge of the individual and their relationship with them.

4. Prepare the reference interview carefully. Decide what the individuals know and the information you want from them. If the issue is ability to withstand stress or integrity, it is essential to know what questions to ask. In this sense, a reference is the result of a structured interview. To give a potential referee a list of poorly-described competences – or, worst of all, a job description – is not enough. Referees do not always understand "HR speak". They need to be asked clear, specific questions about the behavior of the candidate they know something about. For instance, could they describe an incident in which X faced a moral dilemma, a setback, a very important client? How did they behave? It is desirable to think through these questions before the interview with the referee.

In summary, the whole exercise is threatened by a simple, but fundamental problem concerning the referees' willingness to tell the truth. This is why it is advisable to have an interview rather than a written report, and why it is not a good idea to let any candidate nominate his or her preferred referees. Friends of the candidate might well "censor" their responses to help their friend get a job. They may see it as a justifiable support for a friendship. Equally, more and more organizations attempt to prevent people writing references because these documents can be used later in litigious evidence. If people feel confident they are not being recorded and their views are kept completely anonymous, they are more likely to be completely honest about the individual under question.

It is frequently the case that, after a leader has spectacularly and publicly failed and derailed, the press can, it seems, quite easily find a

THE ELEPHANT IN THE BOARDROOM

surprisingly large number of people who were unsurprised by the event because of the information that they had but were never asked. They had often worked for the individual in the past and had extensive data on his or her peccadilloes and proclivities. Importantly, as noted in Chapter 1, it is essential to have a "select-out" set of criteria for the boss, and someone who is to take responsibility for gathering information on things one *does not want* in the leader.

Coaching, counselling and training

All leaders need to be self-aware, with an accurate appraisal of their talents and skills. Derailed leaders often overestimate their abilities. Those who underestimate them tend to appear lacking in confidence and are, therefore, unlikely to be selected for high positions.

Thus, derailment-prone leaders have found it pays to overestimate their abilities. Essentially, developing self-awareness involves:

- knowing actual ability, which may be measured in an assessment or development center
- knowing how others perceive them, particularly peers and subordinates, which can be assessed by 360-degree feedback
- knowing how they react under stress and pressure, which can be assessed by using "dark side" measures that have been developed for the work-place (Hogan and Hogan, 2001).

Thus, classic methods such as development centers, 360-degree feedback, coaching and Cognitive Behavior Therapy (CBT) are encouraged. A paradox here is that, because derailed managers are by definition so often self-absorbed, eager to blame others for all their short-comings and poor learners from experience, they do not benefit from any of these interventions.

Can coaches prevent derailment? Can they spot the signs early enough? Coaches are usually introduced *after* executives have been selected. They come in many shapes and forms, often from a completely unregulated industry. Coaches may help incompetent rather than "disturbed or disordered" leaders. Almost everyone goes though periods of self-doubt, of stress and of indecisiveness: good coaches can act as excellent sounding boards for leaders under those conditions. They may help leader's self-awareness, reduce their stress and encourage healthier, adaptive behaviors.

Yet it is unclear how a coach could prevent leadership derailment from either an incompetent or disturbed leader, given what most coaches say they do. A "talking cure" is unlikely to "cure" incompetence. Self-awareness, an improved sense of self-efficacy and better coping skills are all desirable characteristics, but still not enough to overcome incompetence that is due to lack of ability.

Further, there are three reasons why coaching is unlikely to have any beneficial effects on the disturbed, disordered or toxic leader. The *first* is resistance: paradoxically, those who need it most, resist it most. One cannot force a CEO to take a coach. Neither can one get him or her to follow any directions or recommendations. Whilst some CEOs are happy to sport "a trophy coach", others see no need whatsoever. *Second*, the literature on anti-social and narcissistic personality disorder attests to the poor prognosis for these conditions. Certainly, the average business coach is unlikely to have the training or skills to diagnose and then confront those individuals. The only way they are likely to accept a coach is when they behave in ways that flatter or promote them. In other words, coaches are unlikely to be able to be efficient because the all-powerful CEO – who is, after all, the client – prevents them from doing what they should do.

Third, there is the current evidence. There seems to be no documented case of derailment being prevented or halted by coaching. Indeed, all the case studies of bad leaders suggest the precise opposite: they refused to listen to anybody.

Nelson and Hogan (2009) believe that knowledge of the executive's personality should help both coach and executive be more effective. It is possible to predict who will become quickly disillusioned, who will fake enthusiasm and who will be self-defeating. The idea is that a full understanding of the "dark-side" profile of the executive can help the coach design better and more appropriate intervention strategies, and anticipate the reaction of the particular executive they are working with.

"Transitioning"

This is a polite concept for movement usually sideways, downwards or out. Nearly all derailed leaders have been judged at one time to be highly effective, competent and talented – positions which bring more responsibility and more scrutiny.

Senior jobs are more complex and call for more subtle influencing and persuading skills. Senior managers have to form strategic alliances, empower and delegate. Earlier, lower-level jobs do not call for the same skills. More is expected of senior leaders. It would be wise to give a probationary period to those who try Darwinian sink-or-swim, climb-or-fall solutions in the learning-curve test, to judge their performance potential for the future. Succeed means stay, failure go. But, whilst this may be practical at supervising level, it is not the case with very senior managers.

So, what are the best transitional options? Apart from the obvious issues around selection, there is the issue of integration. Managers tend to be encouraged to use "let go" tactics (technical details) in favor of strategy. They may need special help with soft skills like presentation, negotiation or performance management.

They need help in being integrated with the existing teams and structures. They need to have help in internal networking so that they can build social capital and alliances.

Through various case studies, Capretta *et al.* (2008) listed "interventions" development plans and assignments which helped potentially derailing executives. These included:

- being given various specific and challenging assignments
- repeated 360-degree feedback
- tough, credible specialized coaching
- regular contacts with the CEO.

They list both individual and organizational responsibilities for preventing derailment. At the individual level these include:

- enhancing self-awareness by seeking feedback
- being an acute, agile, willing learner
- observing closely others' reactions; monitoring one's effect
- seeking appropriate coaching and mentoring.

More interestingly, perhaps, they list eight things organizations should have in place to prevent derailment:

1. Have systems that integrate development into managers' work, not what each person could and should learn from each assignment.
2. Ensure that leadership development is a life-long, not one-off, journey.

3. Support risk-taking and be tolerant of experience-learning mistakes.
4. Ensure managers complete jobs before moving them on.
5. Become a feedback culture with mechanisms to ensure formal and informal feedback regularly.
6. Invest in good coaches.
7. Empower those dedicated to talent (i.e. HR, a particular specialist) to do their job better.
8. Look for, rank, strategize and prioritize derailment factors.

THE EMPLOYEES' PERSPECTIVE

Some authors and publishers appear to have discovered there is an appetite – and, therefore, market – for "semi self-help" books that help people identify and deal with their bosses. Here, failed and derailed are called "bad" or "nasty". The books are all about dealing with, or surviving, having to be managed by such people. They belong to the "victim" school of self-help books that relieve one of any responsibility for personal misfortune.

Interestingly, authors of these books have discovered they can write two similar books but from opposite perspectives. Thus, Scott (2005) wrote *A Survival Guide for Working with Bad Bosses* and followed this up with Scott (2007) *A Survival Guide to Managing Employees from Hell*.

Scott (2005) in a self-help book (*Survival Guide*) for those working with bad bosses suggests she can spot various types. She notes, rather inconclusively:

1. Too aggressive	Not aggressive enough (weak and wishy-washy)
2. Too controlling and manipulative	Not controlling enough
3. Too organized and structured	Unorganized and/or disorganized
4. Too rigid and inflexible	Too uncertain and vacillating
5. Too emotional	Lacks compassion and empathy
6. Too much of a micro-manager	Doesn't provide direction or instruction
7. Makes impulsive or bad decisions	Indecisive
8. Too nosy and invasive	Shows a lack of care and concern

Various other qualities are identified as characterizing a bad boss. These include:

9. Yells, screams, and is often rude and insulting
10. Engages in sexual activity in the office by making unwanted sexual advances, or being involved in a sexual relationship with an employee. This means harassment in many forms
11. Involved in criminal activities and asks employees to cover up or participate in these activities
12. Can't be trusted because he/she makes promises and doesn't keep them or lies. Completely untrustworthy
13. Unfair, biased, corrupt in playing office favorites or not giving proper recognition or credit
14. Too much of a perfectionist in all things.

Indeed, there are a growing number of books which started with books from a leader's perspective. Thus, in the book titled *Jerks at Work* Lloyd (1999), in a "question and answer" style, gives advice to leaders regarding the selection, induction and management of employees. However, like all others in this genre, he finds it difficult not to list various "types" who in his words "don't get it". These include the: spreader of ill-will, the noisemaker, the ancient historian, the amateur psychologist, the teaser, the blame defector, the media freak, the bragger, the slug, the slacker, the meanie, the reporter, the perfect one, the vacationist and the linguist.

Pincus (2005) in his book *Managing Difficult People* has ten "negaholic" types. They are: the bully, the complainer or the whiner, the procrastinator, the know-it-all, the silent type, the social butterfly, the "No People Skills" person, the rookie, the over-sensitive person and the manipulator.

Katcher's (2007) book is written for leaders, presumably to help them. His book is catchingly titled *30 Reasons Employees Hate Their Managers*. The 30 reasons are conveniently categorized into five sections. Employees are treated like children (not appreciated, afraid to speak up); employees aren't respected (not listened to but lied to); employees are not receiving the recognition they need (understaffed, undertrained, bound with red tape); employees feel unappreciated (not appraised); and employees have shown no commitment.

Some of these popular books are more conceptual than others. But they do have a formula: *first*, a statement that bad, nasty, sick, incompetent bosses are surprisingly common; *second*, a list of the types;

advice for dealing with them and *finally*, general advice. A good example is the slim volume by Carter (2004). The list includes the carrot dangler, the two-faced boss, the people sucker, the crusader, the chunky boss, the enmesher, the violator, the invalidator, the no-hoper, the analyzer and the me-me boss. They are, however, categorized by the "three mentality system", so bosses with a mammalian mentality try the alpha male way, and those with a cognitive mentality the argumentative and legalese ways. So, later, these nasty bosses can be takers, misers and abusers.

Scott (2005) divided her self-help books into five sections. First, she considers those unfit to command. Here, we have the 'no-boss boss', the 'pass the buck boss', the 'scatter boss', and so on. Then she describes the power players, the unethical bosses, and so on.

Scott (2005) offers reasonable but obvious advice as to how to deal with each type based on an analysis of the organization's size, culture and standards; the boss's personality; your own personality; needs and career goals; the power and position of the boss and, more importantly, how the other employees in the company feel about the boss's behavior.

Scott (2005) wisely lists a number of "other factors to consider and questions to ask":

- Why is my boss acting this way? Is it his personal style? Does he act this way with everyone, or just with me? Is there something I might be doing that is leading my boss to act this way, such as my acting unsure that I can accomplish a task he wants me to do?
- What is my own goal or desired outcome in this situation? Do I want to change the situation? Would I like to make the best of a bad situation? Do I want to get out and get a good recommendation? How would I prioritize these different goals and outcomes?
- How do others in the office who might be similarly affected feel about the boss? What are their goals for change? Would they like me to speak for them? Can I involve others, so we plan to deal with the boss as a group?
- How does my boss prefer to deal with conflicts and problems in the office? Is he open to communicating about them? If so, what is generally the most common or effective way to do this: having a one-to-one meeting, having a phone conversation, sending a memo, or writing an email? Alternatively, does he generally prefer to avoid dealing with problems directly? Would he like employees to handle these issues themselves?

- What's my own personality style? What kind of approach am I most comfortable with? Would I rather have a meeting, phone conversation, or send a memo or email?
- How important is this issue? Does this need attention right away, say, because it is undermining office morale and productivity? Or am I the only one who is bothered and, if so, is there a better time to raise the subject?
- How likely am I to succeed? How likely is it that my boss is going to change?
- What's the political environment like? How powerful is my boss? How much power or influence do I have in my position? How valuable is the work I am doing, and how easily can I be replaced? What kind of support does he have from others, or is he the company owner? Are there any outside factors that might affect my boss, such as a spouse, community influence, or government regulations?
- How would I feel if this situation continues as is? How important is it to me that this situation changes, or can I live with this problem for now?
- What is the risk of bringing up the problem with my boss or others in the company? What is the worse-case scenario?
- Are there any communication problems or flawed assumptions that may be at the root of the problem?

The problem with all these books is that they ignore the fact that it may be the organizational culture, or, indeed, leaders *themselves* that is/are the real cause of the problem. These books are also long on amusing categories for bad leaders, but short on advice as to know what to do.

TOXIC FOLLOWERS

History has shown how "good" leaders have been led astray by the manipulative forces of followers. Followers can heavily edit and censor the information they give to leaders. Others flatter their leaders, appealing to their vanity. Many withhold all forms of criticism leading to group-think.

It is perhaps no accident that 360-degree feedback and coaching have become so popular in trying to give decision-makers honest feedback. It is naïve to think that followers at all levels do not powerfully influence their leaders. Inevitably, influence is a two-way process: different personalities are vulnerable to different types of influence.

Offerman (2004) memorably noted: "caught between the Scylla of follower unanimity and the Charybdis of flattery, leaders might be tempted to keep their followers at a distance" (p. 59). The question is how to get at what is going on because of the censors or ingratiators – any department. Here leaders have to be careful who to delegate to what.

Offerman (2004), in a paper on toxic followers, offers the following advice (p. 58):

Six Ways to Counter Wayward Influences
There is no guaranteed means of ensuring that you won't be misled by your followers. But adhering to these principles may help:

1. Keep vision and values front and center. It's much easier to get sidetracked when you're unclear about what the main track is.
2. Make sure people disagree. Remember that most of us form opinions too quickly and give them up too slowly.
3. Cultivate truth tellers. Make sure there are people in your world you can trust to tell you what you need to hear, no matter how unpopular or unpalatable it is.
4. Do as you would have done to you. Followers look to what you do rather than what you say. Set a good ethical climate for your team to be sure your followers have clear boundaries for their actions.
5. Honor your intuition. If you think you're being manipulated, you're probably right.
6. Delegate, don't desert. It's important to share control and empower your staff, but remember who's ultimately responsible for the outcome. As they say in politics, "Trust, but verify".

LEADERS SELF-HELP

What about self-help for potentially derailing leaders? To some extent this is an oxymoron because many derailed leaders, particularly those with psychopathic and narcissistic tendencies, do not believe they need any help. Indeed, they feel the opposite: confident, capable and talented, and in a better position to help others who need it. However, for those who have sufficient insight and occasional self-doubt, how can they help themselves?

Kellerman (2004), who placed all bad leaders on a two-dimensional (ineffective vs unethical) framework, offered simple self-help tips presumably for good leaders who may go bad:

- Limit your tenure in terms of time
- Share power with others
- Don't believe your own publicity
- Get real and stay real by getting in touch
- Compensate for your weaknesses
- Stay balanced in the work-life sense
- Remember the essential mission of the organization
- Stay physically and mentally healthy
- Develop a personal support system of family, friends and associates
- Be creative by considering all options
- Know and control your appetites and urges
- Be reflective with an emphasis on self-knowledge and control.

She offers further advice for leaders working with others:

- Establish a culture of openness that encourages diversity and dissent
- Install an ombudsman who is a monitor of standards
- Consult and appoint advisers who are both strong and independent
- Avoid group think by encouraging dissent and discouraging cohesiveness
- Obtain reliable and complete information, and disseminate it
- Invite historians and ethicists to the table
- Establish a system of checks and balances
- Strive for stakeholder symmetry, connecting to all constituents.

BLAMING THE SYSTEM

Even the most simple of self-help books acknowledges that bad leadership is not exclusively about incompetent managers and sick employees. To some extent, the problem lies in a company's policies, processes and procedures which are unhelpful, inefficient. Thus, Lloyd (1999) notes the problems caused by poor training, appraisal or reward systems. Equally, Pincus (2005) notes that a company's policies and procedures can be the cause of problems. That is, leaders fail because they follow the inappropriate, inefficient or downright stupid policies set out by companies. By definition, then, the aim must be for any leader or senior manager to change those procedures.

The "system" is more commonly known as the "organizational culture". It is about both the formal and informal, but also implicit and explicit rules that people follow. Sometimes, it is about group processes that occur.

"Group-think" (Janis, 1972) is the term given to the pressure that highly cohesive groups exert on their members for uniform and acceptable decisions that actually reduce their capacity to make effective decisions. The concept of group-think was produced as an attempt to explain the ineffective decisions made by US government officials which led to such fiascos as the Bay of Pigs invasion in Cuba, the successful Japanese attack on Pearl Harbor, and the Vietnam War. Analyses of these cases have revealed that, in each case, the President's advisers discouraged the making of more effective decisions. Members of very cohesive groups may have more faith in their group's decisions than any idea they may have personally. As a result, they may suspend their own crucial thinking in favor of conforming to the group. When group members become tremendously loyal to each other, they may ignore information from other sources if it challenges the group's decisions. The result of this process is that the group's decisions may be completely uninformed, irrational or even immoral (Greenberg and Baron, 2003).

Often there are thought to be eight markers or signs of group-think. *First*, ignoring obvious danger signals, being overly optimistic and taking extreme risks. *Second*, discrediting or ignoring warning signals that run contrary to group-think. *Third*, believing that the group's position is ethical and moral, and that all others are inherently evil. *Fourth*, viewing the opposite side as being too negative to warrant serious consideration. *Fifth*, discouraging the expression of dissenting opinions under the threat of expulsion for disloyalty. *Sixth*, withholding dissenting ideas and counter-arguments, keeping them to oneself. *Seventh*, sharing the false belief that everyone in the group agrees with its judgments. *Eighth*, protecting the group from negative, threatening information. Some of the potential consequences of group-think include:

- fewer alternatives are considered when solving problems; preferred accepted solutions are implemented
- outside experts are seldom used; indeed, outsiders are distrusted.
- re-examination of a rejected alternative is unlikely
- facts that do not support the group are ignored, or their accuracy challenged.
- risks are ignored or glossed over; indeed, risk is seldom assessed.

To prevent or reduce the effects of group-think, managers can:

- encourage each member of the group to evaluate his or her own and others' ideas openly and critically
- ask influential members to adopt an initial external (even critical) stance on solutions (even leave the group for set periods)
- discuss plans with disinterested outsiders to obtain reactions
- use expert advisers to redesign the decision-making process
- assign a devil's advocate role to one or more group members to challenge ideas
- explore alternative scenarios for possible external reactions
- use subgroups (select committees) to develop alternative solutions
- meet to reconsider decisions prior to implementation.

CONCLUSION

Good managers are characterized by various phenomena. Often, they tend proactively to seek feedback from trusted, honest observers throughout their career to see how they are doing; next, they seek out opportunities to grow, develop, learn or upgrade important skills. They also seek a formal or informal coach or mentor to help them over times of acute change or transition. In short, they seek out sources of assessment, challenges and support.

Those prone to derailment do not. Through hubris, anxiety or lack of insight they have to be given "developmental" assignments and coerced to go on. They might go on short, taught leadership programmes, but few cite those events later as crucial ingredients of their development. They need opportunities to examine their style, strengths and weaknesses, with intensive and honest feedback.

Paradoxically, perhaps, an early career failure or mishap can be an excellent learning experience, so that mistakes are not repeated.

Coaching for executives can help a great deal. Some organizations have prescribed mentoring where every manager at a certain level is mentored by a person above them.

Not all derailment can be prevented. However, much can be done to help the stressed leader, crossing over the thin line between poor management and pathology.

The cost of derailment is high: for the individual manager and his or her family, peers and subordinates, and for the company as a whole.

Often, derailment is quite unexpected. Yet, nearly always, a more careful and critical review of derailed leaders' biographies contains all the cues that derailment might occur. By then, it is too late.

Organizations can reduce – rather than prevent or eliminate, the prospect of their senior leaders and managers derailing by ensuring good governance and strong management processes. Leaders need enough "freedom to manoeuvre" but not unlimited power.

All leaders work with "top teams" called "boards" or "cabinets" or whatever. They can easily become highly dysfunctional and themselves be a cause of management derailment. It is desirable to have someone monitor the health of boards from time to time.

There are many stages where derailment may be addressed. The most obvious are recruitment and selection. There is now much more interest in this issue and excellent psychometrically validated tests to evaluate the dark side of personality. These can indicate possible areas of concern when leaders are put under pressure, which they inevitably are.

Coaching and mentoring can help. Paradoxically, those who need it most also resist it most and benefit from it least. It takes a highly skilled coach to confront a very senior manager/leader and help him or her to avoid derailment.

However, because derailment is now "on the agenda", the *Elephant in the Boardroom* may now be acknowledged.

REFERENCES

Ackerman, P. and Heggestad, E. (1997). Intelligence, personality and interests. *Psychological Bulletin, 121*, 219–45.

Ackerman, P. and Rolfhus, E. (1999). The locus of adult intelligence. *Psychology and Aging, 14*, 314–30.

Adair, J. (2002). *Inspiring leadership*. London: Thorogood.

Al-Khatib, J., Malshe, A. and AbdulKader, M. (2008). Perception of unethical negotiation tactics. *International Business Review, 17*, 98–102.

American Psychiatric Association (APA) (1994). *Diagnostic and Statistical Manual of Mental Disorders*. (4th edn) Washington, DC: APA.

Austin, E., Farrelly, O., Black, C. and Moore, H. (2007). Emotional intelligence, Machiavellianism and emotional manipulation. *Personality and Individual Differences, 43*, 179–81.

Avolio, B., Walumbwa, F. and Weber, T. (2009). Leadership. *Annual Review of Psychology, 60*, 421–49.

Babiak, P. (1995). When psychopaths go to work: A case study of an industrial psychopath. *Applied Psychology, 44*, 171–88.

Babiak, P. and Hare, R. (2006). *Snakes in Suits*. New York: Regan Books.

Balthazard, P., Cooke, R. and Potter, R. (2006). Dysfunctional culture, dysfunctional organisation. *Journal of Management Psychology, 21*, 709–32.

Baumeister, R., Campbell, J., Krueger, J. and Volis, K. (2003). Does high self-esteem cause better performance, interpersonal success, happiness and healthier lifestyles? *Psychological Science in the Public Interest, 4*, 1–44.

Becker, J. and O'Hair, D. (2007). Machiavellians' motives in organizational citizenship behaviour. *Journal of Applied Communication Research, 35*, 246–67.

Bedell-Avers, K., Hunter, S., Angie, A., Eubanks, D. and Mumford, M. (2009). Charismatic, ideological, and pragmatic leader. *Leadership Quarterly, 20*, 299–315.

Beier, M. and Ackerman, P. (2001). Current-events knowledge in adults. *Psychology and Aging, 16*, 615–28.

Benning, S., Patrick, C., Bloniger, D., Hicks, B. and Iacono, W. (2005). Estimating facets of psychopathy from normal personality traits. *Assessment, 12*, 3–18.

Bentz, J. (1967). The Sears Experience in the investigation, description and prediction of executive behaviour. In F. Wickert and D. McFarland (eds) *Measuring Executive Effectiveness* (pp. 147–206). New York: Appleton-Century-Crofts.

Bentz, V. (1990). Contextual issues in predicting high-level leadership performance. In K. Clark and M. Clark (eds) *Measures of Leadership* (pp.131–44). West Orange, NJ: Leadership Library of America.

Bertua, C., Anderson, N. and Salgado, J. (2005). The predictive validity of cognitive ability tests. A UK meta-analysis. *Journal of Occupational and Organisational Psychology, 78*, 387.

Blonigen, D., Carlson, S., Krueger, R. and Patrick, C. (2003). A twin study of self-reported psychopathic personality traits. *Personality and Individual Differences, 35*, 179–97.

Borman, W., Hanson, M., Oppler, S., Pulakis, E. and White, L. (1993). Role of early supervisory experience in supervisor performance. *Journal of Applied Psychology, 78*, 443–9.

Brody, N. (1992). *Intelligence*. London: Academic Press.

Brown, A. (1997). Narcissism, identity and legitimacy. *Academy of Management Review, 22*, 643–86.

Burke, R. (2006). Why leaders fail: exploring the darkside. *International Journal of Manpower, 27*, 91–100.

Bushman, B. and Baumeister, R. (1998). Threatened egoism, narcissism, self-esteem and direct and displaced aggressions. *Journal of Personality and Social Psychology, 75*, 219–29.

Campbell, W. (2001). Is narcissism really so bad? *Psychological Inquiry, 12*, 214–16.

Campbell, W., Bush. C., Brunell, A. and Shelton, J. (2005). Understanding the social costs of narcissism. *Personality and Social Psychology Bulletin, 31*, 1358–68.

Capretta, G., Clark, L. and Dai, G. (2008). Executive derailment. *Global Business and Organizational Excellence, 4*, 48–56.

Carroll, J. (1993). *Human Cognitive Abilities*. Cambridge: Cambridge University Press.

Carter, J. (2004). *Nasty Bosses*. New York: McGraw-Hill.

Cattell, R. (1987). *Intelligence: Its Structure, Growth and Action*. New York: North Holland.

Charan, R. and Colvin, G. (1999). Why CEOs fail. *Fortune*, 21 June.

Christie, R. and Geis, F. (1970). *Studies in Machiavellianism*. London: Academic Press.

Cleckley, H. (1941). *The Mask of Sanity*. St Louis, MO: Mosley.

Clements, C. and Washbush, J. (1999). The two faces of leadership: considering the dark side of leader-follower dimensions. *Journal of Workplace Learning, 11*, 170–5.

Cold, J., Yang, M. *et al.* (2009a). Psychopathy among prisoners in England and Wales. *International Journal of Law and Psychiatry, 32*, 134–44.

Cold, J., Yang, M., Ullrich, S., Roberts, A. and Hare, R. (2009b). Prevalence and correlates of psychopathic traits in the household population of Great Britain. *International Journal of Law and Psychiatry, 32*, 65–73.

Conger, J. and Fishel, B. (2007). Accelerating leadership performance at the top. *Human Resource Management Review, 17*, 442–54.

Courtis, J. (1986). *Managing by Mistake*. London: Institute of Chartered Accountants.

Crocker, J. and Wolfe, C. (2001). Contingencies of self worth. *Psychologist Review, 108*, 593–623.

De Clercq, B. and De Fruyt, F. (2003). Personality disorder symptoms in adolescence: A five-factor model perspective. *Journal of Personality Disorders, 17*, 269–92.

De Fruyt, F., De Clercq, B., Miller, L. *et al.* (2009). Assessing personality at risk in personnel selection and development. *European Journal of Personality, 23*, 51–69.

Deary, I. (2000). *Looking Down on Human Intelligence*. Oxford: Oxford University Press.

Deary, I. (2001). *Intelligence: A Very Short Introduction*. Oxford: Oxford University Press.

Deluga, R. (2001). American presidential Machiavellianism. *The Leadership Quarterly, 12*, 339–63.

Dixon, N. (1972). *On the Psychology of Military Incompetence*. London: Jonathan Cape.

Dotlich, D. and Cairo, P. (2003). *Why CEOs Fail*. New York: Jossey-Bass.

Dragow, F. (2002). Intelligence and the workplace. In W. Borman, D. Ilgen and R. Klimozki (eds), *Handbook of Psychology*: vol. 12 (pp. 107–30). New York: Wiley.

Durrett, C. and Trull, T. (2005). An evaluation of evaluative personality terms. *Psychological Assessment, 17*, 359–68.

Einarsen, S., Aasland, M. and Skogstad, A. (2007). Destructive leadership behaviour. *Leadership Quarterly, 18*, 207–16.

Emler, N. (2005). *The Costs and Causes of Low Self-Esteem*. Unpublished paper: LSE.

Emmons, R. (1984). Factor analysis and construct validity of the Narcissistic Personality Inventory. *Journal of Personality Assessment, 48*, 291–300.

Eysenck, H. (1998). *Intelligence: A New Look*. London: Transaction Publishers.

Farson, R. (1997). *Management of the Absurd*. New York: Touchstone.

Finkelstein, S. (2003). *Why Smart Executives Fail*. New York: Portfolio.

Fulmer, R. and Conger, J. (2004). *Growing Your Company's Leaders*. New York: Amacom.

Furnham, A. (2001). *The 3D Manager*. London: Whurr.

Furnham, A. (2004). *The Incompetent Manager*. London: Whurr.

Furnham, A. (2006). Personality disorders and intelligence. *Journal of Individual Differences, 27*, 42–6.

Furnham, A. (2007). Rating a boss, a colleague, and a subordinate. *Journal of Managerial Psychology, 22,* 610–21.

Furnham, A. and Crump, J. (2005). Personality traits, types and disorders. *European Journal of Personality, 19,* 167–84.

Furnham, A. and Stringfield, P. (1994). Congruence of self and subordinate ratings of managerial practices as a correlate of supervisor evaluation. *Journal of Occupational and Organisational Psychology, 67,* 57–67.

Gardner, H. (1999). *Intelligence Reframed.* New York: Basic Books.

Gardner, W. and Avolio, B. (1998). The charismatic relationship. *Academy of Management Review, 23,* 32–58.

Gentry, W. and Shanock, L. (2008). Views of managerial derailment from above and below. *Journal of Applied Social Psychology, 38,* 2469–94.

Gill, R. (2006). *Theory and Practice of Leadership.* London: Sage.

Glad, B. (2002). Why tyrants go too far: Malignant narcissism and absolute power. *Political Psychology, 23,* 1–37.

Goethals, G. (2005). The Psychodynamics of Leadership. In D. Messick and R. Kramer (eds), *The Psychology of Leadership* (pp. 96–112). Mahwah, NJ: Lawrence Erlbaum.

Goldman, A. (2006a). High toxicity leadership. *Journal of Managerial Psychology, 21,* 733–46.

Goldman, A. (2006b). Personality disorders in leaders. *Journal of Managerial Psychology, 21,* 392–413.

Gottfredson, L. (1997). Why g matters: The complexity of everyday life. *Intelligence, 24,* 79–132.

Gottfredson, L. (1998). The general intelligence factor. *Scientific American,* 24–9.

Gottfredson, L. (2002). Where and why g matters: Not a mystery. *Human Performance, 15,* 25–46.

Gottfredson, L. (2003a). g Jobs and Life. In J. Nyborg (ed.), *The Science of Mental Ability.* Oxford: Pergamon.

Gottfredson, L. (2003b). Dissecting practical intelligence theory: its claims and evidence. *Intelligence, 31,* 343–97.

Gottfredson, L. (2005). What if the hereditarians' hypothesis is true? *Psychology, Public Policy and Law, 11,* 311–19.

Gottfredson, L. and Deary, I. (2004). Intelligence predicts health and longevity, but why? *Current Direction in Psychological Science, 13,* 1–4.

Graham, J. (1996). Machiavellian project manager. *International Journal of Project Management, 14,* 67–74.

Greenberg, J. and Baron, R. (2003). *Behaviour in Organisations.* London: Pearson.

Gunter, B., Furnham, A. and Drakeley, R. (1993). *Biodata.* London: Methuen.

Gustafson, S. and Ritzer, D. (1995). The dark side of normal. *European Journal of Personality, 9,* 147–83.

Hall, J. and Benning, S. (2005). The "successful" psychopath. Adaptive and subclinical manifestation of psychopathy in the general population. In C. Patrick (ed.), *Handbook of Psychopathy* (pp. 459–78). London: Guilford Press.

Hare, R. (1999). *Without Conscience*. New York: Guilford Press.

Harvey, P., Martinko, M. and Douglas, S. (2006). Causal reasoning in dysfunctional leaders-member interactions. *Journal of Managerial Psychology, 21,* 747–62.

Herrnstein, R. and Murray, C. (1994). *The Bell Curve*. New York: Free Press.

Hodson, E., Hogg, S. and MacInnis, C. (2009). The role of "dark personalities" (narcissism, Machiavellianism, psychopathy), Big Five personality factors, and ideology in explaining prejudice. *Journal of Research in Personality, 43,* 686–90.

Hogan, R. (2007a). *Comments on the Hogan Business Reasoning Inventory*. Tulsa, OK: Hogan Assessments.

Hogan, R. (2007b). *Personality and the Fate of Organizations*. New York: Erlbaum.

Hogan, R., Barrett, P. and Hogan, J. (2009) *Hogan Business Reasoning Inventory Manual*. Tulsa, OK: Hogan Assessments.

Hogan, R. and Hogan, J. (1997). *Hogan Development Survey Manual*. Tulsa, OK: Hogan Assessments.

Hogan, R. and Hogan, J. (2001). Assessing leadership: A view from the dark side. *International Journal of Selection and Assessment, 9,* 40–51.

Hogan, R., Hogan, J. and Kaiser, R. (2009). Management derailment. In S. Zedeck (ed.), *American Psychological Association Handbook of Industrial and Organizational Psychology*. New York: APA.

Hogan, R. and Warrenfeltz, R. (2003). Educating the modern manager. *Academy of Management Learning and Education, 2,* 74–85.

Horney, K. (1950). *Neurosis and Human Growth*. New York: Norton.

Hough, L., Oswald, F. and Pleghart, R. (2001). Determinants, detection and amelioration of adverse impact in personal selection procedures. *International Journal of Selection and Assessment, 9,* 152–94.

Hulsheger, U., Maier, G. and Stumpp, T. (2007). Validity of general mental ability for the prediction of job performance and training success in Germany. *International Journal of Selection and Assessment, 15,* 3–18.

Hunter, J. (1986). Cognitive ability, cognitive aptitudes, job knowledge and job performance. *Intelligence, 29,* 340–62.

Hunter, J. and Hunter R. (1984). Validity and utility of alternative predictors of job performance. *Psychological Bulletin, 96,* 72–98.

Hunter, J. E. and Schmidt, F. L. (1976). A critical analysis of the statistical and ethical implications of various definitions of test fairness. *Psychological Bulletin, 83,* 1053–71.

Hunter, J. E. and Schmidt, F. L. (1990). *Methods of Meta-Analysis: Correcting for Error and Bias in Research Findings*. Newbury Park, CA: Sage.

Ishikawa, S., Raine, A., Lenez, T., Bihrli, S. and Lacasse, L. (2001). Autonomic stress reactivity and executive functions in successful and unsuccessful criminal psychopaths from the community. *Journal of Abnormal Psychology, 110*, 423–32.

Jakobwitz, S. and Egan, V. (2006). The dark triad and normal personality traits. *Personality and Individual Differences, 40*, 331–9.

Janis, I. (1972). *Victims of Group-Think*. Boston, MA: Houghton-Mifflin.

Jonason, P., Li, N., Webster, G. and Schmitt, D. (2008). The Dark Triad. Facilitating a short-term mating strategy in men. *European Journal of Personality, 23*, 5–18.

Judge, T. and LePine, J. (2009). The bright and dark side of personality. In J. Langan-Fox, C. Cooper, and R. Klimoski (eds), *Research Companion to the Dysfunctional Workplace* (pp. 332–55). Cheltenham: Edward Elgar.

Judge, T., LePine, J. and Rich, B. (2006). Loving yourself abundantly. *Journal of Applied Psychology, 91*, 762–76.

Kaiser, R. and Hogan, R. (2007). The dark side of discretion. In R. Hooijberg, J. Hunt, K. Boal, B. Macy and J. Antonakis (eds), *Leadership in and of Organizations* (pp. 177–97). Amsterdam: Elsevier.

Kaplan, R. and Kaiser, R. (2006). *The Versatile Leader: Make the Most of Your Strengths – Without Overdoing It*. San Francisco: Pfeiffer.

Katcher, B. (2007). *30 Reasons Employees Hate Their Managers*. New York: Amacom.

Kellerman, B. (2004). *Bad Leadership*. Boston, MA: Harvard University Press.

Kelloway, E., Sivanthan, N., Frances, L. and Barling, J. (2007). Poor Leadership. In J. Barling, E. Kelloway and M. Frone (eds), *Handbook of Work Stress* (pp. 89–112): Thousand Oaks, NJ: Sage.

Kets de Vries, M. (1999). Managing puzzling personalities. *European Management Journal, 17*, 8–19.

Kets de Vries, M. (2003). 'Doing an Alexander': Lessons of leadership by a master conqueror. *European Management Journal, 31*, 370–5.

Kets de Vries, M. (2006a). *The Leader on the Couch*. New York: Jossey-Bass.

Kets de Vries, M. (2006b). The spirit of despotism: understanding the tyrant within. *Human Relations, 59*, 195–220.

Kets de Vries, M. and Miller, D. (1985). *The Neurotic Organization*. San Francisco, CA: Jossey-Bass.

Kline, P. and Cooper, C. (1983). A factor analytic study of measures of Machiavellianism. *Personality and Individual Differences, 4*, 569–71.

Kuncel, N., Hezlett, S. and Ones, D. (2001). A comprehensive meta-analysis of the predictive validity of the Graduate Record Examinations. *Psychological Bulletin, 127*, 162–81.

Kuncel, N., Hezlett, S. and Ones, D. (2004). Academic performance, career potential, creativity and job performance. *Journal of Personality and Social Psychology, 86*, 148–61.

Langan-Fox, J., Cooper, C. and Klimoski, R. (2007). *Research Companion to the Dysfunctional Workplace*. Cheltenham: Edward Elgar.

Larrson, H., Andershed, H. and Lichtenstein, P. (2006). A genetic factor explains most of the variation in the psychopathic personality. *Journal of Abnormal Psychology, 115*, 221–3.

Lasch, C. (1979). *The Culture of Narcissism*. New York: Norton.

Lee, K. and Ashton, M. (2005). Psychopathy, Machiavellianism and narcissism in the five-factor model and the HEXACO model of personality structure. *Personality and Individual Differences, 38*, 1571–82.

Lipman-Blumen, J. (2005). *The Allure of Toxic Leaders*. Oxford: Oxford University Press.

Lloyd, K. (1999). *Jerks at Work*. Franklin Lakes, NJ: Career Press.

Lombardo, M. and Eichinger, R. (1999). *Preventing Derailment: What To Do Before It Is Too Late*. Greensboro, NC: Center for Creative Leadership.

Lombardo, M. and Eichinger, R. (2006). *The Leadership Machine*. Minneapolis, MN: Lominger Ltd.

Lombardo, M., Rinderman, M. and McCauley, C. (1988). Explanations of success and derailment in upper level management positions. *Journal of Business and Psychology, 2*, 199–216.

Lubit, R. (2004). *Coping With Toxic Managers*. New York: Prentice Hall.

Luthans, F., Peterson, S. and Ibrayeva, E. (1998). The potential for the "dark side" of leadership in post-communist countries. *Journal of World Business, 33*, 185–201.

Mackintosh, N. (1998). *IQ and Human Intelligence*. Oxford: Oxford University Press.

McCall, M. (1998). *High Flyers*. Cambridge, MA: HBS Press.

McCall, M. and Lombardo, M. (1983). *Off the track: why and how successful executives get derailed*. Report 21. Greensboro, NC: Center for Creative Leadership.

McCauley, D. and Lombardo, M. (1990). Benchmarks: An instrument for diagnosing managerial strengths and weaknesses. In K. Clark and M. Clark (eds), *Measurement of Leadership* (pp. 535–45). Greensboro, NC: Centre for Creative Leadership.

McGregor, D. (1960). *The Human Side of Enterprise*. New York: McGraw-Hill.

McHenry, J., Hough, L., Toquam, J., Hanson, M. and Ashworth, S. (1990). Project A validity results. *Personnel Psychology, 43*, 335–54.

McHoskey, J. (2001). Machiavellianism and personality function. *Personality and Individual Differences, 31*, 791–8.

Menkes, J. (2005). Hiring for smarts. *Harvard Business Review, 83*(11), 100–9.

Miller, A. (1949). *Death of a Salesman*. New York: Penguin.

Miller, L. (2008). *From Difficult to Disturbed*. New York: AMACOM.

Millon, T. (1981). *Disorders of Personality DSM-III: Axis II*. New York: Wiley.

Mumford, M., Espejo, J., Hunter, S., Bedell-Avers, K., Eubanks, D. and Connelly, S. (2007). The sources of leader violence. *Leadership Quarterly, 18*, 217–35.

Murphy, K. (2002). Can conflicting perspectives on the role of g in personnel selection be resolved? *Human Performance, 15*, 173–86.

Neisser, U. (1967). *Cognitive Psychology*. New York: Appleton Century Crofts.

Nelson, E. and Hogan, R. (2009). Coaching the dark side. *International Coaching Psychology Review, 4*, 7–19.

Nelson, G. and Gilbertson, D. (1991). Machiavellianism revisited. *Journal of Business Ethics, 10*, 633–5.

Nettlebeck, T. and Wilson, C. (2005). Intelligence and IQ: what teachers should know? *Educational Psychology, 25*, 609–30.

O'Connor, J., Mumford, M., Clifton, T., Gessner, T. and Connelly, M. (1995). Charismatic leaders and destructiveness. *Leadership Quarterly, 6*, 529–55.

Offerman, L. (2004). When followers become toxic. *Harvard Business Review, 82*(1), 54–60.

Oldham, J. and Morris, L. (2000). *The New Personality Self-Portrait*. New York: Bantam Books.

Ones, D., Viswesvaran, C. and Dilchert, A. (2006). Cognitive ability in selection decisions. In D. Wilheml and R. Engle (eds), *Understanding and Measuring Intelligence*. London: Sage.

Otway, L. and Vignoles, V. (2006). Narcissism and childhood recollections. *Personality and Social Psychology Bulletin, 32*, 104–16.

Padilla, A., Hogan, R. and Kaiser, R. (2007). The toxic triangle: destructive leaders, susceptible followers and conducive environments. *Leadership Quarterly, 18*, 176–94.

Paulhus, D. and Williams, K. (2002). The dark triad of personality: Narcissism, Machiavellianism and psychopathy. *Journal of Research in Personality, 36*, 556–63.

Paunonen, S., Lonqvist, J-E., Verkasalo, M. Levkas, S. and Nisswen, V. (2006). Narcissism and emergent leadership in military cadets. *Leadership Quarterly, 17*, 475–88.

Peter, L. (1985). *Why Things Go Wrong*. London: Unwin.

Pincus, M. (2005). *Managing Different People*. Avor, MA: Adams Media.

Pullen, A. and Rhodes, A. (2008). "It's all about me": Gendered narcissism and leaders' identity work. *Leadership, 4*, 5–25.

Raskin, R. and Hall, C. (1981). The narcissistic personality inventory. *Journal of Personality Assessment, 45*, 159–67.

Rate, C. and Sternberg, R. (2007). When good people do nothing. In J. Langan-Fox, C. Cooper, and R. Klimoski (eds), *Research Companion to the Dysfunctional Workplace* (pp. 3–21). Cheltenham: Edward Elgar.

Ree, M. and Carretta, T. (1998). General cognitive ability and occupational performance. *International Review of Industrial and Organisational Psychology, 13*, 161–89.

Ree, M., Carretta, T. and Teachout, M. (1995). The role of ability and prior job knowledge in complex training performance. *Journal of Applied Psychology, 80*, 721–30.

Ree, M. and Earles, J. (1994). The ubiquitous predictiveness of g. In M. Rumsey, C. Walker and J. Harris (eds), *Personnel Selection and Classification* (pp. 127–35). Hillsdale, NJ: Lawrence Erlbaum.

Ree, M., Earles, J. and Teachout, M. (1994). Predicting job performance. *Journal of Applied Psychology, 79*, 518–24.

Reed, G. (2004). Toxic leadership. *Military Review, 8*, 67–71.

Reeve, C. and Hakel, M. (2002). Asking the right questions about g. *Human Performance, 15*, 47–74.

Rolfhus, E. and Ackerman, P. (1999). Assessing individual differences in knowledge. *Journal of Educational Psychology, 91*, 511–26.

Rolland, J.-P. and De Fruyt, F. (2003). The validity of FFM personality dimensions and maladaptive traits to predict negative affect at work. *European Journal of Personality, 17*, 101–21.

Rooke, D. and Torbert, W. (2005). Seven transformations of leadership. *Harvard Business Review, 83*, 66–77.

Rosenthal, S. (2007). *Narcissism and Leadership. A Review and Research Agenda.* Working Paper: Center for Public Leadership, Harvard University.

Rosenthal, S. and Pittinsky, T. (2006). Narcissistic leadership. *Leadership Quarterly, 17*, 617–33.

Salgado, J., Anderson, N., Moscoso, S., Bertua, C. and de Fruyt, F. (2003). International validity generalization of GMA and cognitive abilities. *Personnel Psychology, 56*, 573–605.

Sankowsky, D. (1995). The charismatic leader as narcissist. *Organizational Dynamics, 23*, 57–71.

Saulsman, L. and Page, A. (2004). The five factor model and personality disorder empirical literature: a meta-analytic review. *Clinical Psychology Review, 23*, 1055–85.

Schaubroeck, J., Walumbwa, F., Ganster, D. and Kepes, S. (2007). Destructive leader traits and the neutralizing influence of an "enriched" job. *Leadership Quarterly, 18*, 236–51.

Schmidt, F. (2002). The role of general cognitive ability and job performance. *Human Performance, 15*, 187–210.

Schmidt, F. L. and Hunter, J. E. (1977). Development of a general solution to the problem of validity generalization. *Journal of Applied Psychology, 62*(5), 529–40.

Schmidt, F. L. and Hunter, J. E. (1984). A within setting empirical test of the situational specificity hypothesis in personnel selection. *Personnel Psychology, 37*, 317–26.

Schmidt, F. L. and Hunter, J. E. (1998). The validity and utility of selection methods in personnel psychology: Practical and theoretical implications of 85 years of research findings. *Psychological Bulletin, 124*, 262–74.

Schmidt, F. and Hunter, J. (2004). General mental ability in the world of work. *Journal of Personality and Social Psychology, 86*, 162–73.

Scott, E. (2005). *A Survival Guide for Working with Bad Bosses*. New York: AMACOM.

Scott, E. (2007). *A Survival Guide for Managing Employees from Hell*. New York: AMACOM.

Sedikides, C., Gregg, A. and Hart, C. (2007). The importance of being modest. In C. Sedikides and S. Spencer (eds), *Frontiers in social psychology – The self*. New York: Psychology Press.

Sedikides, C., Horton, R. and Gregg, P. (2007). The why's the limit: Curtailing self-enhancement with explanatory introspection. *Journal of Personality, 75*, 783–824.

Sedikides, C., Rudich, E., Gregg, A., Kumashiro, M. and Rusbull, C. (2004). Are normal narcissists psychologically healthy? *Journal of Personality and Social Psychology, 87*, 400–16.

Shapiro, D. and Von Glinow, M. (2007). Why bad leaders stay in good places. In J. Langan-Fox, C. Cooper, and R. Klimoski (eds), *Research Companion to the Dysfunctional Workplace* (pp. 90–109). Cheltenham: Edward Elgar.

Spearman, C. (1904). General intelligence: objectively determined and measured. *American Journal of Psychology, 15*, 201–93.

Strange, J. and Mumford, M. (2002). The origins of vision: charismatic vs. ideological leadership. *Leadership Quarterly, 13*, 343–77.

Sutton, J. and Keogh, E. (2001). Components of Machiavellian beliefs in children. *Personality and Individual Differences, 30*, 137–48.

Tenopyr, M. (2002). Theory versus reality: Evaluation of g in the workplace. *Human Performance, 15*, 107–22.

Tracy, J. and Robins, R. (2007). "Death of a (Narcissistic) Salesman". An integrative model of fragile self esteem. *Psychological Enquiry, 14*, 1, 57–62.

Trzesniewski, K., Donnellan, M. and Robins, R. (2008a). Is "Generation me" really more narcissistic than previous generations? *Journal of Research and Personality, 19*, 181–5.

Trzesniewski, K., Donnellan, M. and Robins, R. (2008b). Do today's young people really think they are extraordinary? *Psychological Science, 19*, 181–8.

Trzesniewski, K., Donnellan, M., Moffit, R., Robins, R., Poulton, R. and Caspi, A. (2008c). *Low Self-Esteem During Adolescence Predicts Poor Health, Criminal Behaviour, and Limited Prospects During Adulthood*. Paper under review.

Twenge, J. (2006). *Generation Me*. New York: Free Press.

Van Fleet, D. and Griffin, R. (2006). Dysfunctional organization culture. *Journal of Managerial Psychology, 21*, 698–708.

Van Velsor, E. and Leslie, J. (1995). Why executives derail: perspectives across time and cultures. *Academy of Management Executive, 9*, 62–72.

Van Vugt, M., Hogan, R. and Kaiser, R. (2008). Leadership, followership and evolution. *American Psychologist, 63*, 182–96.

Vernon, P., Villaic, V., Vickers, L. and Harris, J. (2008). A behavioral genetic investigation of the Dark Triad and the Big Five. *Personality and Individual Differences, 44*, 445–52.

Viding, E., Blair, R. J. R., Moffitt, T. E. and Plomin, R. (2005). Strong genetic link for psychopathic syndrome in children. *Journal of Child Psychology and Psychiatry, 46*, 592–7.

Viswesvaran, C. and Ones, D. (2002). Agreements and disagreements on the role of General Mental Ability (GMA) in industrial work and organizational psychology. *Human Performance, 15*, 211–31.

Viswesvaran, C., Ones, D. and Schmidt, F. (1996). Comparative analysis of the reliability of job performance ratings. *Journal of Applied Psychology, 81*, 557–74.

Weierter, S. (1999). Who wants to play "follow the leader"? *Leadership Quarterly, 8*, 171–93.

Widiger, T. A., Trull, T. J., Clarkin, J. F., Sanderson, C. and Costa, P. T. (2002). A description of the DSM-IV personality disorders with the five-factor model of personality. In P. T. Costa and T. A. Widiger (eds), *Personality Disorders and the Five Factor Model of Personality*. Washington, DC: American Psychological Association.

Widiger, T. A., Costa, P. T. and McCrae, R. R. (2001). Proposals for Axis II: Diagnosing personality disorders using the five factor model. In P. T. Costa and T. A. Widiger (eds), *Personality Disorders and the Five Factor Model of Personality* (2nd edn, pp. 432–56). Washington, DC: American Psychological Association.

Widom, C. S. (1978). A methodology for studying non-institutionalised psychopaths. In R. D. Hare and D. Schalling (eds), *Psychopathic behaviour: approaches to research* (pp. 71–84). Chichester: Wiley.

Widom, C. S. and Newman, J. P. (1985). Characteristics of non-institutionalized psychopaths. In J. Gunn and D. Farrington (eds), *Current Research in Forensic Psychiatry and Psychology* (vol. 2, pp. 57–80). New York: Wiley.

Wilson, O., Near, D. and Miller, R. (1998). Individual differences in Machiavellianism as a mix of cooperative and exploitative strategies. *Evolution and Human Behaviour, 19*, 103–212.

Zimbardo, P. (2007). *The Lucifer Effect: How Good People Turn Evil*. London: Rider & Co.

INDEX

273